Dimensions of Grief

Adjusting to the Death of a Spouse

Stephen R. Shuchter

Dimensions of Grief
Adjusting to the Death of a Spouse

Jossey-Bass Publishers

San Francisco • London • 1986

DIMENSIONS OF GRIEF
Adjusting to the Death of a Spouse
by Stephen R. Shuchter

Copyright © 1986 by: Jossey-Bass Inc., Publishers
433 California Street
San Francisco, California 94104

&

Jossey-Bass Limited
28 Banner Street
London EC1Y 8QE

Library of Congress Cataloging-in-Publication Data

Shuchter, Stephen R.
  Dimensions of grief.

  (The Jossey-Bass social and behavioral science series)
  Bibliography: p.
  Includes index.
  1. Bereavement—Psychological aspects.   2. Grief.
3. Widows—Mental health.   4. Widowers—Mental health.
5. Adjustment (Psychology).   6. Death—Psychological
aspects.   I. Title.   II. Series.
RC455.4.L67S38   1986   155.9'37   86-10569
ISBN 1-55542-003-6 (alk. paper)

Manufactured in the United States of America

The paper in this book meets the guidelines for
permanence and durability of the Committee on
Production Guidelines for Book Longevity of the
Council on Library Resources.

JACKET DESIGN BY WILLI BAUM

FIRST EDITION

Code 8630

The Jossey-Bass
Social and Behavioral Science Series

To my wife, Susan,
and my daughters, Naomi, Leah, and Kathryn

Preface

This book is about human grief, the myriad responses to and consequences of the death of a spouse. The experiences of men and women who have had such a loss are portrayed here, presented in their own words over a period of many years. From the hundreds of hours of interviews are developed themes that are universal and variations that are unique. The primary audience is the cadre of health and human service practitioners and trainees who are likely to work with the bereaved in their professional roles: psychiatrists and primary care physicians, psychologists, social workers, nurses, counselors, and clergy. Its broader audience includes all those, especially the bereaved and their families, who may wish to gain a deeper understanding of one of life's ubiquitous processes.

The purposes of the book are (1) to establish a broad, systematic scheme for conceptualizing the multiple dimensions of spousal bereavement; (2) to bring these concepts to life through the use of clinical vignettes that illustrate the experiences of the bereaved; (3) to convey an appreciation for the great variability of human responses to such loss; and (4) to present, in the final chapter, a systematic method of assessing the need for treatment and specific therapeutic strategies for treating the problems of spousal bereavement.

Spousal bereavement is usually the most profoundly disturbing and disruptive event in an individual's life. Its effects are experienced at every level of human existence, and problems can develop at all levels of functioning. Therefore, a clinician must have extensive understanding of the many levels at which such a loss affects the survivor. In working with both trainees and experienced clinicians, I have been aware that their exposure to experiences with the bereaved, and to a broad scope of the problems afflicting the bereaved, is marginal. Consequently, they often do not know how to think about what is wrong with and what will help a given widow or widower at a point in time. What is normal? What is pathological? What requires intervention? What kind of intervention? Such questions provide the impetus for this book.

The phenomenology of and treatment approaches to bereavement have been described in a number of excellent professional books: by Parkes and his co-workers in London and Boston (Parkes, 1972; Glick, Parkes, and Weiss, 1975; Parkes and Weiss, 1983); by Raphael (1983) in New Zealand and Australia; by Silverman and her colleagues, describing self-help groups for the newly widowed in Boston (Silverman, 1969, 1970, 1976; Silverman and Cooperband, 1975; Silverman, MacKenzie, Pettipas, and Wilson, 1974); by Lopata (1973, 1979) in Chicago; and by Schoenberg and Gerber (1975). In addition, the National Academy of Sciences has an outstanding review (Osterweis, Solomon, and Green, 1984) of the field of scientific inquiry into the bereavement processes, which gives the reader an appreciation of what is known and what needs to be examined further in this field. These books are directed toward the explication of different dimensions of the grief process. All are based on research findings, and most make suggestions about the implications of their observations for treatment. What is missing from these books, and what represents the essence of this book, is the clinical richness of the experiences of bereaved people over time, presented comprehensively and systematically in a multidimensional framework developed specifically for the clinician.

The data used here are derived primarily from a study by the San Diego Widowhood Project. This research unit of the University of California at San Diego School of Medicine, Department of Psychiatry, was founded in 1977 and has conducted several studies examining the natural history of spousal bereavement, its consequences for psychological and physical health, the neuroendocrine changes associated with acute grief, and our current efforts to develop a standardized assessment tool for the multiple dimensions of spousal bereavement.

In the study whose data are reported here, seventy people (twenty-one men and forty-nine women) were followed prospectively from one month after their spouses' deaths until some time in their fifth year of bereavement, from 1978 to 1983. The research design involved systematic follow-up every three months for two years (months 1, 4, 7, 10, 13, 16, 19, 22, and 25), then yearly follow-up at 37 and 49 months. At each of these intervals, subjects completed self-report questionnaires and were given semistructured interviews. Details of the research protocol as well as some of the statistical data are presented in the Appendix.

The multidimensional perspective presented here was used from the outset to structure the interviews obtained throughout the study. Two research assistants and I conducted the interviews. Interviews were generally hand-recorded, though all interviews at twenty-five months were tape-recorded and transcribed.

The data initially consisted of over 2,000 pages of interview material covering approximately 500 interviews. Despite the obvious methodological flaws (not all subjects were available for interviews at each interval, and some dropped out completely), all available interview material was utilized for its innate descriptive value. Material was then extracted from interviews and organized on the basis of its relevance to the following six dimensions of grief: emotional and mental responses, coping with emotional pain, continuing relationship with the dead spouse, changes in functioning, changes in relationships, and changes in identity.

Observations and conclusions throughout this book are derived not only from the descriptive material but also from other clinical work with the bereaved—mainly in the Widowed Persons' Resource Group. This organization, established in 1980 in cooperation with the Jewish Community Center of San Diego, has been an ongoing source of counseling, social support, and recreational activity for hundreds of men and women since its inception. My experiences as organizer, counselor, and consultant are discussed in Chapter Eight.

This book is organized on the basis of the multiple dimensions of grief as described by the bereaved. Each chapter examines a specific aspect of the survivors' experiences, attempting to provide the broadest view of human responses. The frequencies of such responses are presented in the most general of ways. Conclusions are drawn, in a traditional fashion, from the immersion of a clinician in a great amount of systematically obtained clinical material. Their validity rests, as clinical observations often do, on the breadth of the material from which they are drawn and the observational skills utilized. For example, while there are data to show the frequency of experiences of guilt, by self-report, for all subjects throughout the study, an interview may not have all the elaborations of all the forms of guilt recorded for statistical analysis. For the purposes of this book, statistically valid frequencies were sacrificed for the sake of the breadth and richness of descriptive material provided by our subjects. Furthermore, wherever possible we made use of our subjects' personal descriptions to illustrate a point, thereby allowing the clinical material to speak for itself. A bibliography of relevant literature is included at the end of the book. All quoted material is from research subjects, and efforts were made throughout the text to disguise this material in order to protect the confidentiality of our subjects.

In Chapter One our multidimensional model of grief is described, and its use in evaluating and treating grief-related problems is explained. A description of the six "tasks of grief"—corresponding to the six dimensions of grief—provides a therapeutic framework for the reader to use throughout the remainder of the book.

Chapter Two presents a detailed phenomenological account of the bereaved person's emotional and mental responses to a spouse's death: the shock, grief, sense of loss, anger, guilt, regrets, anxiety, intrusive images, disorganization, loss of control, apathy, and loneliness. These responses are examined as they first appear and as they evolve over time—both as major themes and as variations on the themes.

Chapter Three discusses the various coping skills—such as rationalization, avoidance, and involvement with others—employed by the bereaved to help them dampen the pain of grief. These skills are looked at from the viewpoints of descriptive phenomenology, their primary adaptive values of protection, and their secondary adaptive values in enabling the survivor to continue living in the real world.

Chapter Four describes the many forms in which the bereaved do continue to maintain a relationship with the deceased: through perceptual contact, symbolic representations, living legacies, rituals, memories, and dreams. These phenomena are viewed not only as inevitable manifestations of the emotional needs of the surviving spouse but also as a precondition for successful "resolution" of grief.

In Chapter Five typical changes in functioning—including increased risks to general health and the prevalence of depression and alcoholism among the bereaved—are described. Changes in work-related and social functioning are examined as phenomena secondary to the mental and emotional turmoil that accompanies grief.

Chapter Six presents the vicissitudes of relationships that are affected by death and the grief process. The potential disruptions, dynamic changes, and improvements in relationships with family and friends are elucidated. The bereaved also describe their problems in developing new friendships and romances, dealing with their sexuality, and considering remarriage—aspects of grief that are seldom discussed in detail in professional books.

Chapter Seven examines the numerous ways in which the bereaved person's identity is reshaped, initially in regressive ways but subsequently in usually positive and often dramatic fashion. The loss of a spouse forces the survivor to adapt. From this task, for which there are no volunteers, evolve some of the more creative and beneficial results of bereavement. The changes in the survivor's identity occur at many levels, including not only role functions and life directions but also personal qualities, belief systems, and esthetics.

Chapter Eight, using the multidimensional model set forth, looks at the therapeutic implications for dealing with the bereaved. The therapeutic tasks associated with each of these dimensions are reexamined in greater detail. In addition to general principles of treatment, specific technical approaches are presented, particularly those focused on desensitizing the bereaved to their emotional pain and helping them grieve more freely. This chapter also contains a discussion of support groups and a structure that the professional may utilize in organizing such a group.

I hope that this book will give the reader a cognitive framework and a "feel" for understanding the experience of bereavement, a perspective on how to assess the problems of bereaved people, and an idea of how to help them.

I want to acknowledge the contributions of those people who have been involved in this project from its inception to its completion.

When the San Diego Widowhood Project began, some of the early groundwork for the research came through consultation with my colleague Richard Avery and with Helen Antoniak, then director of the Widow-to-Widow Program in San Diego. Rose Chait, a research assistant at the University of California at San Diego, helped launch the project in 1978. Certainly, the greatest single contributor in acquiring data has been Carolyn Booth, my dedicated and capable research assistant, who spent almost four years interviewing subjects and distributing and collecting questionnaires for the project. During the past year, Lucy Lyons has worked tirelessly to organize our data for statistical analysis. My lifelong friend and now collaborator, Sidney Zisook, has been a source of advice, criticism, and support in bringing this project to completion. I thank my department chairman, Lewis Judd, for his personal and research support; David Janowsky for research support from a National Institute of Mental Health grant; my secretaries, Dorothy Pakus and Mary Wood, for their steady work with my manuscripts and their patience in the face of deadlines; and Jan Albright for picking up the slack when they were absorbed. Finally, I want to express my appreciation to my wife, Susan, and my daughters, Naomi, Leah, and Kathryn, for their understanding and support throughout the writing of this book.

San Diego, California   Stephen R. Shuchter
September 1986

Contents

The Author

Stephen Shuchter is currently director of the UCSD Gifford Mental Health Clinic, a principal investigator of the San Diego Widowhood Project, and an associate clinical professor of psychiatry at the University of California at San Diego School of Medicine.

He received his B.A. degree (1965) from the University of Chicago in biology and his M.D. degree (1969) from the University of Chicago School of Medicine. After an internship in medicine at Michael Reese Hospital and Medical Center in 1970, he did his residency in psychiatry at Yale University School of Medicine, finishing in 1973.

Since 1975 Shuchter has been on the full-time faculty at UCSD, where he has served as director of the department of psychiatry's outpatient service and as director of the clinical clerkship program for medical students. His research studies have focused on spousal bereavement. In 1979, for his efforts in organizing crisis intervention services following the crash of a jetliner in 1978, he received the UCSD Chancellor's Associates recognition award for excellence in community service. In 1981 he was named as volunteer of the year by the Jewish Community Centers of San Diego for his work with the bereaved.

Dimensions of Grief
Adjusting to the Death of a Spouse

 Chapter 1

When a Spouse Dies: Understanding the Experience of Bereavement

Recorded history testifies to the universality of grief; our literature and poetry speak of its profound impact on the survivors of such loss. Only during this century, however, have systematic efforts been made to understand the process and the specific impact of bereavement; and only in the last two decades have professionals attempted to learn what effect therapeutic intervention might have on this process.

The sensitive professional who encounters a bereaved individual is immediately aware that this suffering person needs help, but the nature of the help that is needed is unclear. The usual questions with which a therapist may struggle revolve around what specific actions to take. Should I deepen this person's pain or help stave it off? Is there evidence of "pathological grief"? Should he still be grieving so actively a year later? Should she be encouraged to put away his picture or look at it, to go to the cemetery or avoid it? Should my therapeutic stance be as a sounding board, or should I be "pushing" him to get out of the house? The family says that she cries every day. What does this mean, and what should I do for her? For the family? How long can depression go on before medical intervention is considered? What is the place of medication for sleep or anxiety? Should I be operating like a cheerleader or a priest? How will I know when grief is over? Is it ever over?

This book takes the position that the clinician who treats a bereaved person must understand the many dimensions of grief,

1

the desirable goals or outcomes for each of these dimensions over time, and the methods of achieving these goals. It is toward these levels of understanding and response that a multidimensional model of bereavement is presented here. In Chapters Two through Seven, these dimensions are described in detail; Chapter Eight looks in depth at the therapeutic approach to spousal bereavement, applying a set of therapeutic tasks to each of these dimensions.

The Dimensions of Grief

Emotional and Mental Responses. The acute reactions to loss, described by numerous observers (Lindemann, 1944; Parkes, 1970; Glick, Parkes, and Weiss, 1975), include an initial period of shock followed by intense emotional pangs of grief. The "shock" may be experienced as a sense of numbness or unreality, it may have a dreamlike quality, or it may be a state of normal thinking and functioning. In this state of detachment, the individual is protected from the impact of a new reality and may remain in this state for minutes or for days—or even, in rare instances, for weeks and months.

Shock gives way to the waves and pangs of intense grief. People become flooded with such emotions, often manifested through autonomic discharge and the experiences of "heartache" or a "knife in the gut." These occur intermittently, in waves, frequently initiated by some concrete reminder of the death. They can occur suddenly and unexpectedly, precipitated by endless sources: contact with mutual friends, a memory or an image, a song or a picture or an article of clothing. Each "trigger" is met with the same pain. Over time such experiences of grief usually become less frequent and less intense; but they are likely to occur, at least occasionally, for months and even years. At "special times"—holidays, birthdays, anniversaries—they may be ushered in with greater intensity.

As the reality of the death sinks in, the survivor often experiences an increasing sense of loss. The sense of loss is not simply for the person who has died but also for the part of the survivor that was "connected" to the spouse, as well as the survivor's hopes, dreams, and plans for a future with the spouse.

The missing, longing, yearning, and searching become a part of the survivor's life. These experiences, too, after a period of great intensity, usually lessen gradually over time.

As time goes on, loneliness becomes an increasing part of the survivor's existence and can evolve into a most painful and inescapable affect. Many of the newly bereaved also go through a period where anger becomes a significant part of their grief. While the essence of such anger probably lies in the loss and hurt, the focus of the anger and the forms that it can take are highly variable. The anger may be felt toward the dead spouse for unhealthy ways of living or as a legacy of anger from the relationship. Usually, however, it is felt as a response to being abandoned and left in the lurch. The survivor may find herself angry at the spouse's doctors for acts of commission or omission; at God or fate; at her family or friends. The anger may also take the form of a sense of exploitation by society and envy of those who have a relationship that the survivor no longer has.

Another frequent and painful affect is guilt, whether in the form of survival guilt or a sense of responsibility for the death or suffering of the spouse. Usually, this sense of guilt, especially the more irrational feelings, is transient. Later, as the survivor makes new emotional attachments, there may appear a new form of guilt: a sense of betrayal. Again, this is usually transient.

Anxiety and fearfulness about both the imagined and real threats to the newly bereaved person's existence become a regular part of life. Those who have been more autonomous and independent may feel better prepared to face the world alone, but even the most adaptive people experience some anxiety while facing the uncertainty of the future as well as the realistic hardships created by long-standing illness, large medical bills, loss of income, lack of insurance, and concerns about the welfare of surviving children.

Among the disruptive legacies of a spouse's death are the intrusive images that force their way into the survivor's mind. These images often focus on the circumstances of the death or the appearance of the dying spouse. Particularly in the early weeks and months of bereavement, these intrusive images can create overwhelming distress.

Mental disorganization is another highly distressing feature of bereavement, one that may interfere significantly with the survivor's capacity to function. People experience varying degrees of distractibility and poor concentration, confusion, forgetfulness, and lack of clarity and coherence. Contributing to this disorganization may be rapidly changing emotional states produced by acute stress. Certainly, such phenomena can be part of a depression; and if they persist beyond the first few months, they are likely to be manifestations of "true" depression. Apathy, independent of other depressive symptoms, may also appear, often after some delay in time. This condition may seem quite foreign and dystonic to a usually on-the-go and active person.

It must be remembered that many people die after prolonged illness, particularly cancer, where there has been significant deterioration, pain, and suffering for both the dying and surviving spouses. Under such circumstances the survivor is likely to experience a sense of relief: from his own suffering, from the suffering of his spouse, and at times from other hardships or conflicts that were an integral part of the relationship. Often a sense of guilt may accompany this relief.

Throughout the early weeks and months of bereavement, survivors frequently find themselves in fluctuating states of turmoil associated with the unpredictable emergence of any of these emotional and cognitive changes. They may feel overwhelmed, out of control, as though they are "going crazy." Healthy, generally adaptive people may never have experienced such an emotional "roller coaster" and find it very disconcerting to be unable to assert control over their internal lives. Some people find this aspect of their bereavement as upsetting as the other changes.

Coping with Emotional Pain. Faced with the onslaught of recurrent, often unpredictable, and usually disruptive emotional and cognitive states, people find ways to protect themselves from such distress. Survivors will utilize their customary defenses where possible; usually, however, they will resort to developmentally more primitive defenses or to multiple defenses.

Numbness has been described as an emotional state, but it also serves as a coping mechanism. Its essence is the extreme of detachment or dissociation between the head and "heart." Accompanying this state, particularly in the early phases, is a sense of disbelief that lasts for months despite the obvious perceptual and intellectual awareness of the death.

Survivors can exert conscious emotional control through suppression in many situations where they deem it socially inappropriate to express their feelings or where they fear "giving in" to their feelings. Others use isolation of affect as their "customary" way of dealing with uncomfortable feelings, albeit on an unconscious basis. The effectiveness of these defenses is highly variable, depending on the circumstances and the intensity of the stimulus. Furthermore, although it does protect the person from his or her affect, emotional constriction also can interfere with the expression and catharsis that are necessary to the emotional and physical well-being of the surviving spouse.

Widows and widowers utilize a variety of "altered perspectives" to mitigate their loss and suffering. Intellectualization and, especially, rationalization serve as major means of protection. Several recurrent themes become prevalent in the thinking of the bereaved: "He is better this way than to be suffering." "Things could have been worse." "We were lucky to have what we had." "I'm better off now."

One of the mainstays of the bereaved is the operation of faith. This is a powerful and effective means of coping with death and seems to operate in a number of ways: it can facilitate acceptance, provide meaning, offer help and support through God, combat loneliness, and offer the bereaved a chance to reunite with the spouse in heaven.

Avoidance becomes a standard in the repertoire of the bereaved. This quickly learned response develops as soon as the survivor perceives, consciously or unconsciously, that a given stimulus sets off the painful feelings of grief. A bereaved person may become unable to tolerate looking at pictures of his spouse, sleeping in her bed, keeping her belongings at home, driving by the hospital where she died, talking with mutual friends, going to the cemetery. In the extreme, avoidance can be as complete as the accidental exposures to reminders allow it to be. More commonly, the survivor's capacity to tolerate such exposure will increase over time. He will find that he can "dose" himself; that is, make efforts to expose himself to such triggers for brief periods when he feels stronger.

Being "busy"—with work, school, housework, hobbies, or volunteer work—is another means of coping, allowing the bereaved to invest themselves, focus their thoughts, and distract themselves from their grief. Such distraction often contrasts sharply with the eventual return to an empty house, where their grief emerges.

Radio, television, or reading becomes a frequent part of the day-to-day efforts of the bereaved to distract themselves—even though material from the media may also serve as a trigger. The media, particularly radio and television, also may provide a modicum of companionship, through sound and pictures, which can combat loneliness.

Involvement with other people can be a productive and adaptive way of dealing with one's grief. Relationships can provide support and comfort or stave off loneliness. They may offer the bereaved an opportunity for the direct expression of powerful feelings and troubling thoughts. They can also distract a bereaved person from his grief; by focusing on others' needs, one momentarily forgets one's own misery. Pets, an often forgotten resource, can be objects of affection and caregiving as well as providers of love, appreciation, and companionship. They may also provide a connection to the lost spouse.

Indulgence in many nonproductive and even self-destructive means of coping with internal feeling states is frequent in the newly bereaved. The use of food, alcohol, tobacco, or even sex may take on compulsive features. The newly bereaved are more vulnerable to such maladaptive behaviors for many reasons. Their pain is powerful, their resistance is low, their sense of entitlement is high, and they often say to themselves, "Who cares?" Manic defenses, on the verge of clinical mania, may be expressed in other impulsive acts, such as spending money or making drastic changes in one's residence, career, or relationships, in frantic efforts to ward off pain.

Continuing Relationship with the Dead Spouse. A survivor may cope with the death of a spouse by completely negating the loss—that is, by keeping the dead person alive through a variety of psychological mechanisms that permit survivors to maintain their ties to their dead spouses. In some instances the survivor visualizes the spouse as continuing to have an existence in another place, most commonly heaven, with the further implications of peace and eventual reuniting. Or the survivor may maintain continuing contact with the spouse—for instance, through an internal sense of the spouse's presence to watch over, comfort, or protect her. Again, some bereaved persons may keep the deceased alive by imbuing certain belongings, creations, or shared experiences with the spirit or memories of the deceased. These are frequently personal possessions that capture an important attribute (a favorite robe, a garden tended by the deceased, tools or equipment associated with a vocational interest, a car) or symbols of the marital relationship (a ring, the bed, or the home). Most of these symbols of continuing contact are, of course, experienced ambivalently: they keep the person alive but also serve as reminders that he is gone and therefore can become painful triggers.

Living legacies also provide continuity of these relationships. Through identification the survivor may take on personality characteristics, habits, esthetic values, or even somatic symptoms of the deceased. Or, on a more active, conscious level, the surviving spouse may carry out the dead spouse's wishes, expectations, or commitments—often through endowments. The most abundant living legacies are children, whose genetic makeup recreates aspects of the dead person's appearance, mannerisms, or personality.

Our social and cultural rituals reinforce the individual predisposition to perpetuate such connections. Tributes to the deceased are incorporated in most services. Afterward friends and family bring the bereaved gifts of their memories and the realization that the deceased remains alive emotionally. The cemetery evokes the painful awareness of death and the emotional connection that continues.

As time goes on, memories—sometimes comforting, sometimes painful—remain the most tangible and available sources of this continuing relationship. During the early weeks and months of bereavement, however, the survivor may be appalled to discover that he cannot conjure up images and memories of the deceased. The fear that one cannot recapture the loved one may be further complicated under circumstances of a prolonged wasting illness, where the only memories and images available are the scenes of illness, helplessness, emaciation, or death. When positive memories appear down the road, they are met with tremendous relief. Similar desperation can occur when people find their memories fading away, intensifying their sense of loss or precipitating guilt for not caring enough.

Survivors' dreams may reveal the status of their relationships with the deceased. Most commonly, dreams about the spouse are retrieval in nature, reflecting the obvious wish that the spouse has returned: scenes of mundane life where the spouse simply exists. Other dreams reflect efforts to separate or to deal with the conflicts that were a part of their lives together.

In each of these psychological phenomena, the survivor tries to bring the deceased back to life, in whatever form this can be accomplished.

Changes in Functioning. Many studies have documented the heightened risks to health of spousal bereavement, particularly during the first year. While studies of mortality (Kraus and Lilienfeld, 1959; Rees and Lutkins, 1967; Clayton, 1974) have yielded variable conclusions, the survivor's risks of depression, alcoholism, drug abuse, cardiovascular disease, neuroendocrine disorders (Hofer, 1984), and suppressed immune function (Bartrop and others, 1977) all appear to increase after the death of a spouse (Osterweis, Solomon, and Green, 1984). Somatic symptoms of distress are a fairly universal part of the acute reaction to grief and may be the source of the increased frequency with which the bereaved utilize health care.

Work performance may be significantly impaired as a natural consequence of a specific medical or psychiatric disorder. Even in the absence of such a disorder, acute grief frequently creates mental disorganization, confusion, anxiety, memory disturbances, and distractibility, which can significantly interfere with the person's capacity to perform a task. Contributing to this dysfunction are intrusive thoughts and images and strong emotional reactions. Later on, if a clinical depression evolves, it may reproduce many of these same disorganizing phenomena. Furthermore, where apathy appears, the loss of motivation about one's tasks will contribute to deteriorating function.

While social activity may be adaptive as the bereaved seek out others for support, involvement, and distraction, at times—particularly in early phases—the grieving person may exhibit varying degrees of social inhibition, withdrawal, and isolation. This withdrawal may be a primitive mechanism to protect and preserve precious emotional reserves in an individual whose survival is threatened. Its effect, however, may be to cut off essential resources.

Other forms of dysfunction involve both role changes and problems—such as difficulties in driving a car alone, writing a check, caring for children, cooking meals, filing insurance bills, or obtaining Social Security benefits—that often seem overwhelming.

Changes in Relationships. One of the inevitable consequences of spousal bereavement is that the surviving spouse experiences significant changes in his or her relationships with other people. There may be greater closeness, a different meaning, an altered role or dynamic. Some relationships end while others begin, but all are affected by the death.

The most complex changes in relationships occur within the family. Where there are young children in the home, the surviving parent will have the task of helping these children in their grief. Where there are grown children, conflicts may arise between these children and the surviving parent because of differing expectations about their relationships and roles. The surviving spouse may also be seen as the major support for older parents or in-laws and may have the responsibility of helping them grieve. With any family member, regardless of the nature of his prior relationship to the surviving spouse, there is an opportunity for growth and greater intimacy or, conversely, the possibility for conflict and disruption.

Friends also may be a major source of support for the bereaved. They can reach out and give or understand and accept the survivor's withdrawal and not be put off. They can offer practical help and emotional support by sharing the pain and allowing its free expression. Sometimes, however, friends may be incapable of empathizing with the bereaved—either because they have a strong need to deny that such a threat to their own marriage could exist, or because they find the person's grief too intense, or, at times, because of fears concerning the bereaved person's sexual motives. As a result, the bereaved may find themselves avoided, treated differently, or rejected. In addition, both family and friends may allot an insufficient period of "permission" for the person's grief.

Out of the turmoil of bereavement, survivors may form new friendships with people who have experienced their own grief and are more understanding and accepting of a widowed person's distress. For some, new romances occur, with both the obvious advantages of intimacy and sexuality and the conflicts caused by feelings of betrayal, comparisons, and the difficult process of dating, as well as the inevitable conflicts inherent in all relationships. Where remarriage occurs, complications may be created by "blended" families; and, even when the new marriage is successful, the experiences of grief do not end.

Many bereaved persons, even if they do not remarry, ultimately enter into new sexual relationships. In some instances—especially when the death followed a prolonged illness where sexuality played a diminishing role—the survivors may have suppressed their sexual feelings for a long interval; the reemergence of these feelings therefore causes surprise and perhaps some guilt. This guilt may lead to sexual dysfunction, which is usually short-lived. For others sexuality proceeds easily and naturally and may become more fulfilling than it had been within the marriage.

Changes in Identity. Some of the most profound changes that occur in the bereaved are those that reflect their personal identity. For most people spousal bereavement is likely to be the most disruptive, threatening, and challenging experience of their lives. Under these circumstances it is not surprising that the potential for dramatic changes exists. The bereaved are "given the opportunity" to think, feel, and behave in ways that may be new and foreign, ways that they otherwise might never have experienced.

Initially, the bereaved may experience an intense regression, what Horowitz and colleagues (Horowitz, Wilner, Marmar, and Krupnick, 1980) describe as the emergence of "latent negative self-images": perceptions of the self as helpless, inadequate, incapable, childlike, or personally bankrupt. Also contributing to this state may be the loss of the "mirror" function of the spouse who has died and whose own perceptions or social status may have contributed to his spouse's sense of self. Over time, these negative images usually give way to more positive ones, as the survivors find themselves able to tolerate their grief, carry on their tasks, and learn new ways of dealing with the world. By mastering their trials and tribulations, the bereaved develop a growing sense of strength, autonomy and independence, assertiveness, and maturity.

The bereaved also go through a significant, and at times radical, alteration of their world view, the set of beliefs by which they operate. After their loss, often well into the second year, the bereaved often feel that they have lost their direction. This loss of direction and meaning is precipitated by the disruption of the plans and hopes they shared with their spouses or by the shattering of belief systems that governed many of their actions: beliefs in controlling one's destiny, maintaining invincibility, a just and merciful God, deferred gratification, unbounded optimism. All such beliefs are challenged, fall short, and leave a vacuum that only gradually becomes filled again—at times with modified reassertions of the old beliefs and at times with totally new ones, reflecting the finiteness and fragility of life and the limits of control. As a result, the bereaved often become more appreciative of daily living, more patient and accepting, more giving. They may develop new careers or change them, enjoy themselves with more gusto, or find new outlets for creativity. On the other hand, some people do stagnate or wither, unable to meet the challenges, unable to experience personal growth.

Treatment Considerations: The Tasks of Grief

What are the implications for such a multidimensional model of grief in regard to treatment? What, in general, needs to be treated? Since all of bereavement seems disruptive, should "all of it" be treated? Should only "pathological grief" be treated? Instead of defining "pathology," the multidimensional approach defines optimal or desirable "tasks" for each of these dimensions. The determination of a need for treatment then depends on how the bereaved are able to achieve the task as defined in each dimension. In all instances the demands on the psychotherapist are also multidimensional, requiring flexibility and the capacity to shift roles as the needs of the bereaved demand. It should be kept in mind that the "tasks" presented here are the products of clinical interpretations and judgments and have not been validated through independent studies.

The following tasks of grief emerge from the various dimensions of grief:

1. Learning to Experience, Express, and Integrate Painful Affects
2. Finding the Most Adaptive Means of Modulating Painful Affects
3. Integrating the Continuing Relationship with the Dead Spouse
4. Maintaining Health and Continued Functioning
5. Adapting Successfully to Altered Relationships
6. Developing an Integrated, Healthy Self-Concept and a Stable World View

In Chapter Eight these tasks are discussed in further detail.

Task 1. Learning to Experience, Express, and Integrate Painful Affects. The therapist who understands the emotional and cognitive processes accompanying grief can elicit these processes through open-ended inquiry or more specific exploration. The therapist's knowledge and anticipation of the survivor's reactions may further facilitate their expression.

"Normalization" is an educational approach that, through reading or discussion, enables the bereaved to understand the normal grief process and therefore to overcome barriers of embarrassment, guilt, or fears of "going crazy," which may inhibit the experiences of grief.

The therapist—by his or her presence, empathic availability, and patience in waiting for emotions that "are not ready"— can provide a partial antidote to the loneliness and isolation experienced by some survivors; and the psychotherapeutic exploration of survivors' developmental conflicts can place many of their current experiences in a historical context. Reality testing may help alleviate guilt, underscore the appropriateness of anger or relief, or allay anxiety about the future.

Task 2. Finding the Most Adaptive Means of Modulating Painful Affects. Initially, the therapist must review, in detail, the mechanisms being used by the bereaved to ward off their pain. Clearly, the bereaved cannot tolerate such affects all the time but will generally "dose" themselves, usually without conscious effort. The therapist should support the defenses that help the survivor cope with the demands of daily life (for example, rationalization, involvement with others, faith) and actively discourage those that are likely to be counterproductive or destructive (for example, alcohol, withdrawal, impulsivity). Where the person is floundering and suffering for lack of sufficient "protection," the therapist may recommend appropriate ways of managing such affects (through volunteer work, hobbies, and the like). Where the person has completely suppressed painful feelings, evocative techniques may be important to "let in" affect, even though the defenses have proved fairly adaptive (see Task 3).

Task 3. Integrating the Continuing Relationship with the Dead Spouse. The bereaved demonstrate a strong emotional need to maintain some form of continuing relationship with their spouse. Evidence of this need is universal; and, as is suggested in Chapter Eight, this phenomenon may be essential to "healing." The therapist's task is not to make the bereaved "let go" of the spouse but to help the bereaved maintain such ties in whatever form they evolve, to help them feel comfort with the means they find for themselves. At the same time, such ties must not interfere with living, and, in fact, do not necessarily do so.

Where the survivor is unable to relate in some way to the spouse—where there is rigid avoidance that will not permit thoughts, images, or feelings about the spouse to emerge—the therapist can help the bereaved person overcome this "phobic" response through the use of evocative techniques, enlisting the agreement and conscious cooperation of the bereaved in such efforts. For instance, the therapist can ask the patient to describe the events surrounding the spouse's death, or to reminisce about poignant periods of life with the deceased, or to bring one of the spouse's belongings to a session. Through these techniques the therapist tries to create a "trigger" and then helps the bereaved person bear the pain when it appears. Occasionally a trip to the cemetery may provide this breakthrough.

Task 4. Maintaining Health and Continued Functioning. Ongoing assessment of conflict-laden areas in any of the dimensions of grief can help to lower stress levels. At the same time, the therapist can help the bereaved person deal with major stressors in the outside world—by, for example, securing access to social support services, medical and legal services, financial services, or other community institutions. The role of medical treatment for insomnia, anxiety, and depression is a controversial issue. Briefly, I will say that my bias is to treat those syndromes that appear to have a "life of their own" or have led to incapacitation or overwhelming distress.

Task 5. Adapting Successfully to Altered Relationships. In some instances of rejection by friends or family, there is no way to know what has happened. The therapist can try, however, to help the bereaved person understand the difficulties that others may have with displays of grief—thereby "softening the blow" and protecting the bereaved from feelings of responsibility for the rejection. In most instances changes in established relationships can be examined, understood, and dealt with by the bereaved or, at times, in the context of some form of relationship therapy.

In confronting a bereaved person's anxiety about forming new relationships of any sort, but especially romantic involvements, the therapist may need to uncover fears and their developmental precursors; cajole the bereaved to risk disappointment or rejection or to face feelings of guilt or inadequacy; support adaptive responses; or encourage the bereaved person to join a support group. Sexual counseling may be necessary, though such problems usually are resolved quickly.

Task 6. Developing an Integrated, Healthy Self-Concept and a Stable World View. Most people who lose a spouse are basically healthy individuals with stable identities. During the early periods of bereavement, however, feelings of inadequacy, guilt, loss of control, and hopelessness usually emerge. At these times the therapist must maintain a strongly held conviction, based on the historical evidence, about the fundamental intactness of the bereaved and the evolution of identity through grief into an even more positive form. Such a conviction serves as a source of reassurance and support in the present.

This outline of therapeutic tasks is not meant to define all aspects of treatment of the bereaved but to emphasize a perspective that may be useful as the reader examines each of the dimensions of grief and attempts to formulate appropriate interventions in a given situation. The demands on a therapist are many: the often exquisitely painful work of joining a grieving spouse in his or her pain, the cognitive task of analyzing the problems being presented, and the need for flexibility and versatility in employing a broad repertoire of therapeutic skills for extremely diverse problems.

 Chapter 2

Emotional and Mental Responses to Loss of a Spouse

The death of a spouse can produce some of the most profound and intense experiences of human emotion and thought. Such a loss elicits a wide range of internal responses, which are at times overwhelming and at times perplexing. This chapter focuses on those responses that are typically seen in the surviving spouse, both in their essential forms and in their unique and idiosyncratic expressions.

Protective Responses

Confronted by the death of a spouse, even where the death may have been expected, most men and women experience some form of initial shock; that is, a period of time during which the impact of their loss has not registered. Although the mechanism is not understood, somehow the "wisdom of the body" sets up a barrier between the intellectual and emotional spheres, which serves to protect people—without their exercising conscious control or making active efforts—from what would otherwise be an overwhelming experience. As a result, the most commonly encountered initial responses of the newly bereaved are states of relative numbness or emotional constriction and detachment. What they experience may seem unreal, dreamlike in quality. Others experience this numbness as a state of normality, where they can think and act quite clearly, apparently unaffected by the death. Under these circumstances people are understandably often surprised by their response, or lack of it, and their capacity to carry on without falling apart.

The most dramatic example of this phenomenon in my personal experience occurred after the death of one of my closest friends, a man in his mid-thirties who collapsed suddenly while playing basketball. During the funeral and the home visits, his wife remained totally composed; and the day after his funeral, she passed her oral examinations defending her doctoral dissertation in Russian literature. Another example is Jacqueline Kennedy, who served as a heroic model of composure following the death of John F. Kennedy. The inner experiences of people living through such ordeals are highly variable but seem to have a common thread running through them.

> Doris awoke early to make breakfast. She returned to awaken her husband, Edwin, but found him unresponsive. She shook him, thinking he was teasing, then kissed him on his forehead, which was cold. Realizing that he was not breathing, she administered mouth-to-mouth resuscitation and external heart massage. She called her family physician, relating precise and concise information, and then resumed cardiopulmonary resuscitation (CPR). The police arrived quickly and confirmed his death. Until that point she was not convinced that he had died. In retrospect she was amazed at herself for demonstrating such control and precision. She had carried on with the skill and detachment of a good physician under great stress.
>
> Daphne's husband, Ray, died after being in a coma for two weeks. He had a brain tumor diagnosed more than two years before and had been deteriorating for the last six months. At the point he died, she began to feel numb. "I remember at my husband's funeral I was standing there sort of looking at it from a distance. I couldn't seem to realize what was happening to me. I felt like I was watching a movie, that's what it felt like."

These states can last for highly variable lengths of time, usually giving way to intense emotional reactions within minutes to hours. However, they can remain for weeks or even months.

> Joanne's husband died rather suddenly and unexpectedly from a heart attack. "I was still going through a numb stage the first holiday he was gone. He passed away nine days before our twenty-ninth anniversary and sixteen days before Christmas. So I fixed the family a Christmas Eve dinner and got through Christmas Day and everything was just fine. I often thought to myself, 'If I loved him so much, how could I be going ahead normally?' But the pain hadn't caught up with me yet."

> Shirley's experience was prolonged for over a year. "I felt like a nervous high, numbness, through the whole year. I giggled my way through it or something. I wasn't feeling."

Emotional Pain of Grief

For most newly bereaved people, the reality "hits home" fairly soon and very intensely. They often experience a "flooding" of emotions, a rapid welling up of tears, uncontrollable crying. There are "pains," which some feel as a wrenching of their insides, "a knife in the gut," "heartache"—all manifestations of the often physiological reactions that are characteristic of grief.

> *Doris:* "I think it was about two weeks when I finally came out of the initial shock. I felt as if I was going to throw up. I felt full up to here and I kept retching and I couldn't vomit and I was just trembling from head to toe."

> When Marie's husband died after a prolonged bout with cancer, Marie was very matter of fact and philosophical. "My husband had a military funeral: the flag-draped coffin, the taps, the firing of the

guns, everything. Do you know I didn't really feel the effect of that until my brother-in-law's death [two months later]. Because he had the same thing. My daughter had gone up there with me. When they blew taps, it was the first time that I felt any effect of my husband being dead. They blew taps and the next thing I knew I felt like my feet were giving out from under me. And everything just seemed to black out."

Such responses can erupt suddenly and unexpectedly, particularly in the first days and weeks; they are usually triggered by a reminder of the person's loss. These reminders can come from a thousand sources, from all of one's senses, from a lifetime of memories, or from the most innocuous-seeming situations.

Melinda had Jim at home throughout most of the final stages of his lung cancer. "Several times he couldn't make it to the bathroom and he'd urinate on the rug. And I tried many times to get it cleaned up, and sometimes when it's really warm in the room the urination smell will come up and trigger me and I'll fall apart."

Shortly after Frank's death, Annette was driving her car when the song "You Light Up My Life" began playing on the radio. As soon as she heard it, she burst into tears. "Every day as I was leaving his hospital room he would tell me that I light up his life."

The men and women in our study described "triggers" coming at them from every direction. We will examine these in greater detail in Chapter Four as we discuss the ways in which the bereaved attempt to cope with them and at times to perpetuate them. What is most striking about these experiences is that they can be exquisitely painful and unbearable yet are almost universal phenomena with which people must contend.

Sense of Loss

Closely associated with the emotional pain and often a major "trigger" to it is the survivor's growing awareness of the emotional fact of death, the sense that one has lost something essential that cannot be retrieved. The widows and widowers in our study had been married for an average of twenty-three years, during which time the emotional bonds between them and their spouses almost invariably formed a broad network of connections. Such couples grow to be a part of each other, regardless of the degrees of autonomy and independence that appear on the surface and in spite of major disruptions and broad areas of conflict. As a result, the tearing and wrenching of these connections create not only painful open wounds at the surface of the survivor but defects in the innermost fabric. Looking at the survivors' descriptions of their experiences, one cannot avoid the recurrent themes of loss, not only of the persons who died—their qualities and characteristics, the intimacy created in the relationship, the gratifications they provided—but also of parts of the survivors that were disrupted and taken with the dying persons. The missing, longing, yearning, and pining are both for the dead and the living.

> *Daniel:* "My relationship with my wife was one of extreme closeness. I would confide in her. . . . She understood and she responded, and I felt comfortable. She gave me the strength I needed when I had weaknesses, and she was there to comfort me when I needed comforting. And I felt that I could go to her with anything. Even though there were plenty of times when there was discord and arguments, I had the feeling of more security and I was comfortable. I never had to be on my toes about what I would say, how I would say it. I don't have that feeling anymore with anyone."

> *Pamela:* "The most difficult thing to deal with has been just knowing that he's not here after thirty-six years. I don't know, you still expect to see him

coming in. . . . At times, even when I'm with other people, there is a big empty hole in the center of my body."

Harold: "I've lost my ideal companion. My wife was always a cheerful, happy, pleasant person. She wouldn't let herself get down. She had the ability to always laugh a lot, no matter how tough it was. Her courage, well it's something I never got used to, something that I always envied in a way—her ability to bounce back after her mastectomy. The following morning she was joking with the surgeon. I've always had a tendency to be a little bit more morose and pessimistic, and her unfailing cheerfulness and optimism were good for me, you know. Now that's gone, and the days look blacker and blacker."

Carol: "Night was terrible. I tell you that other side of the bed was just awful. And I had, you know, some days used to be bad. It just seemed like everything was always all right. At the end of the day your husband gave you a kiss and said, 'I love you,' and it's all, it seems like everything is all right. Regardless of what kind of day, what kind of problem you had, it all sort of settled at night when you and your husband were together. And I missed that. I still miss that [two years later]. I would wake up in the middle of the night and he wasn't there, and it's a frightening experience. That's that total dependency that I talk about. I've never gotten away from that. I really miss that and talking over things, just being able to sit and talk to someone."

Daphne: "I feel like he is slipping away from me. Am I supposed to say 'That's it' and go on? It's like half of me is missing."

Beatrice: "You feel as though half of your brain has died because partners store different sorts of information."

Linda: "You feel that half of your last breath is taken when he took his last breath."

Doris: "We were so close and at first I just didn't feel I could carry on. I just felt half of me was gone and we had such a good close relationship. It's the little things I miss. He'd always kiss me goodbye before he went to work in the morning, tell me that he loved me, and at night at 5:30, I really missed that at first. . . . I think when you're sick is when you really miss them more than ever. Edwin was very kind and understanding when I was sick."

Clearly, the losses experienced when one's spouse dies extend beyond those described here. There are losses of relationships, roles, status, security, styles of living, a sense of meaning, and a vision of the future. These losses are not experienced with the same suddenness or intensity as the losses of spouse and self, though the long-term effects may be as devastating. It is important also to bear in mind the variability among survivors in their early responses to loss—variability resulting from the marital relationship, the nature of the illness, or simply "individual variation."

Several of the marital relationships in our study were described as highly conflictual or "bad" by the survivors. Two of these survivors said that they experienced only "relief" and "release," with minimal remorse or sense of loss. Said Ethel, "You don't miss a headache when it's gone." However, it is not so much the presence of conflict or incompatibility as the existence of detachment, a lack of emotional involvement, that makes a loss relatively painless. To the contrary, turmoil in a relationship usually indicates that people are very involved with each other, and some of those relationships ended with even more tumultuous grief.

A number of survivors whose spouses had gone through a prolonged period of illness, usually with cancer or heart disease, reported a less intense response at the time of their deaths than at the onset of the life-threatening illness. With these survivors the process of detachment may have begun at a much earlier time.

This process of "anticipatory grief" (Aldrich, 1974; Gerber and others, 1975) was not an invariable occurrence, however. For other survivors the terminal illness created even greater degrees of intimacy and intensification of bonding, which made the loss more devastating.

"Individual variation" in responses to loss may result from differences in innate bonding mechanisms, adaptive devices for protection, or personality factors such as dependency or autonomy. Possibly all these factors are essentially the same phenomenon looked at from a different perspective. Regardless of the etiology of such variations, the fact that a spouse's reaction is not intense can be disconcerting and often guilt producing, because of the prevailing view in our society that suffering and pain are evidence of love and loyalty.

However deeply felt the sense of loss is in the first weeks and months, there is an inevitable lessening of intensity over time. Again, the degree and the time course are highly individualized; and a small number of people in the study experienced quite intense and persistent feelings of loss well into their second year of bereavement. The usual evolution is to a sense of sadness and nostalgia without the desperation of the earlier experiences. At the end of five years, this sadness becomes a permanent legacy, though it may only linger below the surface waiting to be tapped.

> *Bobbi* [two years later]: "I still feel sadness once in a while. It's usually fading. I can almost feel a choked-up and teary sensation but it doesn't happen very often. It's happened a few times in the past couple of weeks, but it's almost more like nostalgia or sadness than anything stronger. The intensity is so much less. The first few months the intensity at times would seem almost unbearable, gradually less to the way it is now. I'm sad in a way that I don't remember him more clearly. And it seems sad that I'm not as sad as I was. I wrote a poem shortly after he died, just a little two-liner: 'Don't cry they say, you won't miss him in time./They don't know that's why I cry.'

When the pain went away, part of him went away
too, which is sad but inevitable."

Linda [two years later]: "I will never get over the
feelings of missing him, but these feelings are now
peaceful feelings rather than miserable, unhappy
feelings."

The awareness of this evolution can occur in sudden yet subtle
ways.

Doris [twenty-two months later]: "Just recently I
realized I'd only been using half of the bed to sleep
on. I also became aware of being able to come home
to an empty house without being upset."

As time goes on, the acute sense of loss changes to a sense of
missing the person and of sadness. With further time, these
sensations become less a part of moment-to-moment awareness and
more a set of feelings evoked by special circumstances. "Getting
over" a loss is a misnomer.

Lucille: "The pain is not gone but dormant. . . . I'm
just not wearing it on my sleeve."

Anger

Many of our research subjects went through some period
when anger was a significant part of their grief. As long as five
years after the death, some people in the study demonstrated
significant remnants of anger, even where they appeared to have
made otherwise good adjustments. A common denominator to all
grief is some form of suffering, and both history and our personal
experiences suggest that human beings often get angry when they
are deeply hurt. The forms that such anger takes and the objects of
the anger can be quite diverse. It can be felt as hatred, resentment,
envy, a sense of unfairness. It can be directed at one's spouse,
family, friends, God, doctors, or society's institutions (or at one's

self in the form of regrets and self-reproach). The form and the objects are not random selections but seem to represent the most appropriate vehicles available to the one who is suffering. Even where the grieving person is aware that the particular vehicle of expression is inappropriate, out of proportion, or irrational, the feelings are very real and exert a significant influence over that person.

Implicit to most of the emotional and mental responses associated with anger is a deeply held though often unconscious belief that, magically, one could undo what has happened and the person who died could be returned if responsibility for the death could be located or the right questions answered. This is a theme that occurs over and over in the mental life of the bereaved.

Anger at the Dead Spouse. The most difficult focus of anger to reconcile is that directed at a spouse who is dead. Men and women regularly experience the sense that their spouses have left them, abandoned them to contend with the world alone, or died to hurt them. The survivor frequently feels perplexed or even guilty about harboring such feelings. "How could he leave me?" is the rhetorical question frequently asked.

> *Phyllis:* "The most difficult thing that came up was the tremendous anger that went on for so many months. That he'd gone and died on me. And having to deal with my feelings [that] there must have been something terribly wrong with me or he wouldn't have done that to me. All of the time my mind is telling me this is irrational, but it didn't make any difference. It's something you feel and you have to deal with it."

The survivor's anger is more acceptable if it is focused on the impact of the death—the spouse's avoiding help in raising children or carrying out other responsibilities—rather than the simple fact of it.

> Diane was angry with Alvin because he had not
> finished their income taxes before he died. "I could
> kill him. I wish there was a telephone up in
> heaven!"

Such anger feels justifiable where the survivor believes that the
dead spouse contributed to his or her own demise.

> Ralph's wife, Darlene, had had long-standing prob-
> lems with alcohol but had been getting help and was
> drinking less. During a visit with family, she re-
> sumed her heavy drinking over a period of a week
> and died in her sleep of acute alcohol poisoning.
> Ralph was very bitter about her death, both because
> of her drinking and because she had left him to care
> for a household with two young children.

> Lucille and Arthur had been married for twenty-eight
> years. Throughout their marriage Lucille reproached
> her husband for smoking, but to no avail. He ate and
> smoked when he wanted. "He enjoyed his vices."
> Ten days before his death, he had been released after
> a two-week hospitalization following an acute my-
> ocardial infarction. During that period, on two
> occasions, he insisted that he and his wife have
> sexual relations, and during the second such inter-
> lude, Arthur suddenly lost consciousness and died,
> confirming Lucille's worst fears. Lucille's anger was
> directed at Arthur for his lack of restraint, both for
> pressing his sexual needs (for which she also expe-
> rienced severe guilt) and for his long-standing
> indulgences. "If he cared, he would have taken better
> care of himself."

In one instance the survivor's anger extended beyond her
husband to her infant, whom she regarded as an extension of her
husband and initially as an unwanted legacy that simply contributed to her problems:

Dick was killed in an auto accident, leaving Sharon, twenty-nine, with a four-month-old son and a three-year-old daughter. "There was a lot of anger. If everything would go wrong, like the day the baby fell out of the shopping cart, I would scream in the house, 'God damn it, why did you go away and leave me to do all this by myself?' I hated him for doing this to me. I hated him for giving me a child that, of course, I wanted. I hated the baby. That upset me greatly, that I actually hated the baby. I guess until I realized that I could love him, and then he started becoming a person and then it all changed."

Yet another aspect of the survivor's anger at the dead spouse is related to the emergence of feelings that were an integral part of their relationship but have become more prominent after death because of the specific issue involved.

During their twenty years of marriage, June and Jack had done little socializing together because Jack had a great deal of contact with the public in his work, and he preferred spending his free time alone. After his death June felt isolated and socially awkward. "I had anger at him, but not because he died. We had a peculiar relationship in a way. We never did anything socially, and I used to tell him that I never felt that I was a part of him because he knew all these people and I never knew them. He was home all the time; we didn't go out. But he was a salesman, and he knew a lot of people. There were 350 people at the funeral and I got 36 potted plants, 500 cards, and I thought, 'I don't even know any of these people,' and I resented it."

Other types of angry feelings toward the dead spouse are usually not accessible early in the course of bereavement but are likely to emerge in the second and third years. These—the everyday feelings associated with the normal ambivalence that exists in all intimate relationships—will be explored more deeply in Chapter Four.

Anger at Physicians. The family doctor is the object of wrath for a great many widowed people. The most fundamental and inescapable fact is that the doctor did not save the patient. We all accept the abstract notion that everyone has to die sometime; when one of *our* loved ones is ill, however, we want that person to be the exception to the rule. Physicians are therefore given a mighty task, often in the face of very bad odds, and are vulnerable to criticism and anger on the part of the surviving spouse. Most physicians in a given set of circumstances are limited in their ability to save the patient, to be sensitive enough to the needs of the family, to be as communicative as possible, or to give sufficient time to the family. In some instances the physician may not be competent to the task.

> Glenda saw her family physician repeatedly for abdominal pain. Her problem was diagnosed as benign fibrous tumors. After several months, when Glenda's husband, Bill, finally challenged the physician, he referred Glenda to a gynecologist. "In less than five minutes' visual examination, [the gynecologist] said, 'Lady, you're in serious trouble.' He operated three or four days later, and she had cancer all the way to her liver. I really thought about suing the man but that would bring nothing back and be more frustration and anger just stirred up. I sincerely believe in my heart that a good doctor that knew his business would have given her a hysterectomy and that would have been it. That sticks there all the time."

> Rudy was being treated for severe emphysema that was in a terminal phase. He was hospitalized and being treated by a team of physicians. Several times a day, he was to be given special treatments to help his breathing. His wife, Edith, had also talked with their

family doctor, who was in charge of his overall care; and they had agreed that he would receive full efforts at cardiopulmonary resuscitation (CPR) despite his deteriorating and presumably irreversible condition. During the night Rudy's condition worsened. When he had a respiratory arrest, no effort was made to resuscitate him. Despite her efforts Edith was unable to piece together the events of the night Rudy died. She learned that Rudy had not received the special breathing treatments more than a couple of times, because of the limited equipment and staff compared to the demand, and that Rudy was "short-changed" because of his prognosis. Edith remained furious at the doctors but did not know where to focus her anger. For months she persisted in her efforts to get satisfactory answers. "It was devastating to think he was treated like that."

Harold: "There is a feeling that the people who administered to my wife's health prior to her death didn't do the best they could. Now I know that, if you look at it objectively, you can't expect everybody to go full stop on everyone all the time. [But when it is] somebody you love very much and [who] is very important to you—as far as you're concerned, they're as important as any prime minister and any president of the United States or anybody else—you want the doctors and nurses and everybody else to try real hard and to make them as comfortable as possible without pain. I felt that as long as she wasn't in any pain, the doctors and nurses should make every endeavor to keep her alive as long as possible. And I don't feel they did that. The notion seems to be prevalent in the medical field that they're going to die in a month, well, what the hell's the difference if they die a week or two early. Well, it makes a big difference to you."

Agnes: "To this day [two years later] I have kind of an anger that I harbor toward the doctors in Chicago.

It's probably unrealistic of me, or it's probably an overreaction on my part, but they kind of rushed me into it. I'll always have a doubt in my mind as to whether I should have allowed them to operate on my husband. When this happened, they just told me, they didn't ask me, they didn't give me a choice. They didn't say these are the pros and these are the cons. They just said, 'We're operating, and when we operate he's probably going to be paralyzed on his right side, and maybe he'll get better and maybe he won't. But he's got six months to live.' And I'll never be sure whether I should have allowed the operation or not. He might have died sooner, but he went through six months of agony that maybe he'd have been better off without it. It all happened so fast, and I felt I was manipulated. I even felt that maybe they used him as a guinea pig and experimented on him, because they were so anxious to operate immediately. It was the way the doctors treated me. In fact, the day the doctor told me the results of the brain scan and what was to happen, he just called me on the phone and had a very cold, matter-of-fact attitude. I wasn't even called into his office or offered sympathy. . . . I'll always have a resentment toward the doctors."

Ross: "I was mad at the world, the world in general, Dr. Cole particularly. Dr. Cole was the oncologist. He did what he thought was right, but I can still be angry about it if I want to. . . . He projected a much more rosy picture than there was. I can read, I know what the pancreas is, I know what it does, and I know that if you don't have it you're going to die. And I can read the various success levels of the therapy. I would have felt much better about Dr. Cole had he told me what the chances are. . . . And I'm mad at Smith Hospital. I'll probably continue to be mad at Smith Hospital. They run the place like—the closest thing to their operation that I know of is a large hotel in Vegas."

Melinda fought against Jim's lung cancer with everything she had, determined that together "we are going to beat this thing," despite the grave prognosis and obvious progressive deterioration and wasting that was occurring. Part of her anger at the physicians treating him was that they were not optimistic enough, even though they acknowledged that Melinda's denial and efforts "to win" had helped keep Jim alive longer than would be expected. "They were always taking away his hope." As part of her battle, she wanted to be able to anticipate anything that could go wrong. "They were always one step behind. If I anticipated something, it wouldn't be such a blow." When a complication occurred, the doctors would tell her that it is not unusual but would not predict all the possibilities. "Obviously, he wasn't the first person to have lung cancer."

Anger at God and Fate. Throughout the ages believers have struggled with questions about why there is suffering if God is wise and merciful and determines the destinies of mankind. Such issues are especially paramount at the time of a loved one's death. It is a distinctly human need to know "why" when tragedy strikes. Again, this probably reflects the magical belief that, if we can understand something, we can gain control of it, master it, and not be vulnerable to it. Even where the proximal cause of death may have been determined, regardless of whether or not there is a discernible culprit, God may still be called on to explain "Why now?" or "Why him?"

Melinda: "He brought me nothing but joy, you know. And the first feelings I get when I get like this is I think about why is he gone. Why do you have to go through so much pain?"

Carl struggled with his anger for more than two years after his wife died. He repeatedy asked himself why she was taken. He planned to ask God but was too angry to do so. He was angry that all ministers do not agree and do not have one answer to this question.

When an object responsible for the death cannot be identified, the survivors are left to rail against fate for depriving them of their loved ones, their dreams. They feel that they have been cheated, that life is unfair, and that good lives have been wasted.

Louise: "But you get lonely and I got very angry. I got mad at God, I got mad at Doug for dying. But I feel cheated. I think that's the word. I feel cheated because initially we were broke, and then we got to the point where we were able to do a few things, and then he got sick and died. And it's not fair."

Beth: "The only time I ever remember really feeling angry was about two or three months after the accident. The airline has a little monthly newsletter that they send out, and they sent me a copy of the one that was devoted to the accident. I opened it up and it had a picture of everybody from the airline. And that's when I really got mad because it struck me as such a waste of so many good people. I pounded my fist on the counter."

Doris: "It irks me that it is so unfair. We were so happy and he was such a good man. There are so many people who don't have good relationships, who aren't such good people."

The notion that it should have been someone else is common and runs through many of the themes of "unfairness." Usually, by implication, the someone else is someone who is not as kind, or worked less hard, or was not needed by a wife and children.

Anger Toward Family and Friends. The people closest to the bereaved are often the most likely to bear the brunt of anger that gets expressed outwardly. Widowed persons usually express such feelings because they believe that they are being inadequately supported—emotionally, physically, or even financially—or that they are actually the brunt of others' demands, scorn, or fears. The changing relationships with family and friends are examined in depth in Chapter Six.

Anger at Exploitation. Survivors often feel that large and impersonal institutions (especially Social Security and the Internal Revenue Service), as well as individuals, are exploiting them or are insensitive to their widowed status.

> Shirley's husband, Art, was a construction worker who was killed when a wall collapsed on him. She was forced to go through endless legal proceedings over the next four years to obtain financial security for herself and her children. She found herself furious at the company's lawyers and the frequently "accusatory" hearings. She felt that she was being punished. "I almost wish I had shot my husband so that I'd deserve the suffering I have." . . . "Another thing that really bothered me was stuff coming in the mail. Sometimes I want to send it in and say, 'You're stupid. You're trying to get a dead man to take out a $10,000 loan.' Just the frustration that you're trying to put it behind and you can't do it when things keep coming in the mail."

> Beth was clearly resentful toward the media for exploiting the crash and for the sensationalism, which she experienced as terribly insensitive.

> Earl felt frustrated and angry that the government can spend enough money to send a man to the moon

but cannot support research to provide a cure for cancer, which took his wife.

Envy. Envious feelings arise quite naturally out of the resentment one feels when one has lost love, happiness, security, or money and sees others who still have all these things. This particular emotion is often not one that a grieving person accepts very readily, since it is usually seen as petty or undignified in our culture. Therefore, when it does appear, it can be accompanied by guilt or shame, thereby compounding the discomfort.

> Louise felt envious of her married friends whenever they took a trip or went somewhere special that she and Doug might have gone. Two years after her husband died, she pulled up beside a husband and wife dressed to go out. "I wanted to roll down the window to ask the woman if she realized how lucky she is to have a husband to do activities with."

> Melinda's girlfriend had become involved with a man. Their relationship deepened, and they became engaged to be married. "She would call and be all excited about a letter she's received, and all I could say were very negative things. Then I started to realize that every time she called happy about something, it would make me mad."

Guilt

Many different attempts have been made to explain guilt. In a culture that places a high premium on control over one's own destiny (through science, medicine, law, even religion), the loss of such control—preeminently in death—places the burden of responsibility and guilt on the surviving individual. Another view of guilt, in the circumstances of a spouse's death, postulates that, since we all have innate drives for self-preservation, someone else's death represents an unconscious wish on our part (better him than me) for which we are responsible (magically) and consequently guilty. A variant of this second theme is that all intimate relationships produce ambivalent feelings in both people and that the survivor feels guilty about having (magically) caused the death through conscious or unconscious hostility. All these explanations of guilt suggest that it usually is an irrational feeling. The problem is that a significant part of human nature *is* irrational and that Western cultures (and religions) utilize guilt as a primary motivator. As a result, many people in our culture have a strong predisposition for experiencing guilt.

Few circumstances of living play such a powerful role in evoking guilt as the tragedy surrounding death. Approximately half of our research subjects were troubled by feelings of guilt. The focus of these feelings revolved around three major categories of guilt: (1) survivor guilt, (2) guilt related to responsibility for the death or suffering of the spouse, and (3) guilt over betrayal of the spouse.

Survivor Guilt. Survival guilt is seen in most circumstances involving death and destruction—wars, accidents, major tragedies—especially where a loved one dies. While elements of this type of guilt are supposedly very common in grief states, only one of our subjects explicitly verbalized this feeling.

> *Glenn:* "Why was Eileen taken and I was left behind? She was so good."

Responsibility for Death or Suffering. Much more common were survivors' guilt feelings that reflected a sense of responsibility for the death or suffering of their spouses. Some felt that their actions or decisions led fairly directly to their spouses' deaths.

> Lucille was plagued with strong, unremitting guilt for having been engaged in sexual activity with her husband when he died suddenly of his second heart attack in ten days. This guilt began to dissipate two years later, when she had an affair with a man (who did not die), enabling her to overcome both her fear and her guilt.

Eileen had breast cancer in 1968 and had a mastectomy. In 1978 she was found to have a tumor in her
brain, at first thought to be a metastasis from her old
cancer. In the hospital her doctors found an aneu-
rysm. The operation was a "success," but immediately afterward she went into a coma and never
regained consciousness. Despite his understanding of
the dangers of surgery, Glenn felt responsible for her
death because he had agreed to the surgery.

Bill's wife had been misdiagnosed by her family
doctor, and by the time she saw a specialist and her
cancer was discovered, it was too late. Bill experienced a sense of guilt because "I should have
pushed that doctor harder and sooner—maybe
Glenda would be alive today."

Usually, some grain of reality allows the bereaved person to
seize upon her own guilt and hold on tenaciously in spite of what
is obvious to others.

During the terminal stages of Jim's cancer, Melinda
was with him twenty-four hours a day, ministering to
all his physical and emotional needs: carrying him to
the bathroom, cleaning up his accidents, sleeping in
bed with him and all his paraphernalia. "They
[doctors] all said the only reason why he lasted so
long as he did was because I was so positive and
because I gave him so much attention, and I gave
him so much will to make it. . . . But I think the
only feelings I have, there was a guilty feeling that is
extreme still, and everybody said I'm crazy, but I still
feel there's something else I could have done."
Months later she heard of an herb "that cleanses you
and takes out poisons. Maybe if I had given him this,
I could have cleaned out the cancer."

Several survivors experienced guilt for indirect contributions to their spouses' deaths.

Darlene died from acute alcohol poisoning. Although Ralph had been sober for many years and attended Alcoholics Anonymous meetings regularly with his wife, he felt guilty for having introduced her to alcohol and for contributing initially to her drinking.

Melinda: "I was blaming myself for it [lung cancer] happening in the first place because, see, I had told him when we met that it upset me so much to see him smoke." He would tell her that he was incapable of stopping at that point in his life. "For the first six months after he died, I just kept thinking over and over, 'Why didn't I think of some other psychology to somehow work around the things to get him to stop smoking.'"

Jonathan: "I think there was some guilt in me that perhaps if she had been in a happier marriage situation, maybe it would have been different, because, you know, they talk about the emotional effects upon people, how they bring on cancer maybe. Maybe if she had known a different way of life and if someone else had been in her life, she wouldn't have gotten cancer as quickly as she did."

Guilt was also a manifestation of the survivors' sense of responsibility for having caused their spouses undue suffering—physically, emotionally, or spiritually.

Prior to David's ultimately fatal heart attack, he and Carol had agreed that no extraordinary measures should be taken to keep him alive. When he had his heart attack, Carol administered CPR and David lived for three months with marked brain damage before he died. "During those three months [before he died], I felt great turmoil and guilt. . . . I felt as if maybe I had interfered. So that was a deep-rooted guilt."

Betrayal Guilt. Betrayal guilt is that form of guilt that survivors experienced when they did not remain loyal to their dead spouses. However, loyalty is a quality that can be perceived in very different ways. A number of people felt guilt when they tried to get rid of their spouses' belongings or to change a room in the house. In each of these instances, the particular belongings had become a symbolic representation or personification of the dead spouse, making the act feel as if one were discarding or betraying the person or his memory. This phenomenon is examined in Chapter Four.

Another aspect of betrayal guilt is related to the sense of obligation to suffer in memory of the dead.

After three months of mourning, Ralph felt that he had pretty much recovered from Darlene's death. However, Darlene's parents were still suffering greatly, and Ralph experienced guilt because he was not suffering as they were. "I feel guilty about not feeling even more guilty." Six months later this particular guilt disappeared, but he began to experience guilt again as he became aware that he did not think of Darlene very often. When his wife's friends offered sympathy and help to Ralph and his children, only to learn that it was not needed, his discomfort increased. "Maybe I didn't care enough, or I'd be suffering more."

Donna and Ike had joked about the large amount of life insurance they had and how one of them might "bump off" the other. When Ike died in an auto accident, Donna was fairly well off financially but felt guilty that Ike was not there to enjoy the money. When she bought a new car, she was embarrassed and felt guilty to have Ike's mother see how she spent the money.

Alvin had been home and disabled for a year and a half before the heart attack that suddenly killed him. Diane was feeling considerable guilt: "I feel like I'm free and I feel guilty because I like it." She experienced guilt about "taking over his place and enjoying making my own decisions."

There is an old joke about the woman who dies and in her will indicates that she wants to be cremated and to have her ashes blended in paint, which is to be applied to the ceiling of her husband's bedroom. This story reflects one of the more common conflicts experienced by surviving spouses: that an emotional and/or sexual involvement with another represents betrayal of the dead spouse. Some degree of this sense of guilt occurred in most of those men and women who did get reinvolved, but usually it was minor and quite transient. I am not aware of any subject or anyone from my clinical experience who has suffered in any significant way from this form of guilt—probably because anyone who is still actively involved with and "loyal" to his spouse will avoid involvement with another person. On the other hand, that this phenomenon is so common most likely reflects the reality that almost all widowed people continue to experience significant ties to their spouses (see Chapter Four).

Carlene died at age thirty after a six-year struggle with Hodgkin's disease, leaving behind her husband, Brian, and their two young daughters. During the course of her illness, Brian had told her that he "couldn't live without her." Within months he had married one of his wife's close friends. At that time he was still grieving for Carlene, but he felt that he and the children needed someone else. A major source of his distress was his feeling of guilt because he was enjoying himself "for the first time in six years."

Sharon's guilt extended in many directions. "I'm the number-one guilty person. Guilty that I think I enjoy this marriage more than I did my marriage to Dick. Guilty for contributing to the [fatal automobile] accident by encouraging him to go to work that day. I thought I wanted out of the marriage—guilty about that. Guilty sometimes that my children were his children and that I'm playing a game or at least trying to make a life with Andy and make them Andy's children. Sometimes guilty about Dick's parents' relationship with me, in that I don't let it be the way they want it for his sake."

Interestingly, the only dreams (see Chapter Four) whose manifest content involved guilt were of betrayal guilt.

Ann: "I met this man and I was really attracted to him. We had this conversation, we had quite a long talk and we were interested in a lot of the same things. And I went home that night and had this dream, and it turned into a terrible nightmare. This man was with me, and my grandson called up that something was wrong, and the fellow went over to help him—and just out of nowhere these hands came and grabbed me and pulled me, jerked me back. They were Bill's hands."

While Phil was alive, Susan and her sons always hid things from him to keep him from getting upset and worsening his heart condition. There were also many things that were prohibited from the house. *Susan:* "After he died and anything major happened in our lives—when we got the dog, when we got the cat—I would dream for several nights that he was back and he was not sick. He would just be walking through the house so we would have to hide the dog and hide the cat. It was really weird. I let my son get a motorcycle, and I kept dreaming that we had to hide

the motorcycle, that we had to hide the helmet. I
knew Phil never wanted us to have those things."

Two men who were troubled with guilt for betraying their
wives both had committed these betrayals while their wives were
alive. One had had an affair during the long period of his wife's
deterioration with cancer, and the second described having sexual
fantasies about other women before his wife died. What made these
experiences of guilt so troubling, compared to those of people who
experienced betrayal guilt after their spouses' deaths, may be that,
at a deeper level, forms of "contributory" guilt were involved.
That is, somehow (magically) these men felt that their acts or
thoughts might have played a part in their spouses' deaths.
Clearly, for the group as a whole, contributory guilt was far more
lasting and more intense than betrayal guilt or survivor guilt.

Preempting Guilt. For those whose bereavement came
without warning, there was, of course, no way to anticipate the
loss or mitigate any feelings of guilt that might arise. However,
the majority of people in our study had some knowledge of the
possibility of their spouses' deaths; and these people often made
enormous efforts not only to give the most that they could to their
loved ones but also to avoid future concerns that they either had
not done enough or had done the wrong things.

Marie was forty when her mother died of cancer in
1970. "I missed her dearly when she died. And this is
one of the reasons I went into this job [as a nurse,
working with the elderly], because I felt that there
was so much more I could have done for her and
maybe prolonged her life." When her husband,
Oscar, developed kidney cancer eight years later, she
approached his care in a stoic, almost professional,
way, despite her agony. When he died, "Sure I hated
to walk in that room. I hated to close his eyes. I hated
to try and put his teeth in his head. I hated to have to
take and move his hands and wash him down good
and put his pajama shirt on him and fix his hands so

that there's no marks. . . . When the morticians
picked him up, he didn't have any bruises on him
and his body didn't smell bad. . . . I did the best I
could for him, made his last day as comfortable as
possible."

Merle: "That's where I was very fortunate. I didn't
have any guilt. You see, he was ill there for about
three years. During that time we talked it over. And I
spent so much time with him, you know, and happily and gladly, and we really enjoyed ourselves. So I
don't have any sense of guilt. It's only when you
haven't given people your love that you feel guilty, I
guess."

After Glenda developed cancer, Bill could not allow
himself to have sexual relations with her. "I knew
she was going to die and I just could not, I just could
not have thoughts of—my sex life died, that's all. I
couldn't bear to use her to satisfy my lustful gratification. I couldn't do it. I could not have loved her any
more than I did for the last year and nine months
that she lived, but I had no sex with her at all."

Regrets

Regardless of how many things one can anticipate and
provide for, and regardless of how well or completely or lovingly
a couple may have lived their lives together, when a spouse dies
there are always regrets. The ultimate regret is that the spouse
could not have continued to live, healthy and happily. Beyond
that, survivors often think back to the missed opportunities to do
something or say something that might have enhanced their
spouses' lives or helped with suffering or completed some
unfinished business.

Jeff was dying from a brain tumor. Agnes was
visiting him regularly at the hospital. "I was seeing
him two or three times a day. I'd go back and forth to

the hospital. I had seen him the night before he died; and I knew, we all knew, that his time was short because he had gotten a lot groggier and lost a lot of strength. [At other times] we never said goodbye to each other; we always said goodnight to each other. But that night he looked at me, he gave me a funny look and said goodbye to me. And it didn't dawn on me that he was really telling me goodbye. I looked at him and I wondered, the thought crossed my mind, 'Well, what's he saying that for?' And then another thought crossed my mind to go over and give him another kiss. And then I thought, 'No, if I do that, then I'll be here another half hour.' I was already late getting home, so I just walked out the door. I guess that's the thing that haunts me the most about his death, because he was telling me he knew he was going to die. He knew he was, and I should have known. I should have realized that he was really telling me goodbye. The thing I'll always feel the worst about is that I didn't have the sense to realize. If I'd have gone back to kiss him one more time, I would have felt a lot better for it."

Bill did some traveling by himself after Glenda's death. "I never take a trip without thinking of her, because I feel that this is a trip I know she would have enjoyed, even more than I have enjoyed it, and how wonderful it would have been if I had taken the trip with Glenda. She often wanted to travel more than I was willing to commit myself to travel because I said we couldn't afford it. Sometimes I blame myself a bit for not going ahead and doing these things."

At times regrets may seem trivial. Fay wished that "I had taken him some peanut brittle in the hospital; it was his favorite." Yet, beneath the surface, she was wishing to make up for angry moments and shouting in the past, which bothered her after his death.

In many circumstances the boundaries between guilt and regrets are blurred, and the survivor experiences some mixture of the two.

> Harold was prone to develop depressive moods for several years after his wife died. During these periods he was often filled with self-reproach and regrets that he had not been a more loving and caring husband and more supportive of Rose. If he had taken more interest in her health, he told himself, she might not have died so young.

Anxiety and Fearfulness

The distinction between anxiety and fear is essentially anxiety's absence of an object. Anxiety makes us feel nervous, distressed, uneasy, or unsafe, but we may not be able to identify a source directly; in contrast, we are usually afraid of something: pain, hunger, poverty, illness, humiliation, death.

While its origins may not be clear, anxiety is a universal reality of human existence. Throughout our lives we have developed ways of binding anxiety. The most fundamental and effective means have usually been through relationships; most agree that our early parent-child relationships form models for achieving a sense of security and safety, models that in many ways are reproduced in the intimacy of the marital relationship. Although marriages may have the capacity to provide for a great diversity of needs, virtually all people enter a marriage to satisfy deeply felt needs for closeness and security. Most marital relationships foster the enhancement of such needs because in marriage one's sense of security is constantly reinforced. In other words, whatever their predisposition going into their relationships, people become psychologically dependent on feeling secure. The loss of one's partner and this form of gratification can lead to a major disruption in one's security system, with a concomitant eruption of anxiety. This anxiety can remain free floating and be experienced as physiological symptoms (racing heart, shortness of breath, tingling in the extremities, light-headedness, chest pain, gastrointestinal disturbances, sweating) or psychological symptoms (fear of dying, fear of going crazy, sense of distress or dread). More frequently, however, the newly bereaved are likely to attach their anxiety to something that is reality based, resulting in more specific fears and worries.

Under the distress of the loss, the most fundamental and frightening concern for the bereaved is their own survival.

> After his first heart attack in 1973, Ted's doctors said that he would live two years. His second attack occurred in 1978, and shortly afterward he had open-heart surgery. Two weeks later he died suddenly of another heart attack. Amalia seemed totally unprepared for his death. "For me he was never going to die." Immediately after his death, she became too frightened to sleep alone and had her children—a ten-year-old boy and a thirteen-year-old girl—sleep with her. She had had the same feelings of terror at age thirteen when her mother died. "I thought I was going to die. I was very scared. Worse than now." Four months after her husband's death, she still felt unsafe at night, continued to keep her children's beds in the same room with her, and put a chain against the door at night. She also put up a second fence on her property and was considering having a burglar alarm installed in the house. In the seventh month, Amalia had a dream that her husband was ill and in bed. Someone came to the front door. She went to the door and was shot. Her children remained in the bedroom. "I don't want anyone to steal those children." She then had an alarm system installed and began to sleep better, though her children remained in her room. She kept one of her husband's sweaters on a conspicuous chair so that if a burglar came in he would think there was a man in the house. Early in her second year of mourning, these fears abated and her children went back to their rooms.

While this example is extreme, many survivors, particularly women, experience a great deal of vulnerability, a lack of protection, a sense of not being safe.

> During the first year after Edwin's death, Doris felt insecure and unsafe in her home, especially at night. When Edwin was alive, she had never felt that way, even when she was alone. She had felt safe and protected. On the advice of friends, she rarely told anyone that she was widowed, maintaining her phone listing as "Mr. and Mrs." She became more cautious about her comings and goings, was careful to leave a light on, and asked neighbors to watch for her. "When someone calls asking for my husband, I just say he's not here now and can I take a message and that way you find out who it is." While her insecurity did not impede her functioning, it was nonetheless disturbing. After a year, Doris's fears subsided, as her feelings of self-sufficiency and independence reemerged.

This experience was clearly regressive for Doris in the sense that it propelled her backward to an early stage in her own development, when she had felt incapable of providing for her own security. Yet Doris is a very capable woman who had been quite autonomous and independent prior to her marriage. The emergence of such feelings does not necessarily imply that the individual in whom they occur had only the relationship as a resource of protection. It does point out the extent to which a long-standing and intimate relationship fosters reliance on the relationship while it is there, perhaps contributing to some "atrophy" of the "muscles" of self-sufficiency.

Usually the surviving spouse is clearly aware that the dead spouse provided security.

> *Annette:* "It's a fear because I am basically standing alone. With the support of a husband, whether he

was good or bad, he was there. It was like a wall that protected me from the elements or something."

At times, these basic fears emerge as a direct reflection of the enormity of the loss—that is, that it will happen again.

Ike was killed in an accident one evening after he dropped off Donna at home and went out for groceries. Donna became involved with Cliff shortly after Ike's death, and they had an off-again, on-again relationship in which she was extremely dependent. One night they had a fight, and Cliff was about to leave. Donna felt desperate and told him that if he left, she did not want to see him again. "I realized that I couldn't let him walk out of the house. I was afraid I'd never see him again. Ike left on an errand and I never saw him again."

Here we can see how the sudden death has left its imprint in the form of a continuing fear that another loved one will suddenly die. This fear of becoming involved with another person who will become ill or die is quite prevalent and, for many people, has as one of its major consequences the avoidance of intimacy (see Chapter Six).

For most survivors anxieties interact with real-life responsibilities to produce worries. Everyone has worries and concerns. In a situation that provides us with a general sense of safety and security, we usually face these worries with aplomb except when the real-life demands are overwhelming. For the bereaved the everyday problems and concerns frequently seem overwhelming. To complicate matters, severe economic hardships often are created by long-standing illness, large medical bills, loss of income, lack of insurance, and even disability on the part of the survivor. Among the more pressing worries are those focused on the welfare of the survivor's dependents (see Chapter Six).

Viola had cared for Lyle through six years of illness from cancer. For the last year, he was paralyzed and could not speak. When he died, her only sources of income were her eighty-one-year-old mother's Social Security and a small amount of money from a part-time job. She was constantly worried about her mother's health and about making ends meet. Her mother's eyesight and hearing were failing, and she suffered from depression. Her condition put a tremendous burden on Viola, but she would not consider sending her mother to "a home" for her own convenience. She seemed to be constantly struggling to survive. "I just worry about getting through the month and getting the bills paid and food on the table and the car kept up."

Feelings of Helplessness

Humans are basically adaptive creatures and, as we shall examine in Chapter Three, usually have a large repertoire of coping mechanisms available to them to maintain some internal emotional stability. When these mechanisms fail, when someone is unable to cope, a sense of being overwhelmed engulfs the person. This frightening state, one in which people often feel as though they are "going crazy," is usually transient, though occasionally prolonged, and is commonly experienced by many newly bereaved. It most frequently occurs after the sudden emergence of very intense affect, often the acute sense of loss, at the deepest emotional level. It may, however, follow prolonged emotional assaults of lesser intensity.

Some people tend to contain their feelings, to constrict the range and depth of emotion. For such people the threshold for feeling overwhelmed may be higher.

Doris was very uncomfortable each time she found herself "giving way" to her grief, often berating herself for being out of control. "You know, for two or three months I was afraid to drive the car because I was afraid I wasn't in control of myself."

Some of the surviving spouses had this sense of being overwhelmed or helpless not because of the excessive demands on them or because of their intense feelings but simply because they felt incapable of performing certain tasks or assuming certain roles: for women, writing checks to pay bills, making financial decisions, changing the oil in the car, or disciplining the children; for men, frying an egg, calming a crying child, or asking someone out on a date.

> Yvette and Sal had been married for twenty years, during which time Yvette had never worked and never developed interests independent of Sal's interests. "I was always very reliant on Sal, who was quite reliable and fostered this situation. He made all the major decisions and I went along." After his death Yvette was paralyzed to make any decisions and could not face trying to balance her bankbook.

Forced by reality to face their sense of incapacity, bereaved persons typically experience a great sense of accomplishment and growth (Chapter Seven). Sometimes, however, the *feeling* of being overwhelmed becomes a reality; that is, the person becomes unable to function on an ongoing basis. The person who develops clinical depression (Chapter Five), for example, will manifest a diminished capacity to cope with any demand or feeling.

> Throughout the five-year period after her husband's death, Shirley experienced recurrent periods during which she could not cope with the struggles confronting her: unresolved feelings about her husband, the social stigma of being a widow, manipulation by the legal system, the demands of raising her children. She would frequently bemoan her fate: "God, I wish I had help." For long periods she could only sit and cry. "I'm ready to lock myself in the house. I don't have the energy to cope. I feel backed into a corner, and I don't know where to turn." She felt that nothing would work and that her problems had no

solutions. "Sometimes I don't try. I quit. I just sit. I'll give up, I'll quit. I'll say 'That's it. I'll never try again,' and then I'll kick myself in the rear."

Intrusive Images

The events that occur in proximity to a spouse's death often remain as images in the survivor's mind—a series of photographs with all the detail and color of the experience. Survivors, even those who describe themselves as having poor memories, are often astonished by the details that they can recall with these images. The images can appear spontaneously, "out of the blue," without any clear stimulus; or they can be evoked by any "reminder." They are experienced as intrusive, since people cannot keep them from pushing their way into consciousness and, once there, they are hard to dispel. Their presence and their content may also evoke strong—and frequently painful—emotional reactions.

> *Sharon* [after two years]: "I think about the accident. I think about hospitals. When the situation arises, I'm afraid sometimes to go in, but I do. There is a smell about hospitals that, when I smell it, I start to feel faint. And it's the same smell that was in his room. I can smell it on 805 [highway] if the wind blows the right way. I don't know what it is that smells that way, but it will immediately trigger a very fearful response. I don't think a day goes by that I don't see the accident in my mind—that I don't remember the whole thing in fast-forward motion."

In the early weeks after a death, these images will frequently appear whenever the person's mind is not actively engaged, causing an internal distraction. The bereaved are particularly susceptible at night when they go to bed. At such times, when it is quiet and there are no visual stimuli, there may be a "flooding" of imagery.

Throughout the day (four months later) Gloria found herself replaying the events of her husband's death: his collapse (heart attack), her attempts to help him, the trip to the hospital. "It's especially bad at night. I can't get it out of my mind." She would brood about it until she finally fell asleep, but she would then awaken in the middle of the night with clenched teeth.

Sometimes these recurrent images are focused not on the events immediately surrounding the death but on aspects of the dying process, particularly the change in the dying spouse's appearance. Frequently these images are so powerful that they replace earlier images and memories of the dying or dead spouse. A long period of time often passes before the survivor is able to retrieve more pleasant images of the loved one (see Chapter Four). For some people there is a quality of torture to these experiences.

Melinda: "I would visualize what he looked like toward the very end, because he obviously got very peaked and very, very white, and he was losing the use of his arms and legs to the point where he couldn't move. He physically couldn't move, so I would move him, you know, just so he wouldn't atrophy or anything. All these things, the last two weeks, over and over and over. I couldn't remember anymore, and I still can't to this day [nine months later] remember, the very happy moments we had. They're gone. I can't, I can't. I tried my best, and that's the only way I can picture him."

The replays of these scenes can produce an intense desperation as the survivor tries to change the outcome. Some of the more voluntary retrievals of these images may represent efforts to gain control over what has happened by replaying the scenes with different endings.

A few people reported premonitory experiences related to

their spouses' deaths. These, too, have strong potential to become repetitive and intrusive.

> *Louis:* "Two weeks before her death, I had a dream. She and I were in a car, and it seemed that we were going around the world like this. It was the big world like this [moves hands] and we were on this road going around it, and all of a sudden both of us flew out of the car. I reached for her and she kept drifting away and drifting away and I said, 'Honey, come back!' and I said, 'Oh, my God, she's gone!' Two weeks later, she had her death [sudden, unexpected]. That was the strangest thing that I ever had happen to me. That premonition, you know." Four months after Karen's death, it plagued him. "It's constantly bugging me."

Mental Disorganization

During the early state of numbness or shock, the survivor's mental processes are usually crystal clear, organized, and precise. At times the person believes that he is actually thinking better than usual. After the emergence of painful reality, there are dramatic changes in the mental capacities of many survivors. They experience a state of mental disorganization, a breaking down of many of the processes that result in clear and coherent thinking. They become distractible, confused, forgetful, unclear, incoherent, unable to concentrate. These states are found most frequently in the early weeks of bereavement but may last for several months. Their presence extending past six months is quite unusual and may represent manifestations of depression (see Chapter Five).

Many things may contribute to this disorganization, including rapidly changing emotional states (particularly anxiety), intrusive images, and perhaps disturbances in central nervous system functioning brought about by intense stress (see Chapter Five). This dysfunction often leads people to believe that they are "going off the deep end."

Gloria: "I was very distracted. I'd start one thing and then I'd think of something else that had to be done, like another phone call I should make. So I'd go and make that and I couldn't remember what I was doing when I started."

Lucille: "The worst point was that I couldn't concentrate to read and I've always been a reader. I'd start reading and then before I knew it my mind started off into my own feelings. I became emotional, I couldn't detach myself enough to concentrate on what I was reading."

Phyllis: "I would really work hard and I was very inefficient, you know, and I'd perseverate and walk around and not know what I was doing. I couldn't get stuff done quickly, you know, and I'd get sidetracked."

Ann: "I was just on automatic and, no, I had no goals even for lunch on the same day or any plans. I couldn't make any plans because I would forget them if I made them. I was just kind of like in a vacuum. I was lost."

Relief

Accompanying all the painful, disruptive, and disorganizing emotional and mental processes that follow the death of one's spouse may be a profound experience of relief. It is usually one of the sequelae of death following a prolonged illness. The illnesses commonly encountered in this study were from cancer and heart disease. In these circumstances the couple often have had to live with and share long-standing illness with its pain, limitations, or deterioration of functions and an anticipation of death at some unknown time. Many couples utilize this time creatively and productively, but it is nonetheless a period of great mental suffering. The sense of relief felt by survivors can be as much a result of their own suffering as of their spouses' suffering.

Relief of the Dead from Their Suffering. Regularly, the first element of relief is focused on the suffering of the spouse who has died. Certainly, where pain has been severe, the surviving spouse will invariably experience the relief on behalf of the dead spouse— especially when the couple have grown closer and more intimate during the terminal phases of an illness and when the caretaker has assumed a mothering role (both men and women) and become exquisitely sensitive to the feelings and needs of the dying spouse.

> *Linda:* "You feel like this is the end and he's at rest and he's peaceful now. It is, it's a big relief, because as you're going through this, you have this feeling within yourself and it feels like when it's over, why, you feel happy for him that he's not suffering any more."

Spouses also were aware of other forms of suffering, brought about by progressive body wasting and deterioration of functions, that affect the dying person's sense of self.

> *Melinda:* "You can imagine, as a male and as having a normal ego, [what a terrible blow it would be] to have your wife having to help you by holding on to your penis to help you go to the bathroom . . . or help you make bowel movements or do any of these things."

> *Joanne:* "He [her husband, Larry] liked to swim and ski and jog and go motorcycle riding and bicycle riding and work in the yard and go camping. He would have been a cardiac cripple in constant angina pain."

One can see in Joanne's words that her anticipation of Larry's suffering from chronic cardiac disease has made his death more acceptable, and this theme, that the person is better off dead than suffering, serves as a great source of comfort for many survivors (see Chapter Three).

A sick or dying spouse's personality change also can cause suffering. Such changes can occur from a number of causes. At times they are a manifestation of the difficulties a person may have in adapting to or coping with illness.

> Phil's cardiac condition was a cloud over them throughout much of the ten years he and Susan were together. For the last four years, he had been fairly incapacitated at home. He had always been a rather taciturn, emotionally withholding, and somewhat domineering man; but over the years he became more and more bitter as his illness disabled him. His personality traits became exaggerated. He was increasingly withdrawn, less open and affectionate, and highly critical of his family, unable to appreciate how much everyone had done to accommodate to him. Susan had to struggle to maintain the perspective that his behavior was in part a product of his illness.

Personality change can also be a function of the dying person's illness itself, especially where the brain is invaded by a primary tumor or metastasis or where a disease such as cancer has disrupted endocrine or other metabolic functions. In people who have cancer, there can be striking changes in the personality, including violent or other irrational behavior. Under these circumstances the healthy spouse may feel that the loved one is already gone. Some of these changes may be reversible with treatment (or with discontinuation of some medications that can also produce such changes), but in the terminal phases, death will seem a blessing.

> *Fran:* "You know, it was all so awful. But now, when I look at it, I can see that it was for the best, you know, because it really wasn't him anymore. The doctor told me that in the last stages I wouldn't be able to handle him, but I kept him home the whole time. The last two days of his life I wrestled with him

because he was hallucinating. You know, he was a
fireman all his life and he kept seeing these fires and
he'd want to get me out of the house. So I actually
wrestled him bodily for the last two days of his life,
and I knew he couldn't live like that. I wouldn't want
to live like that."

Relief for the Survivor. The boundaries between the
experiences of the dying and their survivors are probably least clear
in the area of felt suffering. At times the feelings of both are in
synchrony: each feels the other's pain empathically. At other times
the dying spouse may be protected from pain (in whatever physical
or emotional form it may manifest itself) by innate coping
mechanisms, the disease process, or medication, whereas the
healthy spouse still feels pain as he observes the processes of
wasting, dysfunction, and pain in the loved one. In such instances
the only protection available to the surviving spouse is some form
of withdrawal or premature detachment, and the price for this
protection may be quite high in the form of subsequent guilt and
regrets. Thus, the only acceptable resolution for this form of pain
is death, and the subsequent relief can be dramatic.

Ross: "There was relief for both of us. The whole
thing took place over a period of, depending where
you want to start counting, three years, eighteen
months, a year. The last period of about six weeks,
this would be after the chemotherapy and there was
no doubt in my mind. We took her to the naval
hospital and that's when she died. That six-week
period—there was no doubt in my mind that she was
terminal. And it's a relief, yes. Guilt about the relief?
Yes. But . . . it was more relief for her than it was
relief for us. We knew she was in a great deal of pain.
We knew that it bothered her a whole lot. She was
incontinent for the last four weeks. That bothered
her. And the fact that she couldn't take care of
herself. Dying with cancer people are not allowed to
die with any degree of dignity, no way."

The survivor may also experience relief because he is now released from the at times overwhelming tasks attendant upon caring for a dying spouse, among other responsibilities.

> June developed a brain tumor that was diagnosed when she was six months pregnant. She had brain surgery with subsequent weakness of the left side of her body and significant psychological impairment. Perry, a young professional, spent the next two and a half years attending to his wife and infant son, in addition to his own practice. When she died, he experienced a tremendous sense of relief from a huge ordeal. "It was a relief for myself, it was a relief for her. She went through an awful lot. . . . It was killing to me because I was spending all my time in the hospital, and I don't know if you can appreciate how uncomfortable a hospital is for a visitor, but it is—and physically uncomfortable, too. I mean beyond just absolutely spending the time with her until they shooed me out, going home, eating something out of a can for dinner, and then, you know, getting up the next day and doing it again. I was literally exhausted, I think, at the time she died. I was very close to the end of my rope, I think, emotionally and physically and every other way really."

Relief for the survivor can also be focused on the continuing sense of fear and dread with which one may have lived for many years where the spouse had an illness that is potentially but not necessarily fatal.

> *Bobbi:* "I was aware of the absence of fear after a while, after he died. There was a constant fear. He'd had a heart attack. Was he going to get well? Was he going to get sicker? And I wasn't aware of it while it was there, but when it was gone, I thought, 'Gee, I had that hanging over my head all the time,' and it generalized into other areas of money and all kinds of

things. And once that fear was gone, it was a good feeling. Not to be afraid."

Susan: "I felt relieved that he was not suffering anymore, but I felt relieved for myself, that I wouldn't have to watch it anymore. I wouldn't have to wake up in the middle of the night and listen for him breathing, which I did for years practically. He knew and I knew that he was going to die [heart disease] and that it could happen any minute. It's just that it went on for four years, four and a half years, and it was kind of like waiting for the other shoe to drop. You didn't know whether you could do this or that. I'd run out to the store, and in the middle of grocery shopping I'd just feel like I had to run home and see if he was okay. And, of course, he always was. But it was that panicky feeling that maybe I wouldn't be there when it finally happened. After a while it begins to really get to you and you just put on this big show. You're smiling all the time, and inside you just want to scream. It's very hard to live with, terribly hard. So I think that when he did finally die, I think it was a relief, although maybe I didn't admit it for a long time."

Relief from Conflicts. Death also can provide relief for those who experienced highly conflictual marital relationships. On one end of the spectrum are those fundamentally unhappy marriages in which the couple remained together for convenience but where intimacy was long gone and the attachment between the two people was limited. In these circumstances relief was not necessarily mixed with other feelings. More common are the many marriages where two people feel very attached to each other, love each other, and feel a deep sense of commitment to each other but also have significant areas of conflict. In one sense this is an almost inevitable aspect of any relationship; even in the best relationships, areas of conflict will exist. Consequently, when one's spouse dies, one is likely to experience some relief. Where the relief is minor, it will certainly be overshadowed by the tremendous impact of one's grief, but as the tumult subsides, the survivor may begin to experience this relief as a sense of freedom. Where the area of conflict was greater, the sense of relief will be more significant. Under these circumstances the surviving spouse is buffeted about by alternating or coinciding feelings of intense grief and relief.

> Following Phil's death, Susan at first experienced relief from both her constant fears and vigilance about Phil's health and her awareness of his suffering. As months went by and she was less in the throes of her acute grief, she began to examine her marriage, particularly her relationship with Phil, more closely. "I find that I'm beginning to discuss it with other people who have had problems with their marriage. I could never do that before. I always thought it was wrong to discuss a marriage that ended in death. That was something that had to stay inside me." As she looked, she saw problems on both sides, and she experienced relief at being extricated by death from a difficult yet committed relationship.

At times the conflict may be outside the marital relationship; yet it can be just as disruptive, especially when it involves other family members living in the home.

> Lyle was retired and spent most of his time with Viola during their ten years of marriage. Viola had a grown son from a previous marriage, and her mother lived with them as well. "Lyle and I actually did pal around together. We got along famously. There was just the outside influences of my mother and my son that caused our problem. . . . He developed a hatred for my child. Instead of disciplining him, he would hate him more and threaten him. And my boy was scared to death. So many times I repeated, 'How is this going to end?' It was just unbearable sometimes.

Oh, it crushed me. And then as he became more ill, he became more embittered toward my son, and I guess the illness was just part of it. It just seemed like death was the only way out, and I became reconciled to that soon."

Apathy

The problem of apathy—the lack of interest or motivation to carry out one's usual tasks or pleasures—occurs with most bereaved spouses. Its appearance in time is variable, sometimes within days or weeks of the loss, at other times in the second year. It may be transient or may linger for months. People have little difficulty in describing it, but its nature is unclear. At one level apathy appears to have its roots in existential issues of motivation (see Chapter Seven): there has been a fundamental change in the meaning of life and the reasons for doing things.

Seven months after Ray's death, Daphne went through a period of months when she carried out responsibilities but felt apathetic and without commitment toward her job. She often wondered, "What's the point? Why should I try to do well anymore? I have a stack of outstanding performance awards from past jobs, but these now seem meaningless."

Apathy may or may not result in paralysis of action, depending on its severity and other motivational forces. At times the apathy is directed at one's optional activities rather than the "necessities" or the needs of others.

Joe experienced intermittent apathy for over two years. At first, he did only what was necessary and kept revising his determination of "necessary." He felt "no incentive" to do household repairs or housework, even the jobs he enjoyed the most. "When my wife was alive, I used to do a lot of work around the house. She'd say, 'Would you do this?' Of course, I would do it. But that incentive is not there anymore, you know.''

Apathy can also be experienced as the psychological counterpart of a syndrome of depression, with physiological manifestations that accompany it. Most frequently the association occurs between apathy and lack of energy.

Harold: "The overwhelming feeling is that you don't give a damn. It feels like my feet are in lead boots. I have no energy or zest for life.''

At times the apathy will fluctuate with mood alterations.

Shirley: "Well, Monday I just sat down in a chair and looked out the window and had four cups of coffee. Didn't do a darn thing. I just didn't care. Just didn't give a darn. Then I kicked myself and on Tuesday ran out and got my ears pierced and bought a guitar and signed up for guitar lessons. . . . Sometimes you can go for a week and don't want to do anything, and then the next week you just dig in and work, work, work.''

In the extreme, the apathy can evolve into a loss of concern about any aspect of living and leave the way open for suicidal thoughts.

Susan: "I didn't care. I didn't care about anything. There was a point where I didn't want to be on this earth either. . . . But then I would look at the kids, and I've never been one to think, 'Well, I'll kill myself,' and yet the thought crossed my mind, you know, a number of times, but never to the point where I actually planned it or plotted it. . . . It was just a matter of not caring.''

Susan's suicidal thoughts are typical of those evolving from a state of apathy and as such were not a threat to her. Certainly, suicidal thoughts are always a serious manifestation of distress. In the bereaved they are most often seen in the context of significant depression. Depression and depressive syndromes, together with the psychophysiological concomitants—sleep and appetite disturbances, mood and energy changes, and other physical responses—often seen in bereavement, are discussed in Chapter Five.

Loneliness and Being Alone

For most people in most marriages, the marriage relationship provides an anchor to which other attachments, particularly children, connect. At the beginning of the marriage, it may be the only attachment. After children have individuated and left home, it may again assume preeminence as the guardian from loneliness. When death disrupts this attachment, the survivor is vulnerable. Initially, survivors must contend with the profound sense of loss, a specific loss of a specific person. They are alone again in a very specific way, regardless of whether family and friends surround them. What evolves over time is not simply the loneliness that is specific to the spouse one has lost—the yearning, the pangs, the missing—but also a loneliness that is nonspecific, an awareness of being alone and an aching to have an attachment. This is a form of pain that can last.

> *Sharon:* "Well, I don't know if I can describe the loneliness, but it's a glass without water. It's empty and void and . . . [has] nothing to fill it. I remember it. I can't describe it any more than that. It was the worst thing. Not having anyone to talk to or anyone to touch. [After two years] they can still be there [the feelings]. I can feel lonely with a lot of people around. I don't know what it is that I need at that moment, but I know I'm lonely. But it's not the same now because I know I can have it [contact with others] if I make an effort."

> *Lucille* [two years later]: "I'm lonely. I mean, I'm
> still lonely. I have family, I have friends, but I am
> still lonely in the sense of not having a person, a
> human being, who is with you all the time, who
> shares everything with you."

Even as the pain of the loss has subsided significantly,
loneliness may take its place as the predominant form of suffering.
Frequently this suffering serves as an impetus for many to develop
new relationships. Yet for many survivors loneliness remains a
continuing legacy.

Unlike loneliness, being alone is not an emotional state but
simply a fact. For the bereaved it is a fact that can lead to many
responses. Frequently the survivor's initial response is a self-
conscious awareness of being alone.

> *Beth:* "I feel not lonely for people or anything. I've
> got plenty of friends and people to be around, but I
> feel alone without Barry. It's such a big difference."

This awareness of being alone requires adjustment of one's
bearings, especially where one has been unaccustomed to this state.

> *Shirley:* "I've never been alone. Well, when my
> husband went on cruises I was alone, but I'd go back
> home and visit relatives. [And] I knew he was coming
> back. I went right from my family, you know, being
> a daughter. Well, I graduated from high school on
> June 2, turned eighteen on June 12, and got married
> on June 25. So being alone I find very hard to
> handle. I really do."

> *Ross:* "I never realized, I never thought about just
> how couple oriented I was. Not necessarily doing
> things as a couple, but the number of decisions that
> I make, just day-to-day decisions that always consi-
> dered both of us. That sort of pairing. Everything
> was geared to always thinking about two. Nothing

was really geared to just thinking about one. That strikes me, I still feel it."

Aspects of being alone can be very different even where one has had previous experience with it. Concern for safety or security can accompany it.

"Being alone" struck Doris dramatically when she first traveled alone. She experienced fears about traveling alone, concerned about being detached from contact with her loved ones. "For the first time, no one would know where I was."

For some, being alone in certain circumstances can trigger off the strong emotional reactions that any form of reminder about their loss can create.

Bill had a great deal of difficulty tolerating being alone at first, because so many things reminded him of Glenda. "I consider eating alone the worst condition of widowhood. Going to bed alone is not as difficult as eating alone." As time went on and his acute suffering subsided, he became more and more able to tolerate both being alone and eating alone.

After the initial period of suffering, even where elements of suffering continued well into their second year, many survivors experienced being alone in a positive way.

Bobbi: "If loneliness means missing him, I've experienced it. But other than that, I can't say I've experienced loneliness at all, and I can't remember when I ever did. I treasure being alone, my times alone, just as I treasure being with people."

Merle's son was graduating from college, and she gave him a trip to Europe as a graduation gift.

Anticipating his being gone for three months, she thought, "Gee, I'm going to be alone, how great!"

Positive Feelings

Widowhood is often portrayed as the death knell to happiness, now and forever. Certainly, in the early stages of their bereavement, many men and women believe that must be true. At first it may seem that all joy has been taken out of life. In reality, however, most widowed people are capable of and do experience a variety of positive feelings even through the most difficult periods. Grief does not necessarily consume a person's whole existence. People usually have the capacity to operate on multiple levels, at times immersed in grief and at times thinking, feeling, and interacting "normally." Under most circumstances these states will alternate depending on the freshness of the wound, the resources available to the bereaved, the reality demands on the bereaved, and the emotionally laden stimuli confronted.

The usual manifestations of positive feelings, such as joy, peace, or happiness, are experienced as oases amidst the sorrow, associated with particular activities or interactions with family or friends, at work or with hobbies, in distraction or escape. However, they may appear with the death itself and as part of the experience of relief.

> *Linda:* "Your first feeling, even after a funeral and everything, I felt there was a peace and a joy within myself because I knew that he was at rest, you know, and his year of misery was over and I was happy in that respect for him."

Another positive feeling associated with the experiencing of one's spouse's death and the process of dying is the sense of pride that one has given one's spouse as much love and caring as could be given.

> *Louise:* "My husband had a brain tumor and he suffered for about fifteen to eighteen months. By the

time he died, he couldn't move any part of his body
except his right arm from the elbow up and turn his
head. He couldn't blink his eyes, he couldn't swal-
low, and I prayed for over a month that God would
take him. I didn't want him to suffer any more, and
it was hard taking care of him. I kept him home. I'm
glad I was able to because that's where he wanted to
be, and I was surprised that I could. I kept on
working, and my children were a blessing. My
daughters took care of him during the day, and I kept
him nights and weekends. And it was a rewarding
experience. I felt prouder of that than probably
anything else in my life."

The "oases" of happiness are most likely to be with loved
ones if they are available to the newly bereaved (see Chapter Three
and Six).

Pamela: "With my kids, my grandkids, I have seven
little granddaughters—when I can be with them, I
think that's the happiest period. I'm looking forward
to my son coming home the end of June. My oldest
boy will be back. I guess that's the happiest time,
that's when I can be with my family."

Taking measures that remove one from painful reminders
has had a dramatically remedial quality for some bereaved.

Fay felt continuously overwhelmed by the feelings
that were triggered in the home she shared with
Gilbert. Six months after his death, she moved away
and felt "reborn." She cried for joy for two days after
moving into her new house. "I can't believe that
things are so good. It feels so great to be alive!" She
also felt some guilt about being happy.

The bereaved are often faced with a dilemma when they
experience good feelings. Somehow it just doesn't seem right for
them to feel that way, even for brief periods, in the context of their

tragedy. As a result, they may have feelings of guilt, a sense of betrayal; or they may resolve the dilemma by adopting a different perspective: that they have suffered enough, paid enough dues, and now deserve whatever happiness life has to offer. This sense of entitlement may enable the widowed person to enjoy aspects of living with much less conflict.

> Susan felt resentment because her husband was sick during much of their married life and her life consisted of taking care of him. She felt that life was passing her by and that she now wanted some enjoyment. "I feel almost like I've paid my dues, and I just want to do what I want to do."

The bereaved person learns to live with the fluctuations that occur with good feelings and experiences alternating with pain, which can often intrude in the midst of enjoyment.

> *Lucille:* "I've had feelings of contentment. Yes. I can't say no because I've traveled. I've gone to visit friends, relatives. I went back to the East Coast and I went to a wedding. I had a great time. I enjoyed myself with everybody, and all the time I was out there I felt fine. I did have feelings when I got together with some of my husband's relatives, cousins who are still couples who still have each other. So two or three times I felt this great pain inside and I'd say to myself, 'He's missing. He should have been here with this group and he's not here.'"

As time goes on and the wound heals, the likelihood of being able to experience enjoyment and happiness grows. A general state of well-being is unusual, though it can occur, with the first year of bereavement. More often, the achievement of this state is not accomplished until the second and third years of bereavement and at times later.

Effects of Prolonged Illness on Emotional Responses

Because of the prevalence, both in this study and in the general population, of deaths following prolonged illness, it is important to examine the responses of survivors to this situation and contrast them with the experiences of those who lost their spouses suddenly. Obviously, there is no direct benefit in discussing which situation is more or less advantageous, since people have little choice in the matter. At the same time, knowledge of any differences may help to elucidate the processes involving grief. Whatever processes of grief are initiated by the knowledge and course of illness usually begin, at variable time periods, before death occurs, and the role of time becomes an important factor. These processes may be quite distinct from others that do not begin until the point of death.

Initial Reactions. Learning about a potentially fatal or debilitating illness in one's spouse often has the same impact as a sudden death and may have a more intense impact than the subsequent death after the illness. The initial emotional reactions in such circumstances are very similar to those of people whose spouses died suddenly, and include numbness, shock, and disbelief, with great anguish following closely behind.

Anguish and Pain. The periods of greatest anguish are those experienced during the course of a life-threatening and/or progressively deteriorating illness. The spouses of cancer patients in particular suffered tremendously during the course of their spouses' illnesses, often experiencing great relief by the time death occurred.

Glenn found himself overwhelmed at times after learning of Eileen's breast cancer. "I suffered more over that, I think, than I did [when she died], and it could be that that experience was enough for anybody to have to go through, I don't know. But I did an awful lot of breaking down at that time. I mean I had to stop the car on my way home at midnight and stuff because I'd bawl so bad for her."

Susan: "The anguish was when he was alive, that was the anguish. While he was sick, the clenching of the fists and the kind of screaming inside because I was at a loss to help him. And it was the constant trips to the hospital, and many times they would admit him and I'd come home and I would not know whether he would make it that time or not. Those were the times of anguish, not afterwards."

Agnes: "I was told right from the start when he got sick that he had six months to live and that was my worst period. By the time he finally died, it was in a way a relief."

Loss, Loneliness, and Anticipatory Grief. The suffering of the spouse during the illness is probably just as painful as that of the survivor of an abrupt and unexpected death, but it is qualitatively different. During the course of illness, the spouse is contending with the pain and suffering of the spouse as well as the personal hardships of caretaking, maintaining hope, supporting the spouse physically and emotionally, and adjusting psychologically to the impending death. For all the suffering experienced by the caretaker, however, the spouse *is* still alive and frequently available psychologically to share some of the burden. The caretaker may deal with fears but not yet with real loss, or loneliness.

> *Linda:* "I think my roughest period was from the time that I found out until he did pass away. Only I still had him at this point. I could still share with him. The loneliness set in after he died."

The notion of "anticipatory grief" (Aldrich, 1974; Gerber and others, 1975) suggests that prolonged illness prepares the survivor for the loss in a way that eases the grief once death occurs. However, the *loss* of one's spouse does not occur until the point of death, and there is only one way that anticipation can lessen the emotional impact of the actual loss itself; that is, the knowledge of impending death can lead the surviving spouse to detach emotionally in a premature fashion. While this happens for some, for others the prolonged period of illness is at least as likely to intensify the bonding between a couple and make the feelings of loss greater once death occurs.

> Melinda's struggle with Jim's cancer intensified their relationship in many ways. Melinda became inseparable from Jim physically, attending to his moment-to-moment needs on a twenty-four-hour-per-day basis, nursing him with greater degrees of intimacy and greater exposure to his most private moments. At the same time, she fought furiously to deny his illness, to preserve hope, and to maintain a positive spirit. All these actions conspired to make their relationship more real to her and deeper than it had ever been.

> During the years after the onset of his illness and before his death, David and Carol became much closer. They talked about all aspects of living and dying, and they got to know each other's innermost thoughts and feelings in a way that they never had before. "We had a much deeper communication than we had had all of our married life."

Anger. The quality and objects of anger may be different for those whose spouses go through an extended illness, especially where the survivor has held out hope for the spouse's recovery. Under these circumstances disappointment and anger may be directed toward the physicians involved. On the other hand, where death has come suddenly and without warning, anger toward God, the fates, or oneself may be more prevalent.

Guilt and Regrets. Sudden death frequently leaves the survivor with many unresolved and unexpressed feelings, unfinished business, and missed opportunities to say goodbyes. In contrast, anticipation of one's spouse's death offers opportunities for repairing old hurts, giving the most of oneself, and helping the survivor feel that the spouse's death was as appropriate and acceptable as possible. Many survivors felt very proud of their efforts, their dedication to their spouses. Since they had done all they could, they had relatively few guilt feelings and regrets. If life had to end, it could at least end under the best of conditions, with the most fitting expression of shared love.

 Chapter 3

How Bereaved People Cope with Emotional Pain

From the late nineteenth century until today, the fields of physiology and medicine have progressively delineated the processes that regulate the body's internal workings to achieve homeostasis: a state of balance in a complex, continually active system. Changes in the steady state are detected by sensory devices, information is fed to regulatory organs, and changes are initiated so that homeostasis is maintained. Such processes certainly occur within the central nervous system and the brain, and some of these have been defined by neurophysiologists. Those relating to the interactions of mental and emotional states with behavior have not yet yielded to research and remain in the province of observational descriptions. Clinical observations, however, indicate that there is a parallel system of homeostasis for our psychological processes. That is, people are equipped with coping mechanisms that protect them from the impact of psychological trauma and allow them to maintain some internal sense of well-being. We are fundamentally adaptive creatures.

The death of one's spouse brings with it great mental and emotional turmoil with which the survivor must cope. Chapter Two described the many painful feelings of the newly bereaved. The problem of adaptation to such tragedy is complex because the bereaved person must cope with opposing and at times competing forces. On the one hand, there are the psychological assaults of immense and intense emotional pain; on the other hand, there are the realistic consequences of the death—the disruptive changes in the outside environment and the survivor's internal environment. When one is faced with intense emotional pain, the primary task of coping mechanisms is to shut off the pain by any means available; when one is faced with disruptive environmental changes, the primary task of coping mechanisms is to confront these realities directly and continuously until the best level of adaptation is achieved. However, facing reality invariably initiates the pain, and the pain invariably initiates psychological mechanisms whose purpose is to work against reality and dampen the pain. It is in the context of this ongoing dilemma that the grieving spouse must live and cope.

> *Phyllis:* "You're in a black velvet bag, and you protect yourself and shut out all kinds of stuff and only let things back in very, very gradually as you're able to handle it. For me it took two years, two good solid years."

From an adaptive standpoint, what happens practically is that the bereaved person—sometimes consciously and sometimes automatically and unconsciously—seems to regulate the amount of emotion that he can tolerate, using whatever innate or learned coping mechanisms are a part of his repertoire. There is a general tendency for people to use customary styles of coping—that is, the coping mechanisms that they have habitually used to counteract normal day-to-day stress. However, if these mechanisms prove ineffective in the face of overwhelming emotions, some people will revert (or regress) to other coping mechanisms, particularly those that seem less mature or adaptive. An analogy used by Freud to describe these mechanisms or "defenses" is that of a battlefield where the enemy—in this case one's emotional pain—is advancing. The first line of defense is the most powerful and experienced group of troops. If they are overridden, each succeeding line of troops may be less effective and experienced. In the case of psychological defenses, the "front lines" of defense are usually the most tried and true. Once these are overwhelmed, those that are left are likely to be either less adaptive, seldom used, or retrieved from previous discards. At times the bereaved are forced, by virtue of their pain, to "throw everything they've got at them" and utilize multiple levels of defense.

Finally, a number of coping mechanisms are unique to bereavement, although they may be seen in similar form in many kinds of loss. These are the mechanisms by which the relationship with the dead spouse is continued, so that the survivor can negate the pain of loss. Because of the uniqueness and importance of these mechanisms, a separate chapter is devoted to them (Chapter Four).

Numbness

A discussion of numbness was presented at the beginning of Chapter Two, although, strictly speaking, it is primarily a mechanism of protection. Its inclusion as an emotional state is supported by its prevalence among the newly bereaved and by the fact that, even as a defense, it assumes a status that is central to the emotional life of the surviving spouse.

Disbelief

Another form of protection, often accompanying numbness in the immediate aftermath of death, is the sense that what has happened has not happened, a sense of disbelief on the part of the surviving spouse. Our minds are capable of great deception, including the denial of reality, in the interests of protecting us from pain.

> *Doris:* "I didn't believe he was dead. You know, I just didn't believe that. I thought he was teasing me and not waking up."

> Although her husband had been dying of lung cancer over a period of four years, Blanche anticipated that the process of deterioration would be interminable. She had a timetable that involved progressive wasting, incapacity, and confinement to a wheelchair, but it never included death. "I never really thought he would die."

The bereaved express this disbelief in many forms, but all suggest that the enormity of what has happened cannot be fully comprehended or accepted.

Pamela [after ten months]: "It still feels like a bad dream."

While the sense of disbelief subsides over the early weeks and months, remnants of it can persist for years in subtle forms.

Lucille [after two years]: "There's still a thin little something of disbelief, but it's very, very thin. Mostly I have accepted it, that he's dead and gone, and it's just whatever doubt is left is still a little bit of disbelief but it's very, very thin."

One factor that may contribute to the persistence of the sense of disbelief is the experience of knowing intellectually, or by report, that one's spouse is dead yet not having seen the dead body as the final confirmation. This shred of doubt or hope can interact with other forms of denial that are operating to keep the bereaved in that state of continuing, though minuscule, disbelief.

After the plane crash, there were no remains to be identified, and Beth had only her memories of Barry as healthy and happy. While all the evidence surrounding the flight and his presence on it confirmed the reality, even three years after his death, Beth said, "There are still times when I can't believe it really happened."

Emotional Control

Most of us have some capacity to control our feelings voluntarily, at least in certain situations; and some people—by dint of their personalities or through learning or the training they received from their vocation—seem to respond to most emotion-laden situations with control or constriction of their emotional responses. From the perspective of the newly bereaved, this capacity can provide a very effective means of warding off the painful emotions that are prevalent early in one's grief.

At times control is utilized as a tool, for specific occasions, and then put back in its place when not needed, or when one can afford to let in feelings.

> *Bobbi:* "I learned to control it [anguish] while I was around people, while I was working. If I was driving or at home, I'd just let go and howl."

The ability to suppress one's feelings may not occur simply through will alone but may need to be accompanied by further internal dialogue to strengthen one's resolve through some form of rationalization.

> *Linda:* "Well, a lot of times when I'm having dinner in the evening by myself, and I think, 'Gee, here I sit alone,' I begin to feel lonely and I miss Paul. And then I get up and walk around and think, 'Well, this is silly. You're going to be alone maybe for a long time, so why spoil your dinner [over] something that you can't help.' So then I just erase it out of my mind, and I can go ahead."

This defense may work effectively at times and fail at others, depending on the stimulus and its intensity.

> After two years Beth said that she thought about Barry almost as much as she ever did. She was aware that at those times she was likely to be flooded with feelings about him. "Usually I can shut it off fairly easily, but at times they may snowball and it gets much harder."

For people who are predisposed to maintaining control, the defense seems to fall into place naturally during bereavement.

Glenn had spent his career as a fireman. He had taken bodies from aircraft crashes, accidents on highways, fires. He had seen ground-up bodies and "every kind of horror." Except when children were involved, he never had any strong emotional responses. He felt that he had "built a wall" around himself for protection. Throughout most of Eileen's terminal illness and after her death, Glenn maintained a relatively unemotional stance and rarely let in feelings. (As shown in Chapter Two, however, he did experience very powerful emotions when he first learned about his wife's breast cancer.) "I guess maybe I've been more or less of a realist. I've seen so much death and so much discomfort from it that maybe there was a shield built up around me, I don't know. I guess when you are around that sort of thing all your life, you're just kind of in a vacuum. Because if you weren't, you couldn't stand it. I don't think you could anyway." Even so, there were many times during his bereavement when Glenn did experience transitory feelings of sadness and longing, usually accompanied by a welling up in his eyes.

Even people who do not manifest emotional constriction as a generalized state may become constricted under the stress of a particular situation and for a certain time period.

Perry [describing his emotional reactions at the time of June's death]: "I went on very, very tightly at that point. I had pretty much, I think, psychologically battened my hatches down very, very tightly. There was very little give there for me. And I think that when she died, I think I maintained the same sort of posture. And it took me a long while to unwind and to let things flow a little more naturally in my own life."

As with all coping mechanisms, there are advantages and disadvantages in being able to limit the experience of one's emotions. In the extreme, where such emotional constriction is complete, the bereaved person is not actively grieving, and the psychological needs related to facing emotional realities are stymied. Further, while the internal experience of pain may be avoided, the negative impact of the loss in other areas—relationships, health, work—may be profound and perhaps even worsened if the bereaved person is unable to experience the pain or to release it.

> Phyllis became totally constricted after Bradley's sudden death. "I cried once for two hours after he died, and that was it. I shut the door on it. It's like I put it away in the sewer and I didn't open it up until spring vacation [six months later]." She tried to work with everything bottled up inside of her but was disorganized and ineffective as a teacher until she became physically ill for a week. "The next week was spring vacation and I was off anyway. It was like I was a tragedian in an old Greek play. I mean I tore my hair and I beat the wall and I went around screaming. And I did that for four or five days. I absolutely went bananas in my house. And that was it. All that crap I had been handling or not handling, refused to even look at, it all came out in one week."

Altered Perspectives

We are indeed fortunate as humans to be endowed with the capacity to think and reason. Nowhere are these abilities more useful than in dealing with emotional distress. They allow us to figure out ways to alter the meanings of the events we experience and thereby protect us from the impact of the meaning, which we would have perceived as potentially devastating. Through the use of intellectualization, rationalization, and humor, we are able to make life bearable where it may have been miserable.

Intellectualization. Intellectualization is a coping mechanism that is closely related to emotional control. It is the means by which emotional control is frequently obtained. Its essence is a shift in perspective that allows the person who would be experiencing an emotion to step outside of a situation and experience it as an uninvolved observer. This distancing maneuver can help a bereaved person ward off the pain of grief. Sometimes the simple fact of studying and observing one's own or someone else's bereavement can provide a temporary relief from suffering. This form of intellectualization is examined again in Chapter Eight.

Intellectualization was a prominent element in the study described here. An important part of the research design involved the promotion of intellectualization, since we asked people to describe what happened to them and thereby encouraged them to translate emotionally laden material into words and concepts. Some of our subjects actually changed their style of perceiving events from an emotional and painful mode to an intellectual mode. However, a number of the subjects already utilized this mode as a characteristic of their personality and, thus, as one of their "usual" coping mechanisms. This characteristic can be observed not only through the substance of what a person says but also in the style of language, which is distant, impersonal, and often technical or clinical. Furthermore, the content of speech usually reflects or suggests underlying emotions, but the style precludes their emergence.

> *Harold* [discussing feelings of guilt]: "I have [had guilty feelings] but they're not guilt in the sense that—well, of course, a lot of this depends upon one's philosophical or religious outlook. My religious beliefs are that we're all of us prone to do wrong and we do, in fact, do wrong much of the time despite our best efforts not to and that one of the aspects of God's relationship to man is that he does proffer forgiveness of sin for those who believe. I had to accept the fact that where I may have done wrong in the matter of administrating to my wife's health needs, where I might have been a moving force to help improve

things and I wasn't, it wasn't because of bad inten-
tion. I did the best I could at the time. Such mistakes
as I may have made were part of the human condition and that I'm sure she forgives me and God
forgives me and in view of that I'm just going to have
to forgive myself, hard as that might be on myself."

Here Harold is obviously struggling with his sense of guilt and
feels it deeply. At the same time, his perspective and style allow
him to neutralize and obfuscate the intensity of his feelings with
words and abstract concepts, using both intellectualization and
rationalization.

Like all coping mechanisms, intellectualization has its
adaptive and maladaptive components operating simultaneously.
It protects from what may be too painful and wards off what may
be useful or necessary to confront.

Rationalization. Of the purely psychological coping
mechanisms—in distinction to those, such as avoidance or
distraction, that also involve behavior and interpersonal interactions—by far the most prevalent (and, in this study, essentially
universal) mechanism is rationalization. By adopting an altered
perspective, an individual can change an occurrence whose
meaning is painful or devastating into something acceptable or at
least bearable. The application of logical thinking can transform
the most awful truth into a much better truth. One is still left with
something that is a truth and not simply the product of a "trick of
the mind." What dampens the pain is the shift in focus to this
other truth, finding something good in what otherwise seems bad:
"Every cloud has a silver lining." Rationalization is remarkable, a
powerful tool that allows human beings to salvage almost any
situation. This capacity to neutralize pain is an extremely
important form of adaptation.

In the bereaved, rationalization takes many forms but is
mostly represented by a series of variations on a few major themes.
The first such theme is "The deceased is better off this way." By
this particular manifestation of rationalization, the bereaved
person can experience relief when the spouse dies, especially after

prolonged illness and suffering. The pain of loss is mitigated by the survivor's sense that the deceased is free of pain or humiliation, at peace, or saved from a condition of continuous disability or suffering.

> Art's industrial accident left him damaged inside and outside so severely that he never recovered and died in the hospital two months later. Shirley described her daily time in the hospital chapel. "I'd go down and I'd say, 'Let him live. Let him live.' Then a cardio-vascular surgeon, a friend of ours, came up one day. A big man and very active, he says, 'I wouldn't want to live that way.' So I went down to the chapel and I said, 'Okay, I'm not going to be selfish and say make him live, we'll take him any way we can get him. You know what he can handle and You know what my kids can handle and what I can handle, so do what's right.' So I felt at peace, you know."

A second type of rationalization takes the form "Things could be worse."

> As Joe struggled with his feelings of loneliness and longing for Loretta, he searched for a way to rationalize her death. "All I can think of is that maybe I'm better off alone than if she were alive and so sick."

> Phyllis was able to see Bradley's sudden death as an act of love. "His last, greatest gift to me was that he died before I would have to take care of him. It was all meant to be the way it was."

Rationalizations of the "things could be worse" type often are provided by friends, family members, physicians, and others who sincerely desire to ease the bereaved person's pain and cannot think of other ways of being supportive. The bereaved person may reject these offers, regarding them as poor substitutes for genuine emotional support. However, where the bereaved person is receptive, the reasoning can be helpful. Physicians are in a particularly powerful position to provide or reinforce rationalization both prior to and after the death of a spouse.

> Daphne frequently focused on the unfairness of Ray's death. "I talked to my husband's doctor when he was dying, and I was all upset and I said I couldn't understand it. And he said, 'All I can tell you is that there is another patient with a brain tumor who is nineteen years old, has never been married, never had a family. Your husband at least had his career and he had a family that loved him and cared about him.' Looking at it from that point of view, how can I be angry?"

The focus of rationalization is not always on the fact of the death but may be on other areas of discomfort or pain related to bereavement.

> Beth had always been an even-keeled, controlled woman prior to Barry's death. In the first few months, she was distressed by her seeming loss of control, created by the emotional turmoil at the time. She found some relief from this feeling by reading *Widow*. "That was the best part about reading Lynn Caine's book. She was so bad, and that made me feel not so bad."

A third theme is "We were lucky to have what we had." Utilizing this form of rationalization, the bereaved person is able to find comfort by shifting the perspective from the pain of death to the happiness and love that once existed. Again, one sees how the change in focus helps the survivor achieve a very different emotional state. The cliché usually applied to this theme is "Count your blessings."

After six months Viola missed her husband but was no longer experiencing much emotional distress. "I haven't cried for him for two months. I had him with me for those sweet, precious ten years, and I'm reconciled to that."

Carol went regularly to the cemetery to visit David's grave. She always felt better after her visits. When she went there on Father's Day, she saw a Father's Day card written by a small child. "I had a good feeling that at least my kids had their dad. There are a lot of blessings."

Finally, the bereaved may rationalize by saying "I'm better off now." Bereavement brings with it numerous changes, among the most striking of which are the strengths that develop in the bereaved (see Chapter Seven). As a result, many widows and widowers are able to rationalize the deaths of their spouses on the basis of these experiences of growth and personal development. A great number of bereaved, particularly two to three more years after their spouses' deaths, attest to their sense of being more independent, stronger, and more mature by virtue of their experience. Interestingly, and predictably, all of them agreed that they would revert to their former selves, sacrificing this growth, to have their spouses alive and healthy again.

Because of the nature and intensity of the emotional turmoil experienced by the bereaved, the coping mechanisms described here are rarely, if ever, completely effective in dampening feelings. Their success, where it occurs, enables individuals to proceed with the tasks of living without unmanageable duress. At times nothing works, and the grieving spouse is left with his suffering unchecked. At other times coping mechanisms such as rationalization can take hold only after the most acute pain has subsided. There are those who find a partial solution through rationalization but then are unable to accept the results or reject them specifically because they offer a solution.

Ross: "I'm not willing to rationalize it. I'm willing to rationalize it to the extent that she could not have lived. I'll rationalize that her death was good in that it relieved the suffering, took away the pain. That's as far as I'd go and as far as I'm willing to go."

Carol: "I remember one time—I just looked out the window and I happened to see an older couple walking by holding hands. And I just got very, I don't know if it was envious or very angry, you know. I thought, 'Well, now, look. They've got each other and I haven't [anyone]. It's just not fair.' And I would tell myself, 'Well, you know, life wasn't meant to be fair.' " Still her anger and pain persisted.

For all her efforts, Carol could not arrive at a perspective that would ease her mind. Solutions do not always exist for relieving the pain.

Humor. Humor represents an extension of the principles of intellectualization and rationalization, as well as an amalgamation of both. It assumes a stance outside of the experience or as an observer of it and allows one to reflect on what is happening. In addition, humor transforms what is essentially tragic into its opposite—the comic or absurd. The bereaved may utilize humor to ward off acute emotional turmoil (gallows humor) or as an ongoing means of dealing with chronic distress. Frequently a survivor will carry on humorous conversations with or about her spouse, avoiding the painful aspect of the spouse's absence (see Chapter Four).

Carolyn: "I have his [Sam's] truck. It needed three quarts of oil and I said to the girls, 'Oh, wherever your Dad is up there he's saying, 'Take care of that truck. Keep oil in that thing. Check the oil.' Because he was always fussing at me about it, keeping air in the tires and all that kind of stuff."

Humor is used to deal with other issues that may trigger off difficult emotional responses.

> Carolyn's daughters helped her a great deal in staving off her loneliness. She had some concern about being too needy and a burden on them. "They would probably call even if their dad were there. [Jokingly] I wonder if they have been giving me permission to remarry so they can get me off their backs."

> Eighteen months after David's death, Carol was struggling with the idea of having to find direction in her life. "I have no desire to remarry. I'm interested in building my own life rather than duplicating what I had. I've never had to deal before with having to build a new life. I'd like to figure it all out within thirty days."

> Anxious about remarriage, Marie responded to her daughter's inquiry, "I spent twenty-six years of my life making one man miserable and you want me to do it again?"

Faith

One of the more powerful and effective means of coping with a spouse's death is faith, the belief in God. While this belief can at times be shaken (Chapter Seven), where it continues to operate, the bereaved are able to deal with their losses, and the accompanying pain, through a number of different aspects of their belief systems. Religious faith enhances coping in the bereaved by facilitating acceptance, providing meaning, offering help and support, reassuring the bereaved of a continuing relationship with the deceased, and combating loneliness.

Facilitating Acceptance. Religious beliefs can provide a structure within which death has a defined position, and religious training prepares people to accept death.

Marie: "I was brought up in the Episcopal religion to firmly believe that in our lives days are numbered by the hairs on our heads. When our time comes—whether we are sitting down eating a meal, driving in a car, or anything—when it is our time, we're going to go. And there is nothing that is going to stop it, you see. So, therefore, when his time came, with his illness and everything, I said, 'Well, his time has come.' It helped all of us to accept it—through our religious training."

Linda: "I felt that Paul had made his peace with God and that was the most important thing. He was ready to meet Him, and you have to do this in our religion. It's on a one-to-one basis. Somebody can't die for you and go to heaven for you. It's something that you do yourself. It's one to one with God. It's you and God. But I did not feel angry at all about Paul's death because I understood it enough. I knew he couldn't live. His body, his time had come that he had to go. We were born to die."

Furthermore, faith and deep trust in God enable the bereaved to accept what happens as His will.

Agnes had been romantically involved with several men during her twenties but had "passed them all up for one reason or another." After thirty she began to see that time was passing her by, and she wanted to experience motherhood. "If I didn't have children, my whole life would be a waste." She became depressed and withdrawn but after several weeks resigned herself to accept whatever might happen in her life. Shortly afterward Jeff stopped at Agnes's office to meet friends of his with whom she worked. Jeff and Agnes fell in love, married, had children, and were happy for twelve years. "I always felt that it was kind of like a little miracle the way it happened.

Over the years I have developed a real trust in God. Then when my husband got sick I really kind of adopted the same philosophy about it. I felt that, well, he came into my life like that and he was going to go out of my life and there wasn't anything I could do about it. I had to accept it and be grateful for what I had."

Offering Help and Support. Religious beliefs can provide widowed persons with a sense that there is someone there to help them cope with their suffering and with the difficult tasks ahead.

Daniel: "When I feel I have no direction, the first thing I do is to pray, turn it over to God. Ask for help."

Morrie: "The belief in the Supreme Being has helped. She [Pauline] has gone on to another experience. Through my religion I can get assistance with any problem that I might have by simply turning [it] over to the Supreme Being. My belief was strong before she died and has continued to be strong."

Promising Continued Relationship with Spouse. Perhaps the greatest comfort provided for the bereaved by religious beliefs is the reassurance that the deceased will be provided for in the hereafter and that, in many religions, the two will be reunited in heaven. In essence, the relationship will continue and the sense of loss is attenuated (Chapter Four).

Linda: "I feel like Paul has gone on into the heavenly realm and I feel that now I know that he's there and I want to prepare myself down here so that I will be able to—I don't know if I will know him there or he'll just have that peace."

Ann: "It is my belief system that, we believe in reincarnation, and I believe that Billy will be born again. I just hope he waits until I get there and maybe the next lifetime we'll be together all our lives instead of just a small part."

Viola: "There was very little mourning actually because death to me is just the door opening up another forever life and so it was no feeling of an ending, you know."

Combating Loneliness. Implicit in many of these vignettes is the spiritual reality that the bereaved person is not alone, that God is present to share the grief. Religion and prayer can also provide the bereaved with the comfort and support of the church and its congregation, or a forum to promote greater closeness with family.

Ralph: "As far as going to church, we've never been that type. But I've got a deep feeling for some type of Supreme Being. I don't know if it's God. I can remember a couple of times where we'd be sitting, maybe eating dinner, or usually with one of the children I could kind of tell that they were still upset, keeping a lot of it inside. We'd just kind of hug and say, 'Let's say a prayer together.' I don't know, I think just touching and hugging helps."

Avoidance

An integral part of the coping repertoire of most bereaved people is avoidance. Avoidance is a learned response that develops as soon as a man or woman perceives, consciously or unconsciously, that a given stimulus serves as a "trigger" to set off painful feelings of loss. The intensity of this painful experience may be sufficient to develop, rather quickly, an avoidant response for the same stimulus. Thus, if a picture of her deceased husband serves as a painful reminder of a woman's loss, she may learn to avert her eyes when approaching the site of this picture or she may remove it from the wall. Another characteristic of such avoidance is that it may generalize to the point where any reminder will trigger the same response and need to be avoided. For some survivors the trigger may be any symbolic representation of the dead spouse and lead to greater and greater degrees of avoidance. For others there may be only very specific triggers, often a symbol of the "essence" of one's spouse.

The situation often creates a heart-rending dilemma. On the one hand, the triggers are painful and there is a powerful psychological need to avoid such feelings. On the other hand, avoidance itself brings about its own pain because the reminders that are avoided may also be the most important living representations of the dead spouse, the continuing embodiments whose avoidance or discard may heighten the awareness of loss. These objects or experiences may be sought out for their value in perpetuating the sense that one's spouse is still present (Chapter Four). This dilemma is usually resolved by temporizing measures wherein belongings are set aside, and thus are not lost, but remain out of sight.

> *Bobbi:* "I wouldn't look at his pictures. I wouldn't go through his clothes or through his things. It was about a year before I was ready to go through his things, except the things that I had to, personal papers for tax purposes, that sort of thing."

> Lucille couldn't bear the daily reminders of Arthur and very soon after his death disposed of them. "I got rid of everything, all his clothes—everything. All I've got left are just, I've got his watch, I've got his glasses. I have those things in a drawer and I don't want to look at them. Occasionally I take a look. I see the watch and I even tried it on one time. I thought, 'Gee, it would be nice if I could wear it. I should wear it.' Then I'd take it off and I can't wear it."

Lucille is struggling with both sides of the dilemma: trying to free herself from the pain yet unable to relinquish these important belongings and obvious symbols of Arthur's existence. Many bereaved are able to act on one side or other of this dilemma, but others are stymied in the middle, able to go so far with their actions but then forced to retreat. At times friends or relatives carry out tasks which the bereaved cannot.

> *Glenn:* "I had pretty good friends that took care of a few things for me, so I didn't have to clean out her personal effects. They took care of all of that. It probably helped a lot, I don't know. If it had been up to me, the stuff would probably still be there."

When the survivor is confronted by triggers at every turn, there is often a press to make other changes in the home. The bedroom can be a particularly evocative place.

> *Sharon:* "I sold my bedroom set. It was the first thing I did, because no room in the house bothered me as much as the bedroom. I guess I could figure out why, because that was our room. His things were in the dresser and it was his dresser, so I got rid of the whole thing and got one dresser that was mine. Then there was no memory of him standing there or putting something in the dresser."

Occasionally, a survivor finds that getting rid of clothes, furniture, and pictures or making other changes in the home fails to provide relief and therefore takes more extreme steps—moving to a new residence or even a new city—to escape the memories. From such dislocations in the lives of people already in the midst of emotional turmoil and social upheaval, one would expect significant disruption. Yet the sense of relief that often accompanies these moves attests to the intensity of the suffering that precipitated them. This drastic action is not lightly undertaken and is often not successful, since it creates other problems; in particular, the survivor may begin to miss what he has left behind, the very things that he was trying to escape.

During the course of bereavement, the breadth and varieties of experiences, situations, and personal items that serve as painful reminders to be avoided speak to the creativity and symbolic capacity of the human mind. One is continually surprised and enlightened by the myriad forms taken by these symbolic representations (see Chapter Four).

> For years Linda and Paul had spent their weekends at a cabin in the country. *Linda:* "I have gotten in the car and driven out and maybe come within five miles of it, turned around and come back home. That's one hurdle that I haven't gotten over yet [two years later] because he loved that place so much and every weekend we were out there almost, and it was his life, his place." She could not buy persimmons. "Persimmons were one of his favorite foods and I went to get some the other day to make some bread for my son. I went to pick the persimmons up and I had to walk away." She also had to avoid music. "Certain music—this is the reason I stay away from some of the music. Especially some songs, the love songs, you know, the music he played—it'll set me off."
>
> *Phyllis:* "Well, there's one thing I've never dealt with yet, and I don't know whether I ever will. They had a memorial service at the school, and the kids made all of these little folders for me and they decorated them with crayons and painting. They wrote all these nice things—children in his class and other kids that knew him and loved him. I've never been able—I tried to read them once about a year after he died. I couldn't handle it. I just absolutely went bananas. I threw it all back in the box. It was just going to reactivate everything."
>
> *Shirley:* "I haven't been to the hospital for a year. The last time I went by the hospital, it just turned my stomach. I had to get out of there."
>
> *Merle:* "There were certain places that Jonesy and I would go out to eat, particularly breakfast every morning. There's one place in particular we went

very often, because Jonesy liked it, liked the girls that were there. It was just a little cafeteria sort of place, and they knew us there. And it took me a long time—it was over a year before I could go back."

Ross: "We [Ross and son] learned quite shortly to avoid things, places particularly, that my wife liked. We went to a play we'd seen together and had to leave at the end of the second act." Minor changes in tradition also helped to avoid painful memories. "On New Year's Day we had prime rib instead of the usual ham."

Avoidance generally takes several different courses. The first is that, through repeated exposures to painful stimuli, some bereaved are gradually desensitized to triggers and learn to tolerate them. Because of their use of avoidance, they may not initially encounter the most painful stimuli but eventually are able to expose themselves to them as desensitization proceeds with milder triggers.

Bobbi describes the "dosing," or gradual exposure to one of her painful triggers, music: "Music would make we weep—songs that were important to us. Usually I was in the car or at home when I heard the songs that would make me cry and I would just go ahead and cry instead of turning [the radio] off. Some things I would go through and others I wouldn't."

Joanne's approach was even more confronting: "There were times I listened to the radio and it brought back a flood of memories. These were songs that we had danced to. It was very painful. So I turned the radio off. Then there were a couple of times I thought, 'Wait a minute. This radio is going to be here forever. You're going to have to listen to it.' So I turned it back on. I never turned it off again."

Another variant is the spontaneous resolution of avoidance with time. Here presumably as the wound heals, the bereaved sense their lessened vulnerability and expose themselves to the previously painful stimulus, with the resulting less intense response and lessened need for continued avoidance.

> *Gloria:* "I'm a great collector. I have letters that my husband has written to me all my life, including the time he was in the service. I read some of the letters he wrote when I was in Minnesota in '76. About two weeks after he died, I just sort of ran across them. It really made me feel terrible, so I put them back in the drawer and decided I wouldn't do that for a while. I have done it since, and it does make me feel somewhat sad, but at the same time it makes me feel good, if you can understand that. He was a loving and nice person."

> Susan had to go into the coronary care unit as part of her new job. She had been through it often with Phil. She reacted with feelings of great distress and depression, feelings that were short-lived and that disappeared when she went out with friends to a movie that night. Still, she was angry at herself about her reaction. "I thought that I had gotten over it." Months later she returned to the unit and felt proud of being able to accept the "challenge" without fear and with little reaction to the visit.

For some survivors there may be an isolated area of avoidance that becomes encapsulated and continues unabated indefinitely. In effect, a permanent compartment in the psychological life of the bereaved remains emotionally untouched and unapproachable despite the individual's recognition. It is not confronted, and there is no opportunity for it to resolve because of the continued avoidance.

> Early in her grief, Beatrice found herself unable to go walking where she and Fred had frequently walked together. Over time she ceased to avoid these places and felt free to walk anywhere. However, five years after his death, "I cannot open his trunk or read any articles he wrote."

Probably the most striking and at the same time least dramatic form of avoidance is the generalized avoidance response that occurs at the onset of bereavement and continues unchanged. Here, in a sense, the surviving spouse goes forward and "never looks back."

> John and Connie had been extremely close, doing everything together during their thirty-three-year marriage. When Connie died unexpectedly in surgery, John went into shock and could not talk with anyone. His son took care of the funeral arrangements. John felt constant anguish, worse when he confronted anyone they knew, and began avoiding former friends. He could not bear going to church without Connie, because it reminded him that "she should be there with me." At the same time, he could not tolerate being alone and would not go anywhere without company. He could not look at his wife's pictures for two years and was never able to visit the cemetery. After six months he began seeing a woman regularly. He came to interviews accompanied at times by a clergyman or his new girlfriend. During the interviews he avoided emotion-laden material. When efforts were made to examine his feelings, he repeatedly said, "I try to stay out of that." He would not allow himself to think about Connie but "only the good times we had. I try to keep out of these emotional situations. I try not to feel sorry for myself." He and his girlfriend were very active playing golf, taking trips, never allowing him time to think about what happened. Five years after

Connie's death, John maintained the same stance. "I don't think of her much. I'm afraid I'd get all wrought up."

Being Busy

The coping mechanism felt to be the most effective and adaptive by the widows and widowers in the study has been their involvement in useful activity: work, school, housework, hobbies, volunteer work, or any activity in which they could invest themselves, focus their energies, and actively distract themselves from their grief. Clearly, being busy is a form of avoidance, but one with a useful product.

The bereaved are usually able to identify the specific emotions with which they are contending and from which their being busy offers relief.

Marie arranged to have her nursing duties during night shifts because "that's the time you feel for them and you're the loneliest."

During the first weeks after Eileen's death, Glenn was bombarded by self-recriminations, sadness, and tears that he could ward off only by refocusing to something else. "As long as I'm busy, I'm all right."

Bill: "I was interested in my work and I've always enjoyed people. I kept busy, I was doing all the work I could. I feel that kept me from many hours of time that I might have been brooding and hurting much more than I ever hurt. It frightens me to think that I might have had as much as six or eight more hours a day just to let my thoughts dwell on the greatest tragedy of my life. By being occupied with things, making a living, doing something constructive and worthwhile, I think I stole some of that time away from that grieving period. I think it's important to steal all the time you can away from it."

Harold: "In the beginning my loneliness was and still is very much more apparent at night. I used to make a practice of never being home at night because it was so difficult for me to put up with an empty house. I can pretty much stay at home now [two years later] in the evening without getting too depressed as long as I don't let it go on day after day after day."

Primary benefits are derived simply from being busy, no matter what the activity is, as long as the person feels involved in it.

Sharon: "I'm a fanatic about cleaning and I guess I probably polished everything that I could find constantly."

Joanne: "I worked myself to death cleaning the swimming pool. Larry always took care of the pool and so that was a kind of therapy for me. I'd get out and really work, work in the yard planting things, planting new things to take care of."

Earl: "I hadn't started my garden yet, so I went out there and dug a great big hole. I mean I just went out and kept on working out there in the yard to get rid of my frustration. I filled the hole back in again and then I dug another. That seemed to help."

Melinda: "I go to school from 7 in the morning until 3 in the afternoon. I come home. I have a friend that I fly with and we go flying. I go to bed at 9 o'clock, get up at 3 o'clock in the morning, and I start studying. And I just keep myself busy at all times. Everybody says, 'Gee, you're handling this so well.' And I think to myself, 'Little do they know this is a big front.' As far as I'm concerned, the only thing that keeps me going is being totally busy. The moment I'm by myself, I'm dead."

One of the beneficial side effects that accrues from such intense activity is exhaustion, which is frequently welcomed, particularly in helping the newly bereaved to sleep.

> *Carolyn:* "I was working my fanny off, lugging and lifting those guys out at the VA [Hospital] in neurology and neurosurgery. I went home pooped. I went home so pooped that I didn't have time to do or feel a lot of other things other than just get some food down me and maybe look at the paper and fall into bed."

Investment in activities paid off in dividends in many other ways; in particular, it helped people find meaning and direction in their lives.

> Merle found that, during the first few weeks of acute mourning, her work offered her reassurance about herself. "It convinces you that you're still intact at a time when other things don't seem like they're going right. When you feel like, 'Gee, I'm not really working the right way,' and then you're at work and you still function, you think things must not be all that bad."

> *Carol:* "I just don't think I could have made it without work. I got up—it was hard to get up in the mornings and I was really relieved when I got to work. And I worked with children, so I had no time and I got lots of love. You know the rapport from three- and four-year-old kids is delightful. They love you just like you are every day, and I knew that there's no sorrow connected with the kids. So it really became therapy."

> Fran decided to keep the boat she and Boris had spent so much time enjoying, even though Boris thought it would be too much for her to handle. She developed a sense of mastery from the constant work she did in

keeping it in shape. It served as a focus of social activity as she began to charter it for trips. "My life revolves around it."

Earl became politically active in a struggle with the city over a dump site that the local community felt was a danger because of a reported increase in cases of cancer among local residents. He had been involved in a citizens' group before Rita became ill [cancer], but his investment and the anger directed into this project increased after her death. Thus, he was able to stay busy in a cause made all the more meaningful by the nature of his wife's death.

Shirley was floundering for almost a year after Art's death, when she decided to become a race driver. At that point she felt she had "found a niche" that provided her with much activity, interest, excitement, and a new social milieu.

Louis spent almost two years brooding and pining after his wife died. He was retired and had few outlets or interests in his life. On a trip to visit his aunt, he discovered a neighbor of hers who was building porch swings for a living at the age of eighty-nine. Louis was enthralled, suddenly seized on the notion that he ought to build these, and purchased the plans from this man. He felt rejuvenated and began producing porch swings furiously and enthusiastically. "I've sold ten of them already. It's a redwood swing. Wish I'd brought a picture to show you. It's really something. I think I've produced one of the most beautiful porch or patio swings in the country."

Passive Distraction

At some time or other, most people in the general population utilize the mass media—television, radio, newspapers, and books—as part of their day-to-day repertoire of coping with life's stressors and its accompanying emotions. Aside from being informed, we seek out an easy means of being entertained or simply distracted. Such conveniences are also popular means of coping for the newly bereaved, though usually more for their distracting qualities than as sources of information or esthetic pleasure.

> *Bobbi:* "For several months I watched the boob tube, almost anything that was on. I could sit there and watch it. All kinds of crap I wouldn't turn on before or since. It would be like reading fiction. Escape, I suppose, is what it felt like. Now I rarely watch television."

> *Merle:* "I used reading and I didn't read anything worthwhile. I found myself immersed in mystery stories. You didn't have to really use your mind. It was just something that took up time."

> *Linda:* "I have a stereo and I will turn my stereo on. But when I have these feelings of loneliness and I'm not really depressed—but it's just the emptiness that I feel—when I play the music I play light music. I don't go into these sad, sad songs or anything. At other times it doesn't matter what is playing, but during these lonely times I just like to have something light and happy."

At times the media can provide reminders that are comforting, bringing back cherished memories.

> *Doris:* "Well, one thing I will say about television, I think it's good therapy. I really think it takes your mind off things. There are things that I saw with Edwin, especially this family in London at Christmas time, and I saw it on PBS. That's the last thing we saw together on TV. I sort of relived that evening together when I was watching it—in a positive way."

One aspect of the electronic media that may be unique to the bereaved, or at least to people who are alone, is that it provides for many people a form of companionship, a buffer against loneliness or the sense of being alone. This property is described regularly as the basis for using the television or radio.

> *Lucille:* "When I'm home, the first thing I do is, well, in the daytime I keep the radio going so I can hear voices. At night I don't like the radio. At night I like the TV because in addition to a voice I can see faces."

Involvement with Others

Numerous studies have demonstrated the importance of a supportive environment for the newly bereaved. This certainly makes sense when one considers the multiple levels and wide variety of coping mechanisms that are employed by the bereaved through their involvement with others. Involvement with others can help the bereaved cope with their suffering through the emotional support they receive, through the benefits of investing themselves in the concerns of others, through the opportunities for expression that avail themselves, and through partial compensation for their loss.

Support from Others. All the people in our study had either family or friends who were available to them to provide emotional support. This support came in various forms: as understanding and sympathy, shared experiences, or help with life's tasks. At times this support could protect the bereaved from their suffering; more often it provided a temporary buffer, something to ward off the suffering for a while.

> *Agnes:* "I had an awful lot of wonderful support from my family and friends and even strangers in the different hospitals that my husband was in. I drew a lot of strength from other people. People would come up to me that would hear about my situation—and

put their arms around me and sympathize. That
meant a great deal, that was a big help."

Ralph felt that he would have had a much more
difficult time adjusting to widowhood if he had not
had his two children. They were very responsible,
shared in the housework, and provided him with
much-needed company. Of his son Ralph said, "He
is my best friend." They all became much closer to
one another through their loss. "We didn't shut out
the outside, our friends and family, but I think we
kind of drew on each other's strength. I've really been
lucky."

Ann used the telephone frequently to maintain
contact with and obtain support from friends in her
support group. "The telephone I consider a great
therapy. I would call someone up. If I was really sad,
I would call someone else in the group and they'd
talk. And it would take my mind off it."

Investment in Others. In the same way that investment in
work, hobbies, or other activities reaps many benefits for the
bereaved, investment in people-related activities can result in
productive outcomes. Becoming concerned about other people's
needs often precludes focusing on one's own misery. In addition,
helping others provides for the helper a certain sense of mastery
over the situation.

Two months after Faith died, Carl took on a job as
coach of a Pony League baseball team. He spent a lot
of time in activities, including practices and team
parties. He found himself becoming "emotionally
involved with these kids." He felt that he was
contributing something while taking his mind off his
own troubles.

Susan: "I'm working with children in pediatrics. I
never did that before and I find it very, very satisfy-

ing. I find that holding an infant, feeding an infant, is so rewarding. Then again it's that need to be needed, I suppose. Reading a story to a child. One of the most rewarding afternoons I've spent in a long time was taking a child out who had a broken pelvis. Just wheeling the whole bed outside of the hospital because she hadn't been out in two weeks and sitting in the sunshine with her. She taught me how to play backgammon. We listened to the radio and we chatted and she just thanked me over and over and over again. I felt so good for days about that." What made this appreciation for her help more rewarding for Susan was the reality that she had spent years caring for Phil and that he had expressed very little appreciation and was frequently even hostile and resentful.

The most common acts of investment in others occur in those survivors who still have young children to care for. Although caring for their children created an additional burden, it also provided opportunities to get away from their own suffering, forced them to maintain control and mastery where they may have wished to have the luxury of being able to fall apart, offered them intimacy, and gave them a direction and meaning that might not have been there otherwise.

Compensation for the Loss. Nothing can truly compensate for the loss of one's mate; no one can replace that person. However, other people can relieve some of the loneliness, the sense of being alone. New intimacies can develop to fill the need, and old relationships can flower or intensify, to fill in, at least partially, some of the gaping holes left by death. These partial compensations are the products of involvement by the bereaved with others and go a long way in softening or relieving the pain of loss and loneliness.

Gloria: "I missed my husband's love when he died. My friends made me feel that I was still loved. And I

think that's very important. They were very concerned, they were terrific."

There are many needs for intimacy, love, sexuality, and
romance that cannot be derived from family and friends. These
needs drive many bereaved to seek new relationships—romantic
ones. Despite conflicting feelings, the intensity of such needs often
pushes the newly bereaved into romantic involvements far sooner
than custom and tradition usually permit. Many of the widows
and widowers in the study were intimately involved with others
within a few months of their spouses' deaths.

For Harold, becoming involved with another woman
had a dramatic effect in changing his outlook from
pessimism to one of optimism, hope, and confidence.
"Romance improves my state of mind."

For most men and women, many perceived needs were met
by newly developed relationships, but clearly the most intense were
the sense of being alone and consequent loneliness. Of the
relationships into which people were propelled by such feelings,
many turned out to be successful (see Chapter Six).

Pets. The majority of American households have pets, many
of which achieve status as family members, often as quasi-children.
People have long recognized the value that animals possess as
vehicles for relationships, as objects of affection and caregiving,
and as providers of love, appreciation, and companionship. In
addition, particularly after a death, the animal may be an
embodiment of certain characteristics of the deceased or even a
symbolic representation of the dead. For these reasons the ongoing
relationship between the bereaved and a pet may become extremely
important in the process of coping.

Joe: "It may sound silly as hell—but of course
nothing sounds silly to you guys. I've got a bird up
there, one of these cockatoos, and it makes me happy
when he speaks. I take him out in the morning and

feed him, and he crawls up my arm and I talk to the
bird. Put me in cell block number nine, but, you
know, I talk to the bird. I talk to my dog and he
understands me pretty good. It would break my heart
if anything happened to that dog." During the
following year, Joe's dog did become ill and died. He
had the animal cremated and the remains buried. "I
went through the same feelings with him that I did
with Loretta."

Jonathan: "She loved the dog, was crazy about him,
a beautiful Great Dane, and I took good care of him.
And every now and then I realize, when I take care of
him, that I'm taking care of the material thing that
she loved the most—that was the living thing that
carried on from her. I think my relationship to the
dog carries on the relationship with her."

Expression of Painful Emotions

Common wisdom—that is, what everyone's grandmother
would have said—suggests that an important way to cope with
difficult emotions is to express them, to release them, to get them
out of the system. Where the bereaved felt the freedom to release
their emotions directly, they usually experienced great relief from
their loneliness, sadness, frustration, or anger.

Louise: "Oh, I can remember the day I had my
wedding ring cut off. That was the worst one. I came
home and I hollered at everything, all by myself. Just
relief, yes. Boy, I hollered, loud. . . . I had people I
could talk to if I was lonely. If I was by myself, all
alone in that house and I got mad, I hollered like a
lunatic. But I felt better."

Melinda: "I would sit in a chair, feeling lonely and
missing Jim, and sometimes I would just all of a
sudden burst out in tears and turn around, jerk

around, stand up, and just start pounding, just start pounding on the chair."

To attain the benefits of such release, the bereaved often must overcome impediments set up by strong cultural sanctions for people to stay in control of themselves and their feelings.

Melinda: "I'm not a crier. That's my problem. I have a hard time expressing my emotions. And I have turned into a crier because of all this. A lot of times now I'll just go into the bathroom, and I'll sit there, you know, and the tears will come. I never used to carry a handkerchief. I cannot go around without a handkerchief now. I have two of them on me now."

Morrie: "It was embarrassing. I was such a weeper, you know, that it was embarrassing to me to try to talk about it or describe it. [After] twenty-two years in the Marine Corps, a grown man doesn't cry. The emotional level would rise to the embarrassing point, and I would terminate the conversation to avoid that."

Ralph: "I think especially in the first month there would be times I'd just go in my room and cry it out. I guess maybe that's the way I'd release it. Oh, I don't know, when I was brought up, of course, boys never cried. But I think that we never brought our children up that way. I could express my feelings, even if it was by myself, not so much with other people, but I could just cry it out and I'd feel better about it."

Emotional release is a form of expression that deals directly with the underlying turmoil through catharsis. Other means of expression—verbal and written—utilize quite different means of coping with emotional distress and operate much more like those involved in developing perspective. First, verbal or written expression requires a transformation of feelings into words or thoughts, a process akin to "standing outside" of an experience and creating some distance. Second, the communication of these forms of expression is likely to occur, or at least can occur, without emotion. These different forms of expression are certainly not mutually exclusive and, in fact, may complement each other. Verbal or written expression frequently triggers emotional responses through the content of what is being expressed; and, conversely, emotional release is often followed by attempts at achieving perspective.

> *Ann:* "I found that maybe if it was late at night and I didn't feel right about calling someone, I would just get up and write. Just write whatever was on my mind and just write and write until I got it all down. And then I would just fold it up and seal it in an envelope, and it's probably stuck away somewhere. I probably won't ever read it again, but I got it off my mind."

At times people may be reluctant to express their thoughts or feelings because of concerns about the possible effect of such expressions on others.

> *Gloria:* "Initially, I had ample opportunity, and I would have had later if I cared to take advantage of it. But I've known a number of widows who have gone on for a long period of time mourning and wailing, and people get very tired of it. I didn't want to lose my friends. I knew they would listen if I wanted to talk about it because some of them made it a great point to tell me that."

Expressing how one feels and what one thinks can be a very useful way of discharging pent-up feelings and disturbing thoughts. Most of the bereaved, especially in the early weeks and months, find that they do have someone available to facilitate this form of coping—family, friends, clergy, a therapist. At best, however, such mechanisms provide only a temporary catharsis and do not take away one's grief. In this sense, there are real limits to the effectiveness of any coping mechanism.

> *Ross:* "My son and I eventually reached a point where we were just pretty well talked out about it. We'd said everything three or four times. We still wanted to talk, but we didn't want to talk to each other about it any more. It just didn't do any good. We knew how each other felt, and there wasn't anything more we could do for each other or for ourselves by talking to each other."

Indulgence in External Sources of Gratification

Some bereaved persons experience an internal craving for a sought-after object, such as food, alcohol, tobacco, or sex. Frequently the craving is experienced as a compulsion, and the widowed person feels powerless before its beckoning. There is an internal struggle as the bereaved person realizes that succumbing to this desire may result in short-term benefits but long-term liabilities (poor health, guilt, self-deprecation). At the same time, the grieving person tells himself that he is entitled to a certain amount of indulgence after going through such a difficult experience. Besides, regarding the potentially harmful aspects of indulgence, many people have a fatalistic or pessimistic attitude.

There is a specific state of mania in which people utilize many or all of the indulgences described in this section. This manic state may represent a temporary psychological state of "total escape" or a biologically altered mood state in which one may experience elation and expansiveness, a heightened sense of well-being, increased energy and activity, garrulousness, grandiosity, hypersexuality, some compromise of judgment, and an inclination to spend money.

Food. For several weeks after the death of a spouse, the bereaved person usually has no interest in food and consequently loses weight (see Chapter Five). But normal appetite usually returns, and the person may develop continued cravings for food, probably as part of a built-in adaptive mechanism whereby stress stimulates hunger centers in the brain. Struggling with these impulses and worrying about their weight, widows and widowers may experience additional stress, compounding the suffering caused by their grief.

> *Bobbi:* "I have a weight problem. I gained fifteen pounds during that first year and didn't take it off until a year later. I was feeling sorry for myself and pampered myself, which is a response I tend to have. I understood that was what was going on, and I felt that probably it wasn't a good time to try a strict diet. Not then."

It was not unusual for the bereaved to gain weight throughout the first year and then to spend months and years trying to take it off.

Alcohol, Tobacco, and Other Drugs. Prior studies have demonstrated that during the first year of spousal bereavement there is a predictable increase in the use of alcohol, tobacco, and other drugs, including prescription drugs for sleep, anxiety, and depression. By far the most serious health hazard is presented by alcohol. Nor is it an accident that alcohol use and problems are common among the bereaved. The entire history of Western literature serves as a testimonial to the effectiveness of alcohol in dealing with grief: to drown out one's sorrows, improve one's mood, alleviate sleeplessness, help one forget.

> On the day after Jim's funeral, his son came over to help Melinda clean up their apartment. Two days later he returned to dispose of Jim's belongings. He acted on his own, prematurely, but Melinda reluctantly and passively assented. "The only way I could accept it was—I had about four beers before I attempted this. I was heavily on beer for about—well, the night he died, I went over and stayed with my parents that night. And from that moment until

about a week later, I can't even count how many beers a day I had. And the funny thing is I can't get drunk on beer. I just seem to get a little bit light-headed. But it helped. It definitely did. It was not enough to make me drunk or disoriented. I was able to keep in touch with my faculties but high enough where it was kind of an escape a little bit."

When Pauline died, Morrie's first reactions included "a feeling of impending tragedy" and "butterfies in my stomach." He found that alcohol relieved him: "A good vodka on the rocks is best for this."

Merle: "For a while there I did smoke a little more, and now if anything I smoke a little less. What I have been doing is taking a little glass of wine at night. I heard that taking a glass of wine is good for you, helps me sleep."

If people could limit themselves to the beneficial therapeutic benefits of alcohol on a short-term basis, it would be hailed as a miracle drug rather than as "demon rum." Unfortunately, one of the major properties of alcohol is that it is physiologically as well as psychologically addicting and as such requires continued and increasing use. Furthermore, with time the therapeutic benefits diminish and even reverse themselves. Increasing amounts of alcohol cause disruptive sleep patterns, worsening depression, and increasing agitation. As a result of both its beneficial and its addictive properties, alcohol can become a very powerful destructive force in a group of highly vulnerable people.

Regardless of how the initial use of alcohol comes about, it can lead slowly and subtly to significant drinking problems.

Jonathan: "I found myself coming home from work, and it's a very pleasant place where I live. I'd go up and I like to cook, I like to make little things for myself. So I'd cook up something and turn on the TV—and have a bottle of wine. After a while, I realized that 'My God, I'm getting a snoot every night.' Then I'd take the dog out and everything would be beautiful and bright and I'd be kind of a little high and I finally realized I was doing this night after night. So I did something about it because I work around too many alcoholics and drug people and I don't like what I see. I like to drink. It was kind of relaxing. I don't think I was seeking escape. I was in a way enjoying the freedom and the relaxation. But I know how dangerous it is."

The most vulnerable group of people are the bereaved who have had prior histories of alcoholism.

Ross had a drinking problem that had been controlled until shortly after Pamela's death, when he started drinking again to cope with feelings of depression. "It got me away from my feelings. It numbed me. Of course, it does not do a whole hell of a lot for depression, no matter what people think." He knew that he should not have started drinking again, but "I was going through a period of apathy. I just really didn't much give a damn what was going on or if anything was going on." Ross was in graduate school and had been doing well before his relapse with alcoholism. He began missing classes and procrastinating with his work, and his grades dropped from A's to C's. When the school year was over, "it got progressively worse and I drank progressively more all the time" over the next six months until he entered the hospital for treatment. By that time he was already suffering significant medical consequences from alcohol: bone marrow suppression, gastritis, hepatitis, and hallucinations upon withdrawal. Following his hospitalization Ross remained abstinent through the follow-up period three years later and has returned to good health without evidence of chronic damage.

Spending Money. Spending money is an indulgence that many bereaved pursue vigorously in efforts to ward off their grief. At times this indulgence provides short-term relief, as the person experiences a sense of freedom and the feeling of being provided for.

> *Gloria:* "I was very good to myself. I figured that it was a very good time to be nice to Gloria. If I saw a dress I liked, I bought it. I went out and bought a pair of designer jeans, something I would never have done before. I remember buying new shoes. . . . I didn't exactly go crazy doing it, but if I saw something I really liked, I thought about it and decided, 'If this makes you feel good, get it. It's worth the money.'"

Spending money impulsively or frivolously can become complicated when there is additional conflict tied up with the source of the money. The widowed person feels guilt or embarrassment as a result of gaining financially from her spouse's life insurance or pension or another person's legal liability in a wrongful death. Somehow, "it doesn't seem right" to the newly bereaved to enjoy the products of a loved one's death.

Sex. Many men and women deal with their feelings of anguish, loneliness, and desperation for love by engaging in a frantic search to replace their spouses or to find a substitute to provide closeness, warmth, and sex. Since many couples experience the height of intimacy in their sexual relationship, the newly bereaved may turn toward sexual relationships to create the illusion that they have again achieved such intimacy and saved themselves from their pain. Through sexual indulgence they can once again feel loved and needed, regain their sense of self-esteem, stave off loneliness, or simply reexperience pleasure and gratification. While they may actually achieve many of these goals, the intensity of their needs can blind these persons to reality and make them even more vulnerable to exploitation by others or simply unable to make reasonable judgments about such relationships.

Annette described feeling "horny as a toad" since
before her husband died. While they had been close,
they had been afraid to have sex for months because
of his illness. Immediately after Frank died, she felt
guilty about her sexual fantasies and was hesitant
about sex. But within a couple of months, she felt
freer and over the next two years engaged in a series
of affairs. "I have been flying like on a merry-go-
round and partying constantly [one year later]. Last
night I went through old pictures of Frank and me. I
had a gnawing emptiness. I feel an insatiable desire
to be cuddled, fondled, and loved. I don't want to be
old and alone." She wanted to remarry, to find
another relationship that would let her "wipe out"
the memory of her husband. "At first I thought no
one would say 'I love you' again." However, even
after she had many men tell her so and wish to marry
her, she felt that no one could replace Frank. At the
end of her second year of bereavement, Annette found
her sexual drive "simmering down." She had not
found what she thought she wanted but was interested
in settling down, finding someone to share with. She
no longer felt desperate or weak and needy. "Sexual
activity with no meaning is depressing."

Pursuit of Physical Fitness

The pursuit of physical fitness, as a coping mechanism,
operates at a number of different levels. In a manner similar to
indulgence, it offers the bereaved an opportunity to do something
for themselves, to gratify themselves, in a healthy way. On the
other hand, it also serves as an antidote to many aspects of
indulgence that may have already occurred. Successful efforts to
lose weight, stop smoking, and drinking may create a sense of
confidence and control as well as physical well-being. The effects
of bereavement on general health can be devastating, and anything
that is likely to counteract those effects is welcomed. Certainly,
one's personal appearance and attractiveness may become espe-

cially important after the early stages of grief, when the widowed person may be ready to seek out new romantic relationships. Having lived through an ordeal such as the death of a spouse, the bereaved are more likely to be confronting issues of their own mortality and seeking ways to allay some of the anxieties accompanying this awareness. The move toward fitness can calm some of these fears. It may further dovetail with long-standing wishes of the deceased spouse that the survivor make some positive moves toward health. Finally, there may be some beneficial mood-altering properties inherent in vigorous physical activity. Much like any other activity in which the bereaved make an investment, these pursuits also are a means of distraction from painful emotions and may serve as a way of discharging internal stress.

> While Sandra was alive, she was always concerned about Jonathan's gaining weight or being out of shape. A few months after her death, Jonathan began eating more salads and healthy foods and running regularly. He cut down on his drinking. Over the next year, he was running five or six times a week and entering marathons. "Running lets me be alone and free." He thought it ironic that, as a result of his involvement, "I now look the way she wanted me to look" and had forsaken what Sandra had considered his too sedentary life.

Effects of Prolonged Illness on Coping

The anticipation of death through a prolonged period of illness can give rise to appropriate coping mechanisms. To the extent that "hope springs eternal" and feeds into the person's denial, there will be little preparation for the death. It will strike as suddenly and unexpectedly as if there had been no illness in the first place. However, few individuals are capable of such complete denial of reality. The coping mechanism most readily available and one that is relatively imperative is "being busy." Frequently, the physical demands of the caretaking role serve as a major distraction for the sick person's spouse. Furthermore, this task

requires intense emotional involvement, compassion, and support—which may intensify, through empathy, the caretaker's
suffering but will often also distract from and externalize the
suffering.

The suffering and deterioration of the sick spouse reinforce
the rationalization of the surviving spouse to the point that the
relief experienced at the time of death is deeply felt and supported
cognitively. Through the period of illness, many means of coping
are utilized and more effective ones can be identified for use at the
time of death. At the same time, the loss has not yet occurred, and
those mechanisms later used to maintain the relationship with the
spouse are not yet available.

Preparation for Reality. The anticipation of death helps
many couples get their "affairs in order" to lessen the impact of
such loss on the survivor. The most obvious planning occurs
around establishing financial security and expressing wishes about
the rites of passage: plans for funeral, memorial services, burial, or
cremation. In addition, and often more important, the survivor has
time and opportunity to receive training in various new roles—for
instance, in the operation of household functions. Men and
women begin their psychological preparation to take on new roles
as well as guided practical experiences to help them develop
confidence in their newfound abilities. They may learn now to
prepare meals, operate the dishwasher, fill up a car's gas tank,
drive a car, hire a plumber. They have an opportunity to try these
tasks out while their spouses are still around to supervise or
reinforce their learning.

Preparation for Psychological Reality. While the surviving
spouse is learning new tasks and roles, he or she is simultaneously
"trying on" new aspects of identity, new self-concepts: as future
"mother-father," "sole supporter," "boat operator," "single
person," "autonomous functioner," "lonely widow," or "incapable and helpless victim." The anticipation of this future reality
allows the surviving spouse to experiment with such self-
perceptions and work toward realizing those that make the most
sense or are the most desirable. The still-living spouse can also

contribute his or her version of the vision and reinforce the more positive views.

Many people, in anticipation of their own death, will make known their preference or give their blessing for their spouse to become reinvolved and remarried after their death. This can provide a powerful sanction for the survivor's disposition toward new relationships. Such wishes may extend to the development of other kinds of relationships as well.

Acceptance. The anticipation, discussion, and planning that occur around any of the future barriers to be confronted by the bereaved will lessen these barriers and provide a support that can be carried far beyond the point of death and can even include the ultimate acceptance of death. Frequently, the dying spouse may have "come to terms" with death much sooner and more easily than the surviving spouse, and this acceptance can be a parting gift of immense value, enabling the surviving spouse to reach such acceptance. Further, as the survivor enters a period that may seem devoid of meaning or direction, the dying spouse's world view can provide a powerful temporary replacement, something to which the survivor can cling until he or she is able to reestablish a meaning and direction.

 Chapter 4

Continuing Ties to the Deceased Spouse

There are many myths about bereavement and the tasks of the grieving spouse. Prevalent in our culture and fostered by the mental health professions is a concept that the bereaved learn to accept their loss and put it behind them, that they "let go," release the dead, so that they can go on living. The physical facts are that people have no choice but to follow this course of action: the dead are dead, they are buried, and the living continue to live and cope. Emotional realities, however, are far different. Human attachment bonds are established and maintained at emotional levels so deep that the mere fact of physical death cannot truly disrupt these bonds. Our biological and psychological apparatus will not permit it.

This chapter examines the most powerful of all coping mechanisms: those that sustain the relationship. Possibly the most difficult and painful period at the onset of grief is in part a consequence of the survivor's belief that the relationship has been lost forever. Thus, the adaptation that subsequently occurs depends a great deal on the survivor's ability to find some means of integrating the "real" loss and the continuing form of the relationship. An important component of any concept of "recovery" from grief must of necessity include a true emotional recovery of the lost person.

A corollary of the myth is that new relationships, new bonding, cannot proceed until the old bonds have been severed. A survivor's readiness to enter new relationships depends not on "giving up" the dead spouse but on finding a suitable place for the spouse in the psychological life of the bereaved—a place that is important but that leaves room for others. Difficulties in developing new attachments are more likely to occur when the dead spouse's new position has not been secured and the bereaved person fears that a new relationship will completely cancel out the old relationship.

How does the person who has died remain a part of the living? Powerful internal emotional and psychological forces—reinforced by cultural and societal institutions, beliefs, and rituals that tend to confirm the idea of spiritual survival—enable people to continue their relationships with their spouses. These phenomena are examined in the following sections.

There is yet another element to be considered in these continuing ties—namely, that survivors may be intensely ambivalent about them. On the one hand, a bereaved person confronted by the reality that his spouse is gone forever will utilize whatever psychological means are available to sustain the relationship. On the other hand, evidence of the spouse's prior existence is capable of triggering extremely painful feelings. Thus, there is the continuing dilemma: to be comforted by illusions or to avoid reminders. The other option seems psychologically unacceptable: to face reality with its unbearable pain.

Location of Dead Spouse

The great majority of widows and widowers in this study believed that their spouses had gone to heaven or some equivalent "hereafter," reflecting principles of religious faith that helped to sustain them. These beliefs often carried with them the implicit or explicit understanding that the couple would be reunited.

> *Fran:* "I'm sure he's in heaven. I'm a Christian lady, and going to be with the Lord is not a tragedy in our life. I think it's a beautiful thing and that someday that's where I will be. And in the back of my mind, I think that I am going to see all those people that I've lost."

Agnes: "His spirit is alive and floating around up there somewhere. I believe I'll see him when I die."

Glenn: "She's somewhere and I expect I'll meet her again someday. She must be with quite a crowd of our old friends. I'm sure she's got company."

Even when there is no formal concept of heaven, there may be a sense of the deceased spouse's being at peace somewhere.

Susan: "No one has ever asked me that before [Where is he?]. I never thought about it before. I would like to think that he's very quiet and not suffering. [Cries] He's at peace. I don't think about where he is now. I just like to think that he's not suffering."

For some, the spouse's location is simply that—a physical location, with no implications for continuity or connection to themselves.

Lucille: "He's buried six feet under ground."

Bobbi: [Is he in a place?] "No, he's dead."

Continuing Contact with the Deceased

The mind and body of the newly bereaved are so driven to retrieve the loved one who has died that most people, during the early weeks and months of bereavement, have experiences where they believe they have seen, heard, touched, smelled, or felt the presence of their spouses. They may be aware that what they are experiencing is an illusion or a hallucination, but that does not detract from the "realness" of the sensation. The contact takes different forms: searching and waiting for the loved one, experiencing external sensory evidence of his presence, or sensing his presence from within. In other instances the bereaved may talk or write to their dead spouses.

Searching and Waiting. The newly bereaved person who experiences a prolonged sense of disbelief about his spouse's death can remain for weeks and months in a state of heightened arousal—searching for the spouse in crowds, waiting for her return, and looking for evidence that she has not died.

> *Earl:* "A lot of time, if I'm watching the crowds at a football game or a baseball game, a person looks like her and the crowd is just passing by pretty swiftly, but I know it isn't her, but it's a person that looks like her."

> Beth never saw Barry's remains after the plane crash and had trouble accepting the fact that he was really dead. Six months later she still could not move his things and continued to search for him, anticipating his coming home. "I'd hear the back gate open and I'd think, 'Oh, there he is.' Then I'd catch myself and realize."

> Two years after Ted's death, Amalia still felt that he was alive. She maintained a schedule of family meals as Ted had needed them, getting up at 5:30 in the morning to fix breakfast. She would sit in the kitchen having coffee, picturing him drinking his coffee and talking about his job. While she knew the reality, Amalia still made dinner at the same time, as if he might return.

Sensory Evidence of Presence. Mental health professionals— psychiatrists, psychologists, social workers, nurses, and others—are well aware that people suffering from mental and emotional disorders frequently distort reality and thereby create illusions or hallucinations. In most circumstances these clinical phenomena are considered clear-cut manifestations of mental and emotional illness. Bereavement is probably the only common experience where these "symptoms" are not considered particularly patholog- ical. On the one hand, they are distortions of reality and evidence of disordered thinking. On the other hand, in the context of the mental and emotional turmoil of bereavement, they are considered "normal" experiences—regular and normative (statistically) occurrences among "normal" people undergoing enormous stress.

> Amalia frequently felt her husband's presence. "I feel him covering me." At night she was frightened and had her children sleep in her bedroom. "I hear him opening the refrigerator at night like he always did."

> Before Oscar died, he had a collection of coins to be given to his children. One night Marie woke to find Oscar in the room putting away the coins. "I'll tell you, Dr. Shuchter, if I didn't know he was dead, I'd swear to God he was very much alive. It seemed to me he walked in the bedroom and stood in the bedroom door. I looked up and I saw him standing in the door, and he was reaching up like onto this place to get the lighter fluid for his lighter. He looked at me and said, 'Don't worry, I'm just going to lock it up in the desk.' I said, 'A lot of people come in here.' Then one of my kids said, 'Mom, who are you talking to?' Now that's just how much alive he looked to me."

> Fay tried to drive Gilbert's car but couldn't when she saw his hands on the steering wheel.

These perceptual experiences often are interpreted as messages from the deceased.

> After Tom's death Pamela had to go to the hospital for surgery. Following the surgery she realized that she had no husband to take her home and care for her. "It was one of the most horrible feelings I have ever had in my life. . . . Then at one point in the afternoon, it was like somebody was touching my head and patting me on the shoulder. I opened my eyes and there was nobody there. I had been thinking about him, you know, how always before if I had been ill, there was always him when I came home.

And I just felt like he was there, telling me everything was going to be all right."

Eight months after Sandra's death, Jonathan made a special trip to the cemetery on her birthday, bringing flowers and a note. While at the cemetery, he saw a small fawn, the size of deer that Sandra had always enjoyed. "I had the feeling that she was thanking me for coming and telling me that everything was okay."

Morrie remarried several months after Pauline died. At times he still spoke with Pauline, and he wore the neck chain that she had worn when she died. "When I do something wrong, I can feel her pull on the chain." One night the burglar alarm went off, and the next morning he discovered that a fallen picture had set off the alarm. He felt that it may have been Pauline protesting the presence of the fallen picture (a painting he had bought with his new wife).

Daphne was out running when she smelled a flowery fragrance. "I didn't know why, but I felt it was him— telling me 'If you keep on going, good things will happen.'"

Sensing a Presence from Within. Sensing the presence of one's deceased spouse occurs even more frequently without externally perceived stimuli, where the source remains wholly within the bereaved. At times the person has a fairly clear understanding of the forces at work.

Melinda: "I know, I have acknowledged that I will not accept his loss, and the way I make up for that, I just feel like he's with me, he's got to be. Because we were so close and you can't lose someone like that. It's a hard thing because I'm a realist, too. Obviously I know he's not with me, but he and I were so close.

Linda: "Sometimes you'll get that feeling that, you don't hear anything, but it's maybe a peaceful feeling that's in the room. And I feel like maybe he's looking down, or he's around spiritually. It feels like he's there. I think you have that feeling because you're so close to them, and I don't think you want to turn loose of the idea that they're actually gone forever, that they're not coming back."

The "presence" of one's lost spouse provides considerable comfort when it is needed.

When Lucille traveled to New Orleans, "Arthur went with me. He wanted to see New Orleans."

For the first year after Loretta's death, Joe would not sleep in the master bedroom but in the room where she died. "Because of my nature, I feel that my wife is still around in a spiritual way. I feel closer to her in that room." On one occasion Joe felt her presence and was "drawn" to a closet where he found a box wrapped with a scarf belonging to Loretta. It was full of his wife's jewelry. He had been "absolutely sure" that the closet had been cleaned out and concluded this was a psychic experience. Tearful, he said, "I feel like she's still around."

Joe's experience also points to the role that these phenomena play in providing help and protection for the survivor.

Phyllis felt that Bradley stayed with her until it was safe for him to leave. "He didn't leave me until the Sunday after he died. He was hanging around to see if I was going to be okay, and this was a very real experience. I was driving along in the car and I was feeling very sad, and all of a sudden I said, 'Well, you son of a bitch, you're still hanging around. Get the hell out and do what you're supposed to because you may screw it up that we don't meet in the next lifetime. I'm going to be okay. Just go on.' And it was within twenty minutes or so that I was driving alone. The car was empty and I was now alone. He never came back. He got it that I was going to be okay. He knows I'm tough. And he really left and went on to do whatever you do when you die and wherever you go."

Ted stayed around continuously to protect Amalia. She wore his sweaters as a tangible way of keeping him around. When she left the house, she would place the sweater on a conspicuous chair—so that, if a burglar should come in, he would think there was a man in the house. Her fears were somewhat allayed by feeling her husband's continuous presence. Even after three years, "Ted is behind me all the time. I feel him helping me."

Fay got a bee sting, which became badly swollen. She reached for her husband's book on medical treatments but mistakenly got a Bible wherein Gilbert had marked passages about eternal life. She read these passages and then went to bed. The next morning there was no trace of the bee sting. Fay was in awe and felt that somehow Gilbert had contributed to this "cure."

Daphne felt that her entire family benefited from being watched over by Ray. "A lot of times I feel like he's with us. That may sound strange, but I really feel like a couple times a few things have happened." On one occasion she and her children were flying to Seattle for a family wedding, but they forgot a dress at home, turned back, and then got caught in traffic. They arrived late but the plane was held for them. "I told the kids, 'The only reason we're on this plane is because Dad's watching out for us.'" Shortly before this incident, her daughter was found to have a bone chip in her knee and was told that she needed surgery to provide flexibility in the joint. If she had the surgery, she would be unable to play softball and basketball, both important to her. When she went for a second consultation with another orthopedist, the bone chip was gone and the surgery was unnecessary. "She told me afterward that the nuns at her Catholic school sent us home some holy water from Lourdes when my husband was sick. She had taken the Lourdes water and put it on her knee. Now that was the week before she was going to have the surgery. I really think it's him looking out for us."

The "presence" of one's dead spouse is not always a comfort or help but can be experienced as a burden.

Harold was haunted by his memories and his sense of Rose's presence. Many times he would think to himself, "Honey, turn me loose." He repeatedly experienced the image where he would be "waving goodbye to someone who is walking away very slowly. Eventually they get over the horizon but it takes much time. Perhaps they never get over the horizon."

Annette found herself feeling that Frank was looking down at her from a cloud in a place like heaven, observing her behavior on earth. This would happen particularly when she felt that she had been some-what promiscuous sexually, reflecting her sense of guilt.

Joe considered selling his house but couldn't. He believed that Loretta was still in the house and that he would be abandoning her if he sold it.

From these examples, one can see the powerful transforma-tion of needs, wishes, and minimal or no stimuli into vivid and dramatic experiences that have often been interpreted as evidence of either mental illness or the supernatural. Certainly, many of these people might have understood their perceptions as manifestations of ghosts, albeit usually friendly ones. It is difficult not to be impressed by the capacity of our minds to create such experiences in tragic and stressful times.

Communications to the Deceased. Here the fundamental dynamics of the situation are the same—that is, the survivor wishes to maintain contact with the dead spouse. However, the transformation of these wishes into experience is not so dramatic and does not involve psychological distortions. For the most part, communications from the living to the dead proceed more easily, since the bereaved realize that the person with whom they are communicating is dead and that the image is a product of their minds.

The most common form of communication between the bereaved and the deceased involves sharing information about important events that the deceased has missed or about trivial, mundane matters of day-to-day living. Such communications usually reflect a sense of loneliness or longing that is stimulated by life's events, but they may also come "out of the blue" as a mood settles over the bereaved and a desire for contact is there.

> *Bobbi:* "After it first happened, in the evening I'd have a drink. I'd pour the drink and say, 'To you.' And then I wrote to him. Every once in a while I'll come across something, I'll see something interesting and say, 'Gee, Nate, you should have seen this.'"

> *Lucille:* "I talk to him. If I read something in the paper that I think both of us would have gotten a kick out of, I'll say, 'How do you like that? Isn't that something?'"

> Annette used her communications with Frank as a humorous counterpoint to periods when she felt frustrated. "Frank, where are you this week? I need you to come down and clean up the garage."

Survivors also may communicate with their loved ones through prayer, which is a regular part of many people's lives.

Ann: "It's just a nice warm feeling, and I just feel good when I think about him and the time we had together. I don't have that feeling of utter loss anymore. I have a feeling that it is just something I'll always remember, and now I feel if I want to talk to him, he's just a prayer away."

Daniel: "I communicate with her in prayer. I see visions of her. I can create that vision in my mind. Where I associate her with something or I feel like I miss her, I can visualize her physically, her face."

Bill: "Often in the first year I would, whatever you want to call it, I would say, 'Glenda, I miss you.' I might say it out loud, when I was driving by myself or when I got on my knees to pray when I went to bed. I would thank God for her every day."

In a marriage decision making is frequently the product of a joint effort. When one spouse dies, the survivor is often left feeling inadequate or unsure about decisions. In these circumstances communication with the deceased will take the form of a consultation or request for advice about decisions.

Merle: "When it's an important decision about our son or what should I do about the house, then I feel that, although I'm just thinking it over, I'm also communicating, telling him about it. Well, you know how when you have a problem, if you're thinking about it yourself, sometimes you can't come to a decision. But if you talk it over with somebody, it helps. So when I'm having these problems of any kind, I feel that by thinking about it and talking with him, it brings back the sort of things—decisions he would have made on it, you know. And it's a help to me."

Lucille preferred seeking out confirmation for her decisions rather than Arthur's decision. "I will talk to

him and say, 'Yes, Arthur, that's how you would
have done it.'"

Another role of the lost spouse may have been a protective
one. Even where it may not have been so, the survivor may feel the
need for protection or assistance and call on the spouse for help.

Shirley: "I always say my prayers when I go to bed. If
I'm really asking for something real important or
big, I'll say, 'Art, make Him do it. Tell Him I need
that.'"

Sharon: "I used to talk to my father who is dead, and
I would wish that he was there. Now I do it with
Dick. I don't know, it seems like a guardian angel
type of thing. 'You are all-knowing and you are up
there watching me, so just protect me because you
have an in.' If something happens, if the kid is sick,
or I'm worried something will go wrong, when
Mother had the surgery, I call upon him to intervene.
There were two instances that happened in the past
two years where I fantasized that he intervened. I
can't possibly know, but in my mind I told myself
that's what happened. One was when the baby
couldn't walk and fell down a flight of stairs and
suddenly on the third step from the bottom before he
was ready to crack his head open on the cement floor,
he sat up. To me there was just no logical explanation for it. I'm sure there probably is, but at the
moment I said, 'Thank you, God, and thank you,
Dick.' In that order."

Sharon's experience suggests how, when people are psychologically ready, the communication flows in both directions. It
also demonstrates a theme that has run through many of these
examples: that for many bereaved there is a close association
between God and those who have died. This association is not
only of location and spirit but includes some overlapping

functions that involve overseeing, loving and caring, protecting, and helping. It suggests a fluidity between the roles of parents, God, and spouses—a psychological readiness to embrace whatever form of all-knowing, all-caring, and all-protecting being is available. Conversely, this fluidity makes it easier to understand how people are able to move into a state of mind where their spouses "come alive" for them, contrary to what logic and reason would dictate. Our spirituality arises from those magical qualities of our parents that protect us from our earliest helplessness, qualities that are then transferred to God and, to a lesser degree (and certainly less consciously), to our loved ones, especially our spouses. The death of a spouse rekindles the vestiges of our helplessness and once again primes us to experience and embrace phenomena that appear to transcend our usual realities.

Symbolic Representation

Unlike the location of and continuing contact with the dead spouse, which develop after the fact of death, symbolic representation—a process wherein belongings, creations, or shared experiences somehow become imbued with the spirit or memories of the deceased—evolves during the life of the person, essentially becoming a psychological fact by the time of death. The objects of symbolic representation are much more likely to be experienced and dealt with in an ambivalent way: as painful reminders yet means of continued contact, things that the surviving spouse often cannot bear to confront yet cannot get rid of.

Personal Possessions. Personal possessions, usually clothes, can be most expressive of the intimate day-to-day contact that is gone.

> Bill could not decide whether to keep Glenda's clothes or get rid of them but finally felt that it was too painful to keep them. "Well, I suppose because it was a constant reminder. You know, I could almost feel like I could hold the sleeve of the dress and say that was her. At one time she was in this." When he

tried to get rid of her nicer clothes, he found no takers among his family and friends and did not want to give such good things to the Salvation Army. "You know, fine stuff, you just hate to see it go down to the Salvation Army and go away to somebody for $2.50—somebody that has no appreciation. They have strong memories of her and I just can't quite do it." So he kept them in her closet, where they maintained their value but where he was not constantly confronted by them.

Fran: "I kept his old bathrobe for a long time. I used to put it on, and I could smell him because he smoked a pipe and it was in that bathrobe for a long time. It was ready for the rag bag long before. And he had a lot of hats that he gave to my son. My son hung them up in his den, and when I'd go up there to visit I'd take the hat and smell it because I could smell him—you know, with that pipe and his hair. My son asked me what I was doing one day and I felt kind of silly, but I don't know, it was just kind of nice."

Symbols of Pleasure. The passions, pleasures, and hobbies of loved ones reveal aspects of their personalities that the bereaved cherish. When confronted with these things, the bereaved again experience both sides of the struggle to hold on and to avoid.

Louis: "I had one of the most beautiful places in the neighborhood because of her green thumb. Karen spent every day out in the yard, and . . . I would keep her supplied with anything she wanted. She was so devoted to [gardening]." After Karen's death Louis became more interested in the garden, trying to maintain it as best he could yet feeling sad when he looked at it. "I know this is an attempt to keep close to my wife."

A month before she died, Rose wanted to work from her wheelchair in the garden, her pride and joy. *Harold:* "She said, 'Hal, wheel me out to the chrysanthemum bush. It needs cutting back.' A year later, I cut that thing back again. It took me about three hours. It was a very heartbreaking experiment in trying to cope with the memory of it, as it was one of the last things we had done together. But if I didn't have the damn chrysanthemum bush, if I didn't have the yard, if I lived in a different house and had a different yard, I'd be cutting plants that she never planted and she never tended. To me it would be just yard work."

Daphne: "Ray had a silvery motorcycle outfit that was supposed to show up better on the highway. I don't know why but I can't give that away. I think that whole thing represented something to me of his vitality. [After he was sick] he said he'd be back to riding his motorcycle someday. He finally decided that he wasn't going to be able to, so we sold it. But that outfit is still hanging up in the closet. I just couldn't give it away. Maybe I will someday, but it's still hanging there."

Joe: "One of the things she always wanted was a piano or organ. One day we had an opportunity to buy this nice Hammond organ. It wasn't a brand-new organ, but it's a very good organ. . . . One thing that does upset me, well, I mean, it just brings back something to me and I feel sad for a moment and then I'm all right—but on the organ, the last piece of music she played was 'Let the World Go Away.' And it sits there [two years later]. When I see that and the circumstances that happened, it bothers me."

Beatrice kept many of Fred's favorite possessions in a trunk. These included the products of his creativity:

his thesis and various writings. Laughingly she muses, "I think of Fred as being in the trunk."

Jeff was always involved with his ham radio and electronics equipment. He enjoyed fixing things and had installed a little computerized digital clock in the dashboard of Agnes's car. Six months after Jeff died, Agnes asked his brother, who had similar interests, to repair the radio in her car. When he fixed the radio, he also took out the clock, saying that it did not work. When she learned of this, Agnes started crying and was inconsolable. "I guess it symbolized to me that somehow or other in my own mind I felt that my husband, his presence was with me in the car because when I could see that clock working, I knew he put it in. He just loved little gadgets like that. It must have symbolized his presence to me and when my brother-in-law took it out I thought he just really killed him all over again. It was like he just died, and I really just couldn't stop crying over it. So one of my boys called him up and told him what happened, so he came over and put it back in again. Then I felt better. Now it's not working at all, but it's there in the car."

For each of these people, the loved one's belongings or interests represented an important part of that person: devotion, courage, vitality, creativity. Every symbol is unique, evolving from the individuality and interests of those who died. The grieving spouse finds these symbols without looking or trying. They are simply there.

Symbols of the Relationship. These items are important for their ability to keep alive not just the person who has died but also the relationship that was lost with the death. They are symbols of the existence of the relationship as well as specific qualities and shared experiences that were a part of the relationship. The bereaved experience some of their most intense ambivalence about these symbols.

Wedding rings are probably the ultimate symbol of the marital relationship, inasmuch as their purpose is primarily symbolic and they are universally understood to represent this union. After the death of one's spouse, the surviving spouse is often in a quandary about whether and how long to wear the ring. Some survivors feel bound by cultural and societal expectations to wear the ring during an "official" mourning period of a year; others remove the wedding ring within weeks of the death; still others keep it on forever. Because of the value—both in money and meaning—of such rings, they are usually kept by the spouse or given to family members, at times made into other jewelry. Since we live in a society where people are little bound by tradition, individuals' preferences are the rule, usually based on their emotional attachments or reactions to the ring. One evening before the meeting of our weekly support group for the newly bereaved, an elderly woman approached me, trembling, requesting my advice. She had spoken earlier that day with an acquaintance, who had criticized her for continuing to wear her wedding ring several months after her husband of almost fifty years had died. "Doctor, what should I do?" When I reassured her that there was no need to take off her ring unless and until she was ready to do so, she gave an enormous sigh of relief and thanked me profusely. Clearly, she was grateful that I had given her permission to maintain the relationship with her husband.

A couple's bed presents another highly charged emotional situation. For most couples the marital bed was the site of their greatest intimacy as well as the place where most of their time together was spent. Many of the newly bereaved avoid the side of the bed where their spouse slept, while others move to that side to feel greater closeness to the lost spouse. Where the bed serves as too painful a trigger, a new one is purchased. The conflicts increase if a new partner enters the picture. The bed is a frequent locus for "ghosts," the presence of the dead spouse.

An important symbol for a woman is her married name. She may wonder whether to retain her husband's name, Mrs. John Doe, or to go by the name Mrs. Jane Doe, or to drop the Mrs.

Fran: "I feel like I'm still Mrs. Boris J. Thomas. I haven't even been able to sign my checks Fran yet. And maybe that's a way of clinging to him, I don't know."

Other symbols of the relationship can be in the form of love letters shared, special places visited together, songs that conveyed a meaningful theme, or occasions of significance.

Home. Home epitomizes for many the person, the marriage, and the family and as such carries with it both the feelings of loss and the capacity to keep alive all those things that have been lost or changed when a spouse dies.

Living Legacies

Living legacies are not symbolic but actual representations of the personality, ideas, appearance, and other features of the deceased. The incorporation of these aspects of the deceased occurs through a number of different mechanisms: identification, perpetuation of wishes, and genetics.

Identification. Identification is a coping mechanism that works at various points throughout our lives to help us deal with separations and losses. We are accustomed to seeing its manifestations in growing children as they incorporate the characteristics, habits, and tastes of the people closest to them. It represents a form of adaptation in which people are able to retain elements of their loved ones at various points in the life cycle: during the child's early separation and individuation phases, during adolescence as the young person prepares to leave the nest, and at any point where a loss occurs through death. It is clearly an unconscious learning process, inasmuch as the participants are not aware of making any efforts to take on these traits or ideas. In the bereaved, identification with the deceased can produce striking changes in personality traits, habits, tastes, and even physical symptomatology.

The most common way in which identification operates to keep alive a loved one who has died is by way of personality changes in the survivor, who gradually adopts fairly specific traits of the spouse. The process is somewhat complicated by the fact that some traits are often "borrowed" from a spouse in the course of normal relationships. Also, the death of one's spouse might demand that the survivor develop more of that trait. For example, one spouse may be frivolous and the other practical. In situations that call for practicality, the frivolous spouse might defer to the practical one, rather than exercising his or her own practicality. In this situation there may be an "atrophy" of the one's practicality and accompanying "hypertrophy" of frivolousness, with the reverse process occurring in the spouse. Widowhood confers on the survivor the need to deal with the world alone as the sole bearer of both practicality and frivolousness when each is needed; accordingly, both "roles" would need to be developed and integrated in one person. Nonetheless, the diversity and complexity of the features seen in bereavement strongly suggest that identification also occurs.

> *Doris:* Edwin was a perfectionist, and I find myself becoming that way. Especially when my father painted my bedroom and bathroom. It would have been fine, but I could see things that would have annoyed Edwin and it annoyed me. . . . I thought, 'My gosh, this is awful. You know you would have accepted that.' I used to think, 'Do it as quickly as you can, as good as you can, but not take too long.' That used to aggravate me with Edwin sometimes, that he took so long—because he was a perfectionist. Now I've become that way."

> *Harold:* "I'm certainly more like Rose. I think I'm a lot less likely to be cross. I think I'm a lot more tolerant of people than I was before."

When a survivor becomes aware that she has developed the habits of the deceased, she is usually comforted and at times amused. Some of these changes remain permanent fixtures; others are transient.

> *Bobbi:* "One thing—he used to run yellow lights. It would just frighten me sometimes when he would do it. After he died, I found that I was doing it, and I did it for several months. I don't anymore, and I was aware of what I was doing after a while. There were similar, trivial kinds of behavior, things I picked up from him but now are gone."

> *Beth:* "I can see it when I travel. A lot of little things I catch myself doing that he always did and I never did before. We had a picture of every hotel we stayed in, and a couple of other things I catch myself doing that I had never done before. I can't even think now what they were, but I remember commenting on them at the time."

> *Lucille:* "I find that I conduct my life, I do things— my decisions about daily living—I find that I do them the same way that he would do them. I make the same decisions that he would have made."

> *Sharon:* "I thought about that the other day when I thought that my patience was going on me and I've become much less patient over the past two years. And I wondered if I sounded like him. When I would not be able to tolerate the kids screaming or some- thing like that. Sometimes I say things and I hear him. I'm startled. It's almost like he said it. It's the same phrase or the same way he would say it."

One of the more enduring and often inflexible aspects of human personality is one's sense of esthetics, or taste. Yet changing tastes, especially those that reflect the tastes of one's spouse, are not uncommon.

Sid and his wife were both avid readers. While Iris
was alive, he made numerous efforts to appreciate her
interests. "She was a particular fan of Theodore
Dreiser. I could never understand it. He leaves me
cold." Six months after her death, Sid was enjoying
Dreiser's writings immensely. He was astonished.

One form of identification occurs with relative frequency in
bereavement, in contrast to its rarity elsewhere. Here the survivor
develops symptomatology that either mimics the symptoms of the
deceased or lends itself to interpretation as the same disease
process. As a result, the survivor becomes afraid or even convinced
that he will die as the spouse died. Somatic symptoms are a
common component of grief (see Chapter Five), and the circumstances of a spouse's death will frequently dictate how the
symptoms are perceived and interpreted.

Oscar died after a long battle with cancer. Several
months later Marie became aware that she had gained
a lot of weight. Even though she had been overeating
regularly, her first thoughts were that she might have
a tumor.

Blanche felt a "burning" in her chest and thought of
Julius's lung cancer. Her fear that she would die as
he did prompted her to quit smoking.

Daphne: "I started having headaches, which was an
unusual thing. But I thought it was more than just a
headache. I really thought I had a brain tumor, and
I started thinking all the things—my husband's
symptoms, and pretty soon I was thinking, 'Well, I
can't concentrate.' Well of course I couldn't concentrate because I was still depressed. That was one of
the things that happened to him. He was taking
trigonometry at night school and he lost his powers
to compute. That was part of his illness. I had myself
convinced that I had a brain tumor." Her doctor

recognized the problem, examined her thoroughly, and reassured her repeatedly before she felt relief.

Nine months after Edwin's fatal heart attack, Doris began having chest pain and difficulty in breathing. She thought she was having a heart attack but was told by her physician that it was anxiety.

Morrie experienced difficulty in breathing. "I think it's a sympathetic reaction. I remember how much trouble Pauline had breathing toward the end of her illness."

Active Perpetuation. While identification operates as an unconscious process that perpetuates in the living certain aspects of the deceased, there are also quite conscious and deliberate acts on the part of the bereaved that have the same purpose and effect.

As a person prepares for death, he may ask the surviving spouse to carry out certain actions after death. Even where there is no direct expression of a wish or expectation, the grieving spouse may act on a presumed expectation to keep that part of the deceased alive.

Melinda: "When he dies, you lose your purpose. I've just started getting a purpose [nine months later]. And my purpose I suddenly realized was to do the things Jim wanted me to do."

Phyllis: "And the deal was, the agreement was that we had such a wonderful relationship that as soon as the surviving partner was able, they were going to go out looking for another nice person and recreate this beautiful love and this nice experience that we had created with each other. And that was the memorial we wanted."

Joanne remarried during the second year of her bereavement. "I did what I would have wanted Larry to do—to be with somebody else and be happy. I knew that Larry would have been very unhappy with me if I did not get out again and form a new relationship. He wouldn't have wanted me to be alone at forty-eight. I felt he was watching over me and guiding me."

At times these wishes translate into rather mundane though important tasks and are even carried out to some degree before the death occurs. This preparation then continues, and the bereaved person still, in a sense, has the dead spouse's directions on which to rely.

Amalia: "I was getting ready because some women, when their husband dies, they don't know anything. He said, 'Remember, one of these days I am going to die and you have to be taking care of the children, you have to be taking care of the house. So I want you to learn now.' For example, he sent me to the gas station to get an alignment for the car. 'I want you to do it,' he was telling me. 'Go and do it.'"

This "educational legacy" is manifested as the surviving spouse carries out actively the lessons in living learned either specifically in preparation for the death or as one of the incidental benefits of a good relationship.

Fran: "I had a period of four months with him, with just nothing but constant talking and [his] telling me what he wanted me to do, and he showed me how to do all kinds of things. . . . He passed away the first of May, and in August I was already going to a sailing club [because] he told me to get out and meet people. But he didn't know that I was going to keep the boat because he didn't think I'd be able to handle it and I'm learning to do everything. Fixing the car—I put a battery in the car. I fixed my blinkers, because it's all interesting for me. You know, I'd watch him do it and so I thought, 'Well, I think maybe I can do all these things.'"

Harold went through difficult periods of depression, when he felt that life was not worth living. "I'm able to combat these feelings by thinking about how Rose would have dealt with widowhood." His memories of her courage keep him going.

Carl: "Oh, things she taught me, like the cooking, you know. She'd sit there and help me. I don't dwell on it, you know, it doesn't make me emotional or anything. I might say to my daughter or we'll be doing something and she'll say, 'Dad, I don't think you do it that way.' And I'll say, 'Wait a minute. Mom said this is the way you had to do it.' Often-times I can remember her telling me, 'Don't do this, don't do that.' But I don't get emotional with it."

Survivors also may perpetuate the deceased by continuing their good works or sustaining their memory through endowments.

Sal was a local sports celebrity. After his death a special memorial trust fund was set up in his name, which was also used for a Christmas tournament. Furthermore, his team used his name for a trophy. *Yvette:* "They didn't forget about him. It was very reassuring and comforting to me."

Many of the books written about bereavement have been dedicated to a loved one whose death has led to the author's own bereavement and subsequent wish to inform others.

Living On in Progeny. Children and other close relatives often bear a striking resemblance to the deceased—in appearance, personality, mannerisms, and abilities. These characteristics provide living legacies similar to others in their capacity to stimulate distress in or provide comfort for the bereaved.

Five years after Jeff's death, Agnes talked about her middle son (now age fourteen). "He is so much like his father in his interests and mannerisms. It's comforting but it's sad, too—sad that his dad couldn't be alive to see him growing up."

Dick's twin brother, Len, was initially the source of great distress for Sharon. The first time she saw him after Dick's sudden death, she relived the horror over again. Over time, she looked carefully to see how much she would see Dick in Len, using her reactions as a yardstick for measuring how much distance separated her from the tragedy.

Marie: "I don't feel that he's dead, and the main reason is that every time I look at my kids I see him. Through them he's living, so I can't say that he's dead. Physically, yes, but spiritually he lives through the children."

Ralph's daughter was only eleven when her mother died, and Ralph had worried that she did not get enough from her before her death. As she grew up, she became the embodiment of her mother. It was wonderful for Ralph to see his wife recreated.

Rituals

Social, cultural, and religious customs and traditions evolve over great spans of time and generally express both the belief systems and the collective wisdom of the group. Such rituals display the group's knowledge of the grieving process, and the rituals themselves become vehicles to facilitate grief, among many other functions. Our society has numerous rituals related to disposing of the body of the deceased—deemed necessary for public health reasons. In contrast, among certain tribes in New Guinea, the body lies on the dining room table for the first year. Most Western religions have utilized burial as the disposition, contending that the body must be intact for the soul to ascend to heaven.

However, more and more people now utilize cremation, which was quite common in this study.

Many cultures have had a prescribed course of behavior for the newly bereaved, especially widows. In some cultures she jumped onto the funeral pyre because she was deemed useless. In others she automatically became the new wife of a relative; or she was expected to spend a year wearing black and being socially inactive; or she became an object of scorn and was rejected by society altogether. Great changes have evolved as people in a relatively free and open society create their own ways of expressing their grief, including the avoidance of rituals and traditions. This freedom can lead, on the one hand, to greater personal fulfillment and satisfaction in the ways that the bereaved are able to express their farewells and maintain their relationships with their spouses. On the other hand, the rituals serve important purposes, and their avoidance, in the absence of other measures, can leave a vacuum that makes the grieving process more difficult.

All these customs, traditions, and rituals have evolved as a means of dealing with human mortality, and each has as a major component the purpose of achieving some form of immortality, some way of keeping alive parts of the deceased.

Funeral. The funeral or memorial service is the first formal, public acknowledgment and display of a person's death before family and friends. As such, it underscores the reality and the finality for the bereaved in a way that cuts through certain aspects of shock, numbness, and disbelief. The bereaved can begin to grapple "officially" with the tasks of dealing with the loss. By virtue of the people who are brought together for the occasion, there is also some tightening of the bereaved's social support system. Finally, there is the tribute paid to the deceased through the eulogy and through the show of concern by friends and family.

> At Frank's funeral Annette was calm. "Frank was holding my hand and commented on his enjoyment of the service. Then he faded." There were many people at the service, a beautiful ceremony held at sea. "I felt it was a great testimonial to Frank—like

another 'award' like the night before." (Frank had died the day after an award banquet in his honor.) She felt buoyed by the comments about Frank and about their "special" relationship. "Weeks later people were still talking about the funeral."

An audiotape was made of Alvin's funeral service. Diane reminisced a lot about the funeral as a tribute to Alvin. She and the children (three months later) listened to the tape together, using it as a vehicle to talk about him. "All the kids talked about special times they had with him."

The importance of the funeral to the rest of the family became apparent when David decided not to have one, and Carol supported his wishes. "We had no funeral arrangements. That was his arrangement, that he did not want a big funeral. My kids had some problem because even now they say that maybe it would have been better, it would have been easier for them, if they had finality."

Remains. The remains of the deceased are either buried or cremated. Burial in a cemetery creates another means of keeping aspects of the deceased alive, through the symbols of the marker and its inscription as well as by designating a "place" where the deceased is located.

For Jonathan, Sandra's headstone served as a way of keeping an important part of her alive. "There was a phrase that she often said when I left for work: 'Take my love and pass it around.' I put that on her headstone."

Viola was left with a different kind of "marker." "Lyle was buried at sea—military. I donated his flag to the mortuary and they fly it twice a year now. I went to the service, and [it] gave me a proud feeling to know that . . . his flag will be flying twice a year from now on. I think of him at times like that."

Where cremation is utilized, the location of the ashes offers the bereaved another opportunity to carry on the wishes of their spouses or to express other sentiments by deciding where the ashes will reside.

> *Ross:* "My son and I took the ashes and scattered them ourselves. That was a time of intense grief. It was also a period of 'Well, we got through it,' a period of feeling good about it. We flew from here to Montana, took a car, and spent the afternoon with my father and spent the night in a little town at the base of the mountains. The following day we drove to a summit and scattered her ashes in a particular spot that we knew that she liked. We had a lot of time together and a lot of time to talk. It was the right thing for us to do even though there were a lot of emotions, the whole gamut of emotions. . . . We did this for ourselves."

Fran kept Boris's ashes at home with her for a while and experienced great comfort. "He died in May and I had him cremated. My son was going to have a vacation in the middle of June, so I told him not to come down until then. So until then I had Dad on the nightstand right next to my bed, and it didn't seem to bother me, it calmed me. Everybody else thought it was so grotesque that I did that." A month later her son arrived; and, with him, she threw her husband's ashes off the fantail of the boat that he had loved.

Visitation. Following the memorial services, most cultures and religions designate a period of time during which the bereaved spouse and family have some form of reception wherein family and friends visit the home of the deceased and pay condolences.

The visitation or Catholic wake or Jewish "sitting shivah" (seven days) or informal gathering provides a vehicle that serves several important functions. In addition to providing a reminder of the reality of the death, and at the same time keeping the loved one alive through reminiscences, it opens the door for the emotional and practical supports that are needed by the newly bereaved. Friends and family can rush to the side of the grieving person, not only with their warmth, caring concern, and sympathy but also with practical services: food, arrangements and transportation for out-of-town guests, and suggestions for carrying on, which they may have learned from their personal experiences with grief.

> *Ross:* "I don't know what I expected, but what I got was not what I expected. The neighborhood I live in is not much different from any other. Most of us know each other. I've lived there for fifteen years. We don't see each other socially very much. There are only three that would fall in the category of close friends even though I know all of them and I see them on a daily basis. But the support from all of these people was—I wasn't prepared for that. I must have gotten enough food after my wife's death to last the three of us for, God, I don't know how long."

Cemetery. For most widows and widowers, the cemetery plot and marker become the major ritualized memorial for the deceased. With the exception of those whose ashes are scattered or who have been buried at sea, the cemetery has become the true final resting ground for most Western societies. For many people it retains a pivotal position in their ongoing relationship with their lost loved ones. The cemetery is the site of their most poignant emotional experiences or the central focus of their avoidance, either of which speaks to the presence of their loved one. To this site many make regular pilgrimages to seek comfort, solace, and peace, to experience communication, or to fulfill an obligation. For some, over time, it may remain the only place where they "feel" their spouses' presence and where they are flooded with emotions.

Bill: "The cemetery really brings things crashing in on me. Even if I happen to be on business driving near it, it bothers me. I always cried when I went to the cemetery until the last couple of times [four years later]."

For Carol the cemetery was important because it was the only place where she was able to cry—something that she wanted to do, particularly her first Christmas without David.

For more than two years, Linda visited Paul's grave every other week. "It's a peaceful time without tears."

Joe went to the cemetery every couple of weeks to visit with Loretta. He would put flowers on her grave, cry "a bit," and put out bird seed to keep living things around. He would return to his house, say "hello" to his wife's picture, and feel that he had made contact.

Some people who have been to the cemetery cannot return because the experience is too painful.

Susan: "I've been to the cemetery once, after a year, and that was when I was feeling really, really down and I thought it would help me. When I came home, my younger one looked at me, and my face was all tear stained and he said, 'Thought you'd feel better, didn't you?' And I said, 'Yes, I really did.' He said, 'Do you?' and I said 'No.' I will probably go out again and take some flowers. But the one time that I did go, it was really so painful that I couldn't go back again. I just kind of fell apart. Maybe that's what I needed. Maybe it was so bottled up inside of me that that's what I needed. So maybe I should go out now that I feel I've got it all together, maybe I should go out again. See if it would be good for me."

Some bereaved persons do not experience their loved ones at the cemetery, so that their visit seems "hollow."

> After three years Sharon still went to the cemetery every two months. At times her purpose was to seek comfort or ask Dick for assistance. She would say hello, but no one ever seemed to be there. "If I go to the cemetery, I have a conversation with me and the stone. But I never feel any satisfaction."

> After one year Lucille went to the cemetery but could not believe that Arthur was there. "How can it be that he is under that stone? That can't be Arthur. How can he be in a hole rotting away?"

Anniversaries, Holidays, and Other "Special" Days. "Special" days are frequently experienced with a heightened intensity of all kinds of feelings associated with the loved one and his or her death. The symbolism of these occasions reawakens painful feelings that may have been successfully suppressed for weeks or months. The anniversary date of the spouse's death can be a particularly evocative time, especially for the first few years, bringing vivid memories of the time of death. It can be like reliving the experience of trauma.

> Susan had a difficult time as the first anniversary of Phil's death approached. "May was awful. The whole month of May I cried continuously. I became fearful about drinking alcohol, that if I started I wouldn't stop. The same with tranquilizers. I thought I was going bonkers. My head felt like it was going to explode, my eyes were constantly bloodshot from the continuous crying, my voice was not the same because my nasal passages were plugged." Susan went to the cemetery three days after the anniversary. "Everything came back afresh. I relived every minute of May 20 last year." She started marking off days on the calendar to get out of the

month of May. "May 20 would have been our twentieth anniversary."

The first anniversary of Barry's death was made more painful for Beth because of the media coverage of the plane crash, with vivid pictures on television and daily newspaper articles commemorating the event. Beth's anniversary reaction started about one month before and built up to the date of the crash. "I had vivid memories of how things were, the last things we did. My feelings were very intense. I couldn't get rid of them. I don't think I even tried." On the day of the anniversary, Beth became physically ill with diarrhea and vomiting. She experienced great relief the next day, though her feelings faded only gradually.

On the second anniversary of Tom's death, Pamela, who would have gone to the cemetery, was lying in the hospital thinking of "how good Tom was to me when I was sick. I felt he was in the room with me. I felt his hand on the back of my neck and then rubbing my incision. I've been afraid to tell anyone about this. People would think I was cracking up."

Joe felt miserable around the second anniversary of Loretta's death. He was quite tearful anticipating the date. His birthday was the day before, and his children called him, which took his mind off the loss. The next day he went to the cemetery, feeling sad and missing her. For the next month, Joe was unable to talk about her. When he saw something on television that reminded him of Loretta, he felt numb—just as he had immediately after her death.

Around the second anniversary of Frank's death, Annette experienced some suicidal feelings. The trauma she felt at the time of his death came back. She looked at the ocean, where he was buried, every day and continually looked over their pictures. "I felt

like I was paying homage. He would know I was
thinking about him. I had to let him know I had not
forgotten him. It felt like Frank came down, and his
spirit was hovering."

There is tremendous variation in what people experience on
such occasions, ranging from severe and dramatic to mild or even
minimal responses.

On the anniversary of Dick's death, Sharon heard
"their song" on the radio and missed him. She had
anticipated the date with dread, but once it arrived
she didn't feel too bad. She took Dick's mother to the
cemetery. Afterward, while they were having lunch,
her mother-in-law fell apart, and Sharon helped her
feel better.

Usually the intensity of reactions during anniversaries
diminishes over time.

Lucille's first-anniversary reaction started a week
early. She felt "miserable" the entire week, reliving
the traumatic events of Arthur's death and the same
feelings of guilt and helplessness. She cried a great
deal, repeating "Is this really true?" and wondering
whether she would be alone forever and whether life
was really worth living under such circumstances.
Her memories on this occasion triggered depression,
anger, and resentment. The following year she began
to feel sad, though not depressed, two weeks before
the second anniversary of Arthur's death. She did
relive the day he died but with less intense emotions.
A friend asked her to stay with her on that weekend
and accompanied her to the cemetery, so that the day
became more bearable. On the third anniversary,
Lucille felt sadness and a sense of futility during her
visit to the cemetery, but by this time she had
accepted Arthur's loss. "I can momentarily feel sorry

for myself and wonder 'Why did it happen to me?' but I don't dwell on those thoughts. I get up and do something."

After Susan's terrible first-anniversary reaction, when she cried for a month, she worried about the approaching second anniversary, but trouble did not materialize. "On May 10 I had a lovely day. I went to lunch with friends. The specific events of Phil's death went through my mind. I remembered it clearly but didn't feel threatened by it. It was like it happened to someone else. It's becoming less and less real to me. It's not as vivid." Unfortunately, just before the third anniversary, Phil's mother died. Everything about Phil's illness and death reemerged after the funeral. Susan felt as though she was going to fall apart. "It blew me away." For the next three weeks, Susan was moody and depressed. But then she returned to normal and was feeling good again. While her original wound had healed fairly well, her mother-in-law's death had stripped off the scar, leaving Susan exposed and vulnerable until she could seal over the new, shallower wound.

Holidays, particularly Christmas, Thanksgiving, and New Year, are times when families are together and memories are shared. These are special times of the year with "magical" qualities for most people. Because losses are more noticeable at these times, holidays frequently evoke strong reactions in the newly bereaved. When they coincide with the anniversary of a loved one's death, the size of the response is additive.

Edwin died a week before Christmas. The following October Doris began planning and preparing for the holidays and the anniversary. She had planned to have Thanksgiving at her home; as the time approached, however, her anxiety increased, and she "got out of having it at home." That day she went to

church and cried a great deal. For the entire week
between the anniversary and Christmas, she tried to
stay busy. Christmas was difficult, and the tension
continued until January 1, when she felt dramatically
better. Her mood and outlook improved, and she
began to think about travel for the first time since
Edwin died.

Doris's improvement on January 1 was quite striking and
underscores a common attitude among the newly bereaved—
namely, that the first anniversary of a spouse's death should serve
as an indicator that mourning is over. Another of the prevalent
myths about bereavement is that grief should last *one year*. It
derives from social customs and traditions that seem to prescribe
one year as the period of time in which the mourner should
display the trappings of grief in dress and demeanor. As a result,
the bereaved—as well as families, friends, clergy, physicians, and
mental health professionals—have come to believe that a grieving
person should be "fully recovered" within a year. Although some
people do appear to "recover" within this time period, the vast
majority of bereaved spouses require considerably more time to
"get over" their grief, and even then they will be likely to
experience aspects of their grief intermittently and indefinitely.
Where such misconceptions are held, and when magical transformation does not occur after the one-year milestone, both the
bereaved and those who support them are likely to feel considerable disappointment and impatience.

Just as anniversaries and holidays evoke strong psychological reactions in the bereaved, so do any special occasions whose
meaning touches on the loss of one's spouse. These include
birthdays, wedding anniversaries, and other deaths, births, and
marriages—all the important markers in the life cycle.

As her youngest daughter's wedding approached,
Diane thought a great deal about Alvin, who had
died over four years before. He would have wanted to
be there and to dance with his daughter. For several

days Diane felt that Alvin was in the room with her. "It was so real it was frightening."

Memories

Most of us ultimately hold on to what we have lost, or what is now gone, through our memories. These memories, retained images, are in turn often capable of stimulating feelings that accompanied them at some time in the past. These vital links allow the relationship to continue. As with other multifaceted vehicles, the bereaved experienced their memories in a variety of ways.

Comforts. To the extent that memory serves well, it provides comfort and peace to the bereaved, offering continuing connection with their beloved, who is otherwise lost to them. Memory can be selective, so that the images and feelings are good ones, or at least bittersweet.

Ralph [three years later]: "When I think about Darlene, it's the good memories that come to mind. It's easier to talk about her with friends, easier to reminisce."

Viola [two years later]: "I'm making my memories pleasant ones, of our time together. From time to time something funny that he has said will come up, and I'll chuckle about it over again. There's a terrific sense of humor that he did have. Things will come up now and I'll remember. I speak of him freely to people who knew him. 'Remember when Lyle said that?' But I don't say it with any remorse or longing or feeling bad. He's just somebody that was in my life and isn't there now."

Joe [five years later]: "I happened to read an article today about Mt. Shasta. I thought of the trip we took there. I think about Loretta fairly often—memories of places we visited. I don't get as emotional as I once

did. I still miss her and I sure would like to have her
here.''

Bill [four years later]: [Seeing her clothes] ''I remember buying this or buying that for her and the
thrill she had when she opened it up. Seeing it on her
and hearing her friends compliment her. They'd say,
'Boy, you sure have a pretty dress,' and she'd say, 'Bill
bought that for me.' She was always very
appreciative.''

Triggers. Memory becomes a burden when the bereaved
person has not achieved sufficient distance from the acute sense of
loss or when the memories lead to the emergence of painful
emotions.

John did what he could to avoid all painful affects
throughout his bereavement: staying very busy and
distracted, quickly becoming involved with another
woman, and avoiding associations to or thoughts
about his wife, Connie. Even almost five years later,
John would not let himself dwell on thoughts about
her: ''I try to pass off thoughts of my wife real quick.
I might get emotional.''

After two years Harold felt continually tortured by
memories of Rose. In his unhappiness he would
remember how much she enjoyed life and then rue
his fate: ''It's been months since I've heard laughter
or saw anyone enjoy life.''

Blocked Memories. Particularly in the early months after
the death of a spouse, a survivor may be able to summon up only
the most rudimentary memories of the dead spouse. This is yet
another unconscious protective device to prevent the vulnerable
survivor from being overwhelmed by the emotions that might
accompany such a memory or image. To the extent that these
blocked memories are experienced as a loss, they will be quite

distressing for the bereaved person, who is already feeling the pain of loss.

> During the weeks after Larry's death, Joanne ached for him. She tried to imagine him holding her and being intimate, but she could not do so. "I can't remember what it felt like to have his arms around me. I need that."

For Glenn the emergence of memories and, later, dreams of Eileen occurred slowly, over a long period of time. For the first year, he could not remember much of anything about her or picture her face. At thirteen months: "I miss her more now than I have for some time. I'm now starting to remember some of the things I couldn't remember before—some of the good times. I miss them." At nineteen months: "The memories have increased, and she's appeared in a lot of dreams. She's in my mind much more in the past few months than she was the whole first year." At twenty-five months: "I realize every day the longer she's dead, the more I think of her, so to me that's good. I mean, I have good memories of her. And I'd rather think of her than forget her by a long shot." At three years: "Eileen is in my thoughts more now than ever before—in good memories and in dreams that seemed very real on several occasions. There's no time when I'm overwhelmed by emotions. I am moved by feelings about her." At five years: "I can bring up Eileen's name now. All of my friends have known her for many years, and she's always part of the conversation." Glenn's initial inhibition of memories gradually gave way to the increasing presence of Eileen in his mental and emotional life, to the point where, five years after her death, she had become an important part of his daily life again, even though he had remarried quite happily and well.

Memories of one's relationship may seem irretrievable because of inhibition, as we have just seen, or because of traumatic events—such as prolonged illness, with its catastrophic consequences for both the deceased and the survivor—that overshadow these memories and stake their claim to the survivor's mental and emotional life. Almost no circumstances in life bombard one with such heart-wrenching emotions or such powerful images as the vigil over one's spouse who is dying of cancer or another chronic debilitating illness. As a result, those bereaved spouses who emerge from such experiences may have great difficulty in retrieving earlier, more positive and comforting memories of their spouses and their lives together. The pictorial images of debilitation and death may be even more distressing as the survivors try to replace them with greater beauty from the past. In many ways the reactions of the bereaved under these circumstances parallel those of other victims who develop traumatic neuroses from experiences in war, concentration camps, rape, or other disasters. It may take much time—years—to override the horrors and reclaim the earlier memories.

> After June's death from a brain tumor, Perry was at times exasperated by his inability to remember what their lives had been like before her illness of two years. He would have to look at her pictures to remember certain features of her appearance. "It's odd. I blocked out the essence of six years but not the last two years."
>
> *Morrie* [twenty-two months later]: "It's now hard to recapture my relationship with Pauline. I can't identify or get the emotional aspects of our good times—the time before her illness. The period of time when she was ill was so traumatic that it drove out the good memories. The image which always comes back is when she was so ill. The terrible routines, her gasping for breath—I try to turn off these memories."
> At three years: "Whenever I think of her, at this point, I have pleasant and loving memories. The

unpleasant days of her illness seem like a very distant memory."

After nineteen months Earl continued to have vivid memories of Rita's suffering, accompanied by his own anguish. "I can't stamp this picture out of my mind—how she suffered. I felt helpless while she was dying. The hardest part is to see an active person deteriorate." All he could do at these times was to look through their picture albums to remember the good times they had together.

Every night Amalia prayed to Ted. In her mind she would picture him in his blue pajamas, ill and suffering, sitting on top of his gravestone. After twenty-one months the image changed. She still pictured Ted as sitting on his gravestone in his blue pajamas, but now he was feeling well and smiling.

Fading Memories. Since memories serve an important psychological function by sustaining the widowed person's contact with the deceased, the bereaved are understandably distressed when they find that their memories are fading. At the same time, the fading of a once clear memory is probably a manifestation of a diminishing need on the part of the bereaved to keep alive the memory. Not needing it is not the same as not wanting it or as missing it if it were to fade.

Sixteen months after George's death, Gloria became involved with another man. One weekend she found that she was having a hard time picturing her husband. This caused her to feel guilty. She felt an obligation not to let his memory fade too soon. "It doesn't seem right that he should slip from my memory so fast after thirty-three years."

Doris [two years later]: "Sometimes I think things are getting faded—that's the word I'm using. I remember everything, but it seems as if it's, well, it's farther away since he died and I don't know—I don't really think I want it to be that far away. Maybe that's because I feel that I'm getting over his death."

After two years Shirley's memories were fading. "Thinking about Art coming home—and he did that every day. Okay, so you can remember that. And you try and visualize it, you know, and him walking up the sidewalk or walking into the room. You can do that until you get to a certain point and then you're getting closer. [Then] it just shuts off like you flipped a light switch, or it may go back to the distance again. You know, back into the truck and take him back out again. It gets to a certain point and it just shuts off. So I'm really foggy. It's like he didn't—like he was a dream. I have to look at the kids. He had to exist, you know. I've got two kids to prove it. It's just like a dream, but you know it happened."

Idealization. One of the characteristics of memory is its selectivity. We all know from our own experiences that we remember best what suits us, that maintaining our version of reality saves us from much internal conflict and distress. The distortions, our self-deceptions, can be minor or major, subtle or blatant. Many of the bereaved have a significant investment in maintaining a memory that portrays their deceased spouses as paragons of virtue, ideal in all ways, without fault. Given the tendency for people in good marriages to overlook or downplay the faults of their spouses, this idealization is understandable. However, it forces those people to deny any feelings about the spouse's shortcomings or almost any negative feelings at all that are directed at the spouse. How could one be angry at someone who is perfect? And dead besides? Yet a grieving spouse often has many such feelings, which may have to be experienced, recognized, and dealt with in order for the person to achieve optimal adjustment. Usually such idealization is easier for someone else to recognize than it is for the person who utilizes this mechanism.

> *Louis:* "Looking back over the past—what a perfect
> woman she was. [Any flaws?] No, as a matter of fact,
> we were married for thirty-five years and never had a
> bad argument. Never had a bad argument during that
> thirty-five years. Because I'd get mad sometimes at
> something she might do, you know, or something
> she had done. And she'd always smooth my ruffled
> feathers and I'd be ashamed of myself. [She didn't
> have any faults?] I never knew of any. Working too
> hard. That was one of her faults. She worked too
> much."

As a result of such views, Louis felt that all the shortcomings were his, even though there were obviously things about
Karen that angered him. Anger is an inevitable and legitimate part
of all intimate relationships. People are aware of its destructive
potential and are inclined, where possible, to minimize it in a
relationship, even when it might serve constructive ends. Regardless of how people contend with it or even attempt to deny it, at
some level it exists and is operating in the relationship, at times
expressing itself in ways that people "don't mean"—that is, in
ways that people would not rationally choose. A fairly universal
form of angry expression is "Drop dead." It reflects the one way
that a child learns to contend with angry feelings—by wishing that
the object of its wrath would disappear or die. Most adults
recognize feelings of anger and accept the "Drop dead" sentiment
as a manifestation of the feeling but as something they "don't
mean." In a relationship where anger is unacceptable, because
one's partner is too perfect to warrant being an object of scorn,
these feelings will of necessity remain below the surface, unrecog-
nized by their owner. If that spouse dies, regardless of the cause,
the surviving spouse will often contend with these unconscious
feelings of hostility by irrationally assuming (still unconsciously)
that the hostility (and perhaps a childish death wish) contributed
to this death. What finally becomes conscious is a sense of guilt,
which the bereaved does not understand. Louis was plagued with
unrelenting guilt. He somehow blamed himself because his wife
had "worked too much," even though he recognized that she loved

to work hard and that working hard probably did not cause her death.

Often people will recognize their tendency toward idealization and will take corrective psychological action.

> Beatrice became aware that, as time went on, she tended to forget about Fred's bad qualities. "I was sort of making him a saint. Finally, I had a dream of him getting extremely angry, and then I started to remember him as he was."

> After almost two years of bereavement, Jonathan felt that he could be more objective about Sandra. It was easier to talk about faults. "I would have felt too guilty to discuss her shortcomings."

As Jonathan experienced, dealing with one's anger or one's less than flattering opinions about the deceased often runs counter to an individual's sense of what is appropriate or fair. After all, the person is dead. Isn't that enough? Yet the living must deal with all their feelings about and opinions of their dead spouses. Correcting one's internal distortions becomes a prerequisite to living effectively with oneself and others in a relatively new world.

> *Gloria:* "I had a tendency to canonize him after he died. But I think I have a very realistic view of him now. I remember consciously trying to do it—because I wanted to see it realistically. If you canonize someone after they die, you're just painting a pretty picture and it's not the way it was. I wanted to see it the way it was, and it was good enough the way it was."

Dreams

Throughout our lives dreams serve us as a means of coping with the stresses of living. We utilize them to express our deepest wishes and our darkest fears, to replay situations of helplessness in the hope of developing mastery, and to try to resolve our oldest conflicts. At times they are so bizarre and complex that they seem indecipherable. At other times their manifest content is an obvious reflection of the important issues with which one is contending, and the meaning is clear.

Bereaved people's dreams are not different, in their nature and purposes, from other people's dreams. Although the issues with which they deal are quite focal—usually related to the loss— they reflect the wishes, fears, and conflicts of the bereaved, just as other people's dreams do. Whatever other purposes they may serve, these dreams do bring the spouse to life for a while.

Retrieval Dreams. The most frequent dreams by the bereaved are those in which their spouses are not dead but are with them. These dreams can appear at any time after the death, but there is often a delay of weeks to months, the latest in this study appearing first at sixteen months. Most of these dreams are quite mundane, simple, and straightforward: there is an obvious solution to the widowed person's pain, the return of the spouse. Usually there is no awareness, in the dream, that the spouse was ever gone.

> *Doris:* "I had a crazy dream a couple of months after he died. I opened this door, maybe to the bedroom, and here he is vacuuming. It didn't seem natural, and I said, 'Hi,' and I went to put my arms around him. You know, we always put our arms around each other and kissed each other when we saw each other or said goodbye or got up in the morning. And I said, 'Oh, I'm tired,' or something. And it sort of ended as soon as it began. It was kind of disappointing, and I thought, 'Oh, gosh, it was nice to dream of Edwin.'"

> *Merle:* "One of them [dreams] was maybe six months after Jonesy died. We were just getting ready, we were going to get in the car and go somewhere. We never did get in the car, but we were getting ready. And there was just nothing to it, you know. After I woke

up, I remembered. I had a little difficulty orienting myself, you know, because I had just come fresh out of that dream and I said, 'No, I'm not getting ready to go.'"

Pamela recalled her first dream sixteen months after Tom died. It was a scene where she and Tom were on a picnic with their kids.

Glenn, who had been blocked in his efforts to think about Eileen or remember their lives together, did not dream about her at all for the first six months after her death. Then she began to appear in dreams as his wife. "When she comes back to me, it's always in a dream and it's always when we're doing something— either getting ready to go on a trip or maybe we're traveling or maybe we're going to a dance. Like nothing happened." These experiences would bring her alive again briefly and then stimulate the painful realization that she was gone. "I'll never see her again."

Most of the time, the bereaved cannot identify any specific stimulus to such dreams other than the continuing sense of loss. However, at times an identifiable event or emotional reaction may trigger a dream.

Over the five years since Jeff's death, Agnes recalled dreaming about him only once a year. Her most recent dream occurred after she had had a fight with her new husband. In it "Jeff was smiling at me, getting out of a car. I was so happy to see him."

In some retrieval dreams, the bereaved are conscious of their loss, even in the dream. This consciousness heightens the drama of the experience and the emotional reaction to the returning spouse in the dream.

Eighteen months after Frank's death, Annette was going through a period of intense loneliness. Her dreams reflected her loneliness. She would be looking for Frank and then would find him and plead with him to return because "I'm so lonely."

Beth: "When I have a dream about him, it's always good. You know, I haven't seen him in a long time and then he just reappears. It's always the same. He just comes back from wherever he was. A miracle!"

Even where the manifest content of the dream is not obvious, it often takes little unraveling to determine the meaning of many thinly veiled dreams. There is some alternative explanation, contained in the dream, of what has happened to the spouse.

Two years after Nathan's death, Bobbi had a dream about him. "He was in a hospital bed and had grown a beard. I thought, 'So that's why he left me—to grow a beard.' "

Sharon dreamed that Dick was hiding in a box. In the dream she said to him, "What are you doing here? You're missing everything."

In the fifth year after Pauline's death, Morrie had several dreams in which he had been in the service and was not receiving any letters from Pauline. He felt that he should phone home to find out why she was not writing. He was aware, in the dream, of feeling upset by this lack of contact.

Separation Dreams. Separation dreams are a group of dreams in which the bereaved deal with the loss not by compensation through retrieval but by somehow acknowledging the process of loss and participating, usually passively, in the parting. Understandably, these dreams can be painful and frightening, and they are frequently disguised to lessen their impact.

Nine months after her death, Daniel had a series of dreams about Ellen. "In the first one, I dreamed that she left and everyone knew where she was except me, but no one would tell me. In the second dream, I kept insisting that someone tell me where she went. I found out that she deserted me for another man. I looked for her, found her, and then she disappeared. I remember waking up, crying, yearning for her. In the third dream, she came to me, and I only saw her for a few minutes. I asked her to come back, but she said no, that she couldn't. The fourth dream was that she saw me again, only for a short time, and said that she had found a place with another man and that she wanted to stay there and I wouldn't see her anymore. Then the dreams were discontinued, and I haven't had any since." [Meaning?] "Well, if I could draw a parallel, if that's what you mean, I suppose my subconscious was telling me that she was deceased, dead, and that she wasn't coming back."

Earl: "There's a funny dream I had about her. She came in a white car, and then she wanted to drive the car that I had. And I said, 'How come you want to drive my old car when you've got this here beautiful white car out there?' She says, 'I can't be here very long, but I want to drive the car.' She couldn't stay because she had to go back. And that was it." When asked about its possible meaning, Earl responded, "I don't know. See, my father died when I was seven years old and he died at night. And when my mother woke me up that morning, I told her, I said, you know, 'They came and got my father on a white horse,' and then she said, 'Yes, he's gone.' I can always remember that." Using the grown-up imagery of his childhood, Rita had returned to say goodbye to Earl.

Conflict-Laden Dreams. The most common conflict-laden dreams are those that express the guilt of the bereaved. They can be fairly nonspecific but are usually expressions of feelings of betrayal.

> When Annette was involved in a series of affairs, Frank appeared in a dream to tell her that she was "living in sin."

> After obtaining pets, which would not have been allowed in their house while Phil was alive, Susan had recurrent dreams of Phil's returning. "He would just be walking through the house, so we would have to hide the dog, hide the cat."

> After meeting an attractive man, Ann dreamed that her husband's hands grabbed her and pulled her away from the stranger in her dream.

Premonitory Dreams. Two men in the study group reported premonitory dreams, both of which predicted their wives' deaths. While these obviously were not consequences of their bereavement, each had a significant impact on the course of their grief.

> Karen had a seizure disorder but was in otherwise good general health when she had a prolonged seizure that ended in a cardiac arrest and death. *Louis:* "Two weeks before her death, I had a dream. She and I were in a car and it seemed that we were going around the world like this [moves arms]. It was a big world like this, and we were on this road going around it, and all of a sudden both of us flew out of the car. I reached out for her, and she kept drifting away and drifting away, and I said, 'Honey, come back! Honey, come back!' And I said, 'Oh, my God, she's gone.' Two weeks later she had her death. That was the strangest thing that I ever had happen to me." Louis was subsequently haunted by this dream,

trying to understand it yet powerless to deal with it or his loss.

Throughout his life Earl had had many dreams that became reality. Before he met Rita, he dreamed that he would marry a girl who wore glasses—and she did. He had dreamed of his father's death on the night he died. Several years before Rita died, he dreamed that she would die at age fifty-four, the age at which she died. As a result, when he dreamed (twenty-two months after her death) that he was in a car accident, he became very agitated, took his car to be serviced, and avoided taking a trip to visit his son by car.

These incidents are difficult to explain fully as coincidence, as indications of someone's ability to "feel" impending doom, or as experiences that transcend our understanding of the physical universe. When paranormal experiences do occur, however, they have powerful effects on those who have such experiences.

 Chapter 5

Effects of Bereavement on Health, Work Life, and Social Functioning

People whose spouses have died are exposed, particularly during the year after the death, to heightened risks to health. Changes also may occur in their functioning at work and in their social activities.

Health

Bereavement represents a hazard to health. Many studies have demonstrated that, during the first year after a spouse's death, the surviving spouse is at greater than normal risk of dying: "dying of a broken heart" can occur—literally (Reich, De Silva, Lown, and Murawski, 1981). The stress and distress of loss can lead to medical and psychiatric illnesses (Parkes, 1964a, 1964b; Maddison and Viola, 1968; Clayton, 1979). Researchers have been uncovering some of the heretofore unknown connections between emotional stress and the development of symptoms and illness. Some of these changes in the body and mind may be mediated by abnormal production of steroids, particularly cortisol (Hofer, Wolff, Friedman, and Mason, 1972; Hofer, Wolff, and Mason, 1972), the stress hormone, which has marked effects on almost every system in the body. While the most dramatic early responses to bereavement are usually associated with mental and emotional disruptions, disturbances also can be found in the cardiovascular, respiratory, gastrointestinal, dermatological, musculoskeletal, neuroendocrine, and immune systems of the body.

Somatic Symptoms. Following whatever period of numbness or dissociation may occur initially, the newly bereaved are likely to experience the effects of sudden, repetitive autonomic nervous system discharge, which produces symptoms of general anxiety as well as potentially body-wide distress. These symptoms can include anxiety, tension and agitation, "butterflies," chest pain and palpitations, difficulty in catching one's breath, deep sighing, nausea or wretching, diarrhea, dizziness, and headaches. Most newly bereaved experience some initial loss of appetite and weight loss as well as insomnia.

> *Phyllis:* "I learned how completely at the mercy of my physiology I am. This is definitely a physiological thing that you go through. You hold pain, any kind of pain—physical pain, emotional grief—in your body, you know, and you are at the [mercy] of it. And while you are processing it physiologically, it affects your mind."

One of the acute symptoms, which often persists for months, is insomnia. Widows and widowers often have difficulties in falling asleep, may have very restless sleep, and frequently awaken in the middle of the night or early in the morning. Insomnia can be very distressing at any time, but it is worst during these late-night or early-morning hours because there are few external stimuli to distract the bereaved person from intrusive thoughts and imagery or the painful feelings associated with loss. The number of maneuvers to get away from this turmoil may be limited at these hours, so that the person's pain just sits there. Aside from the predictable problems with sleep, our research subjects also had some unusual experiences.

> Following Julius's death, Blanche had problems falling asleep and soon developed the fear that she would be unable to sleep at all. Within weeks she was able to sleep well, but the fear persisted. Throughout the first year, she went to bed punctually at 9:30 P.M., convinced that she would not fall asleep.

Weeks after his wife's death, Ralph developed brux-
ism—the grinding of his teeth while he was asleep—
to the extent that after several months he had taken
the enamel off some of his teeth.

Joanne: "I used to wake up every Saturday morning
at the very same time Larry passed away."

Medical Illnesses. The long-term effects of the continuing
stress of bereavement can emerge as medical illnesses in almost any
system in the body. During the first year of bereavement, the
surviving spouse is particularly vulnerable to the onslaught of
illness—much more susceptible than at almost any other time in
life.

For the two years after Tom died, Pamela, fifty-four,
had constant and continuing medical problems. She
was always preparing for or recovering from major
surgical procedures. Except for a minor back ailment,
she had always been in good health prior to her
husband's death. First she had surgery on her back
two months after he died. She subsequently developed bladder problems requiring surgical repair. As
the second anniversary approached, she was hospital-
ized for pneumonia. While she was in the hospital, a
kidney infection was discovered and, despite treatment, progressed to the point where the kidney
needed to be removed surgically. During the third
year of her bereavement, she had abdominal pains,
hip pain, and eczema as well as headaches and severe
depression requiring hospitalization.

Shirley, thirty-six, developed an enlarged ovary and
lumps in her uterus a year after Art died. Her mother
had died of uterine cancer, and she had heard of
many widows who developed cancer. When she
learned about her condition, she became tearful and
frightened, especially for her young children. After a

minor surgical procedure, she was greatly relieved to find that she did not have cancer.

Six months after Karen died, Louis, sixty-six, had chest pains while visiting family. He was examined and told that he had suffered a mild heart attack. During this period he had increased his smoking and drinking. He also developed arthritis, dizzy spells, and occasional night sweats. He noticed that he healed more slowly when he would get a cut. Also, he found himself depleted of strength and energy and had to take naps during the day. Before Karen's death he had been a vigorous man.

Many of the newly bereaved were able to associate their various ailments—such as shingles, psoriasis, hair loss, stuttering, and menstrual pain—with periods of stress. Frequently these ailments had occurred at some earlier point in their lives when they were under great stress.

Depression. Depression is the single most common medical disorder encountered by widows and widowers (Clayton, Halikas, and Maurice, 1972; Shuchter, 1982b). As it is usually described, the term "depression" refers to a transient state lasting from minutes to hours, often in response to an acute upset, and consisting of lowered mood or sadness accompanied by general pessimism or apathy, self-depreciation, and a lack of pleasure or energy. In the person who has lost a spouse, the mood shifts may be "triggered" by any reminder of one's loss or by loneliness or by other distress. This state of mind will usually persist until some other intervention occurs to create a shift in the mood through the use of one or more coping mechanisms.

Beth found herself in a "blob state" regularly. It would be set off by thoughts about Barry or the events surrounding his death. "I don't get depressed for long—maybe for an afternoon. I feel like a big blob. I just sit and don't think about much besides

Barry—feeling bad." Beth was almost always able to end these states by a conscious decision to do something active, either with others or by herself.

Depressive responses are often seen dramatically under circumstances where the bereaved shift from a setting where they are busy and involved to one where they are unoccupied, alone, and at home with reminders of their loss.

Diane: "At seven o'clock in the morning when I walk into the hospital, I'm one person. When I walk out at 3:30, I'm another person. I like my work, I really do—very, very much. Everybody in the hospital is my friend. It's like a second home. I'm very happy there. I get along with everybody. I enjoy it, I enjoy the entire eight hours. But the minute I walk out, it's like somebody turns the lights off and I just feel depressed, and I go home and shut the doors and there I stay."

These depressive responses, although they appear more frequently in the earlier months and years, are seen regularly as anniversary reactions and may persist indefinitely.

Ronald's wife and three-year-old son were killed instantly when an airplane exploded into their home. Over the years the pain of his grief seemed to get worse. After five years "Emotionally, I don't think I really have accepted it yet. Every time I think about them I feel depressed." His depressive moods were frequent, lasting for a few minutes up to one or two hours. He would combat these feelings and his loneliness by reading and staying busy. "I've become a reading addict."

The acute stress created by tragedies of many kinds activates psychological and biological processes that result in a great deal of intense symptomatology, in which depressive and anxiety features predominate (described earlier in this chapter). At times these symptoms of acute grief mimic depression so closely that it may be impossible to distinguish this grief from depression except for the presence of the other psychological manifestations of acute loss: intense feelings of loss, pining, and the like. One can still connect the painful affects and symptoms *directly* to feelings of the loss.

> *Melinda:* "I was going off the deep end for the first two months. It was horrible. I mean, I was depressed. People could see it in me and I'm a very, very high person, and a go-getter and very independent. People were very concerned about me. People were always calling me up, or people would stop me. 'Are you sick? Are you feeling okay?' Because I just lost—I had no reason to smile. I refused to sing. I'm a professional singer. And I didn't do anything. I stopped smiling, nothing. I mean, you wouldn't get any response out of me, and so an outsider would just see me dwindling away. I lost weight very rapidly. I had no reason to eat, you know. You just lose all your functions. The things that you take for granted were efforts."

While virtually everyone whose spouse dies exhibits some signs and symptoms of depression, the majority of these people experience the depressive features as an integral part of the loss, usually in the acute stages and/or in direct association with thoughts and feelings stemming from the loss.

The hallmark of depression as an illness is in its evolution into a state that has a "life of its own." Regardless of the events or stresses that initiate depression, it can persist and progress to the point where its effects continue unabated and independent of its precipitants. At that point the original precipitant may no longer be as potent a stressor, but the altered biological processes that manifest themselves as depression have already occurred and can exert their influences over every aspect of the individual's mental, emotional, physical, and social life. The signs and symptoms of full-blown depression include biological alterations in mood with

persistent feelings of sadness, despair, helplessness, and hopelessness. Appetite disturbances can be in either direction, with
resulting weight loss or gain. There is a depressive syndrome of
"retarded" depression, which includes increased appetite with
weight gain, excessive sleeping, lack of energy and interest in life,
loss of anticipated and perceived pleasure, and slowing down of
physical and mental processes. "Agitated" depressions encompass
loss of appetite, weight loss, sleep loss, excessive rumination and
agitation, irritability, and an inability to concentrate or focus one's
thinking. With either form of depression or mixtures of such
pictures, a person may also display features of social withdrawal
and physical symptoms, including pain, constipation, lethargy,
and weakness. The person's outlook becomes very negative, and
suicidal feelings may emerge. These are not transient states, but
persistent, progressive, and often recurrent for periods of weeks
and months; at times they may continue for years. It is important
that depressive illness be recognized because it can cause pain,
dysfunction, and even suicide and because it is generally easy to
treat (see Chapter Eight).

Depression often seems to descend on the bereaved unexpectedly, in the second year or even later, when the most acute
aspects of their grief have subsided. Furthermore, depression is an
illness that tends to be recurrent and to run in families, so that
people who have experienced depression in their families or earlier
in their own lives are likely to be predisposed toward developing a
depression during their bereavement. Current scientific thinking
about depression is that the onslaught of significant and continuing stress and distress in a vulnerable person (a person predisposed
by heredity or personality) leads to the biological changes
manifested as depression.

> Carol went through a depression in the middle of her
> second year of bereavement. She lost all sense of
> pleasure and found herself withdrawing socially,
> becoming further constricted and closed off to her
> feelings. Nothing that she did felt right. While her
> work as a teacher and her relationship with the
> children seemed to have sustained her during the first

year, all this changed dramatically. "I just walked through my work, pushing myself to do it. I didn't feel any enjoyment." She felt that she had nothing to look forward to and was always on edge, unable to relax. She could not sleep and was unable to read because her concentration was poor and she was easily distracted. Unlike her usual self, she became impatient and intolerant in her dealings with others. It was also striking to her that all this was going on without any significant ongoing experience of grief; the pain of David's death had subsided.

As depressed people often do, Carol attributed her depression to some existential anxiety. Unable to get sufficient distance to see that the depression has developed a "life of its own," depressed people grapple with its consequences, seeking explanations through their already disturbed means of perceiving things, frequently blaming themselves for what is happening to them and thinking "If only I would do something differently, the depression will go away." Only rarely does the depressed person recognize that this is a *disorder,* which is exerting its effects on most aspects of thinking, feeling, and functioning.

After two years Shirley was experiencing one of the several periods of depression that recurred regularly over the first five years of her bereavement. "I'm ready to lock myself in the house. I don't have the energy to cope. I feel backed into a corner and I don't know where to turn. I don't have the energy to go out the door and then be shoved back—I expect to be shoved back." She had lost interest in keeping up her house. She felt anxious, unable to concentrate. Her pessimism was profound. "Nothing will work. There are no solutions."

Alcohol Abuse. The bereaved frequently attempt to cope with depression (as well as many other grief-related states) through alcohol use (see Chapter Three). Here Shirley describes the way in which her drinking developed insidiously into a significant problem.

> *Shirley:* "I could see why there are alcoholics, because it comes up behind you. You don't even know it. You know you're doing it. You know you're drinking and you know that you're drinking more than you've ever drank before, but you say, 'I've got the will to control it,' but you don't. So all of a sudden—I don't know about other people, but it hit me one day. 'Wait a minute!' It was when at 10 o'clock in the morning at the bowling alley, I was really hyper that day and she [the owner] was willing to sympathize with anybody, not realizing she's doing you more harm than good. She put a drink down in front of me and sighed, you know, and you drink the thing. 'Wait a minute!' Maybe I wasn't too far gone. And I just quit."

Although alcohol is seductive in its immediate relief, the long-term effects are to compound and worsen the problems of depression. Alcohol can also mimic or produce depression when consumed over time. Furthermore, alcohol and depression can become a deadly combination, leading to suicide. When the disinhibitory effects of alcohol combine with the extreme pessimism and hopelessness of some depressions, people may act on suicidal impulses that would otherwise be contained.

Suicide. Suicide is an uncommon consequence of bereavement (MacMahon and Pugh, 1965; Clayton, 1974) despite the fact that depression, the most common cause of suicide, frequently occurs. Suicide in depression is more likely to occur if the person experiencing this disorder believes that there will be no relief from suffering, that the pain will be continuous and unremitting. While a bereaved person's emotional suffering may equal or surpass that of a depressed individual, the bereaved person generally realizes that this suffering will be time limited, even though in the very acute stages of grief that premise may not be easily accepted. The likelihood of suicide increases with a history of chronic depression and with a history and concurrent use of alcohol. In our study almost one in five people experienced some suicidal ideation at one time or other, but only one woman, Julia, did commit suicide eighteen months after her husband's death.

> Julia's life seemed always to have been filled with traumatic separations. Her parents traveled con-stantly, and she was in thirty-two different schools by the time she graduated from high school. She lived with her grandparents for two years while her father was in prison. At age sixteen she married a man who was bisexual and violent. When she was seventeen, her nine-week-old son died suddenly. She had severe depressions in her early twenties and was hospitalized on one occasion when suicidal. After divorcing her first husband, she married Richard, seventeen years her senior and an alcoholic. During their twelve years of marriage, Julia felt that she had held Richard together. She cajoled him about his drinking, living in fear that something would happen to him. He died in his sleep of a heart attack, leaving Julia, age forty, alone. Her grief was very intense for three months, marked by loneliness, longing ("Nobody will ever love me like Richard did"), and intense guilt for having wished him dead at times. Initially fearful and insecure, she made a number of changes that helped her greatly. She became active in her church, bought a new car, refurnished her apartment, changed her job and hair style, and lost a lot of weight, first without and subsequently with effort. Four months after Richard's death, she became involved with a man, feeling guilty, "as though I'm cheating on Richard." She tried to deal with her grief by writing a novel about a widow and then tried, unsuccessfully, to get her book published. Five months after Richard's death, Julia became aware of her progressively increasing alcohol intake and joined Alcoholics Anonymous. Despite her frantic

efforts to override her depression with activity—she worked full time, swam daily, went to book clubs and symphonies, played tennis, and dated "a dull, dull man"—she became more anxious and depressed. She had periods of being afraid to be alone because of suicidal feelings. She was involved in twice-weekly psychotherapy and was being treated with antidepressant medications. Her life of tragedy was further complicated by the deaths of eleven people—relatives and friends—within a ten-month period after Richard died. "It feels strange that I'm alive. It seems too painful to think that I will go on living like this." She did get some emotional support from her mother and her three grown children as well as from the "dull" man, who wanted to marry her. After a year of bereavement, Julia's depression continued to wax and wane, and she had intermittent suicidal feelings. Sixteen months after Richard's death, she was considering moving from San Diego to start over because there were so many bad memories. However, she made a decision to stay and felt better: "Up until now I've always had the tendency to run away." She developed new enthusiasm and began to feel more self-sufficient, more in control of her depression. She stopped counseling, though she continued going to AA. She had some residual feelings of guilt about Richard, continued to miss him, and often reminisced. After eighteen months Julia's depression returned, and she did leave San Diego to try to escape from her pain. She moved to Washington State to be near her eldest daughter. Two months later we received a letter from her daughter. "I found these papers among my mother's things. I am returning them to you. My mother committed suicide last month. She took over thirty sleeping pills and died before we could get her to the hospital. She did not seem to have any reason for living anymore. She was depressed and despondent for the six weeks she was

here before she died. She talked a lot about Richard,
and I believe she didn't want to live without him.
Strange, because I never really thought they were that
close the last few years."

Although, on the surface, Julia's suicide appeared to be the
result of her unresolved grief, it was largely the product of the
effects of depression. While aspects of her grief continued
throughout the year and a half after Richard died—as one would
expect of any widowed person—Julia's suffering in many areas
fluctuated consistently with her depressions, which colored
everything. Undoubtedly, her bereavement contributed greatly to
her depression, but once the depression began to operate independently, she experienced an intermittent struggle with her suicidal
feelings. Unfortunately, one can never know, for certain, what
ultimately determines the final desperation from which suicide
becomes an escape.

Work

Throughout our lives the capacity to do productive work
provides us all with numerous benefits: financial security, personal
satisfaction, enhanced self-esteem, rewarding relationships, and
activity free from aspects of living that may be filled with conflict
and distress. With the death of one's spouse, all these dimensions
of work remain important. To them can be added the opportunity
to distract oneself from the emotional turmoil of grief and often
the provision of a sense of direction or at least obligation around
which to organize a significant part of life. The capacity to work
provides reassurance to the newly bereaved that they are still intact
despite their loss, pain, and sense of lost control in their lives.

The major effects of bereavement on work functions—
whether specific for-pay jobs, schooling, housework, or volunteer
activities—result from the bereaved person's altered and shifting
mental and emotional states, especially in the early weeks and
months after a death.

Performance. The ability to work usually requires that one's mental faculties are operating efficiently. Acute grief frequently creates degrees of mental disorganization, confusion, anxiety, memory disturbances, and distractibility, which interfere with the widowed person's capacity to perform. Contributing to the dysfunction are intrusive thoughts and images and strong emotional reactions. Later on, depression may reproduce many of these same disorganizing phenomena.

> *Ann:* "Immediately following his death, I don't think that my friends realized the state of mind I was in. I could no longer perform the small, everyday tasks that everyone does. I couldn't type, I couldn't—I really couldn't even grocery shop. I would go through the store and get ready to almost check out, and I would look down and I would have all the things in the cart that he liked. When I would realize this, I would think, 'Oh, I can't even buy groceries. I can't face this.' And I would just shove the cart aside with the groceries in it and walk out of the store. Then [friends] would call me and they'd say, 'Have you had dinner? Did you eat lunch today?' I honestly couldn't remember whether I'd eaten or not. And this went on for two or three months. I guess my sons didn't want to interfere or make me think they were interfering in my life, but I look back now and wonder why they couldn't have realized that I just didn't know what I was doing half the time."

> Carol describes her work as a teacher: "I ran through the motions and I didn't make any serious mistakes or anything. I just went through it, but it was just like I was in total space. It was like I was just walking through a pattern. I had never had that before. You know, it's kind of like you're in a trance. You're in a box. Just automatically. Sometimes I'd have a coffee break or we'd sit down, and I'd hear all

this talking going on and I don't think I listened to what was going on."

Linda: "When I first went back to work [as a dental assistant], it was very hard to concentrate. When I would come back to work the next day, there would be errors. I do my own work. Nobody comes along and checks me, so I would find these mistakes, or addition errors when I was doing the bookkeeping. I told the doctor, 'I don't know whether I should really be working for a few weeks or not. I'm making so many errors that I'm not even aware of it.' And he said, 'Well, I think it would be better if you didn't run away from it, just keep checking.' My mind would be wandering off or I would be working and not really paying any attention to what I'm writing."

Phyllis: "I really worked hard and I was very inefficient, you know, and I'd perseverate and walk around and not know what I was doing. I'd get side-tracked, and it wasn't like I was sitting around crying or anything. I was just like a lump, I guess. Kind of like a zombie is the way I was functioning at night, and then I would put on the mask and put makeup on and dress nice and go to work and try to do the job. I went through all the motions, but I couldn't cope with the job for a long time—the first six months."

Doris had problems driving her car. One night she backed into another car and was upset by her lack of judgment and attention. Two months later, when she was beginning to feel better about her driving, she got a ticket for running a red light. She was following an ambulance, which brought back memories of Edwin's death. She was lost in thought when she ran through the intersection.

One of the most difficult "jobs" facing the newly bereaved is the completion of all the financial, legal, medical, and insurance

"business" that is required following the death of a spouse. These
difficult tasks are complicated by the emotional problems involved
in confronting the loss so directly in doing this work.

> *Annette:* "I spent my first year fighting: fighting with
> companies, looking at papers. I could never escape
> from the trauma of the situation, and it was very
> difficult. It was just like a daily job—doing these
> things, calling the attorney, finding out this, going
> through papers. It's like crawling around in the
> grave. It was difficult fighting to get out of it. I'm a
> strong person and I know others who can't handle it
> or couldn't face it or don't have the motivation to
> take care of it."

Motivation. In addition to changes that impair the bereaved
person's capacity to perform, many attitudinal and other motivational changes—such as apathy or depression—also alter such
functioning.

> After a year Lucille still found it difficult to get
> started in the morning. Arthur used to get breakfast
> and then wake her up. Now she felt like "Why
> bother?" Each day she would have to force herself to
> get dressed and go out to look for a job or go
> shopping.

> *Carol:* "I went right ahead [with work]. They never
> complained. I must have done my work. I did
> function. It wasn't anything new. I did just what I'd
> always been doing. But I didn't have the interest,
> though, the fulfillment. My work did not give me
> the fulfillment it used to."

> Beth let the housework go for a long time. "I hired a
> cleaning lady for a while. I just didn't feel I could, or
> I didn't want to bother."

Some motivational changes can contribute to the effectiveness and satisfaction of the bereaved person's work.

> *Linda:* "After Paul passed away, I found that I was staying a little bit longer. I wasn't as anxious to get home because it was empty. Why rush into it? So maybe I would be working another hour later than anybody else. I knew why I was doing it, because I didn't want to go home. I felt more secure at the office because there was somebody there."

> *Jonathan:* "I think I'm more devoted and work better now because I was always torn before between the divided attention to work and to her. I always used to think that I needed more time for her. My job has always been satisfying, and I think I . . . derived more from that satisfaction after my wife died because I needed something to do and it was there and I liked it."

Besides changes reflecting the more immediate results of loss—disorganization, confusion, apathy, emotional suffering and efforts to cope with it—longer-term attitudinal changes, such as changes in attitude toward work, sometimes occur (see Chapter Seven).

> *Perry:* "I certainly don't care as much about my work as I did five years ago or three years ago. I'm still very good at my work, I think, and work hard when I'm there. I think this whole thing has tended to give me a little perspective, and I just don't tend to get buried in [work] to the exclusion of my family, for example. I'm just not highly motivated the way I probably was when I was younger. I maintain my practice and I do a good job. I think there were times during the time she was sick, particularly, that I don't think I was so damn good when I look back. I wasn't as motivated

as I had been. There was a little more apathy. Now I think there are more important things."

Social Functioning

As noted in Chapter Three, social involvement often helps people cope with the emotional turmoil of bereavement. The bereaved seek out others for support, involvement, distraction, and compensation. However, during certain periods of time (particularly the earliest period of acute grief) and states of mind (such as severe depression), some widows and widowers are unable to function socially. In these circumstances the bereaved may experience varying degrees of social inhibition and withdrawal. This withdrawal is more than an avoidance of interactions that may trigger painful emotions. Instead, it is probably a very primitive primate behavior that occurs following separation and loss and has as its main function the conservation of precious emotional reserves in an individual whose survival is threatened. It is instinctive in nature and a powerful force when operating. During these times it may seem impossible to extend oneself to others, to develop a two-way relatedness.

> *Carol:* "I didn't have any desire really socially, I didn't even care about things socially. In fact, socializing sometimes caused me to run. My sister-in-law would insist that I would go sometimes or some places. I went to the movies, and, my gosh, I'd come home and be literally sick afterwards."

> *Carl:* "Mainly I just wanted to be alone, away from people, just to be by myself. The only ones really who could break that barrier were my son and daughter." Carl had a number of friends who took him out fishing and allowed him his isolation and withdrawal even while they were with him. "They stayed with me and we did a lot of fishing, and they gave me a lot of time to get away by myself and just relax."

Social customs often support these innate survival mechanisms by sanctioning social isolation and even prohibiting certain
types of social interaction. Vestiges of these sanctions are still seen,
if not in the outward behavior, then in the attitudes of some
bereaved.

> *Sharon:* "For a while I was quieter and wasn't my
> bubbly self. I think that was probably for two
> reasons. One, because I didn't feel that I had a right
> to be happy at that point. And probably the other
> reason was that I didn't have anything to be happy
> about at that point. You know, I have to play the
> widow. How can I be laughing and having a wonder-
> ful time when three weeks before my husband just
> died? For a long time I felt guilty about any social
> involvement. It depended on who it was doing the
> inviting or who it was asking [and] for what reason.
> On New Year's Eve that year, I remember one woman
> at the party that I went to—I did go, but these were
> such good friends that I didn't feel intimidated—and
> I remember this one woman saying to me, 'Your
> husband died when?' and when I told her she said,
> 'My God, when my husband died, I was still laying
> in the bed at this point in time. How could you have
> gotten up?' She wasn't saying it maliciously. She was
> thinking how wonderful it was of me to be able to
> actually function. I thought, 'Well, it's no big trick
> actually.' You just tell yourself you're going to do it.
> But that was *that* moment, and I was up and I was
> able to handle it. Of course, when New Year's itself
> rolled around, everybody started kissing each other,
> and I headed for the bathroom as fast as I could and
> locked the door because I didn't want to stand there
> with nobody to kiss 'Happy New Year' to."

 Chapter 6

How Relationships with Family and Friends Change

The death of a spouse will invariably alter, in some ways, the survivor's relationship with family and friends and to society as a whole. These changes can occur on many levels of a given relationship. The loss will create both immediate and long-term demands on the family member or friend because of the bereaved person's shifting needs. Furthermore, the family member or friend's personal response to the loss may influence the way in which this person is able to interact with the surviving spouse; and the way that the spouse deals with the emotional turmoil also will influence others' abilities to relate to him or her. Needs and expectations may intensify beyond the wishes or capacities of others to deal with them. Regardless of the degree of "protection" afforded the newly bereaved by virtue of their self-reliance or their network of support, or by the good will and availability of their friends and family, the dynamics of these relationships must change. At times relationships will be deepened and strengthened. At other times they will break under the weight of each person's turmoil, and new relationships will develop to replace the old. Grief will force on the survivor new ways of looking at relationships and at times difficult decisions about what kinds of relationships to pursue.

Family

The most complex changes in relationships occurred within the families of the bereaved. This is easily understood since family members are themselves most likely to be experiencing their own

183

grief, and these relationships are characteristically more intense, more conflict laden, and of greater duration than others in the lives of the bereaved. The specific changes that may occur depend a great deal on the previous structure and nature of the relationship as well as the changing demands and needs experienced by both people in the relationship. The relationships examined here are those of the bereaved spouse with young children, grown children, parents, in-laws, and others, including siblings and grandparents.

Young Children. Twenty percent of the people studied had young children (some as young as one year old) living with them at the time their spouses died. The shifts in family dynamics reflected the age-specific and need-specific demands and abilities of these children in relation to their surviving parents. Predictably, the surviving parents expressed their greatest concerns about the welfare of their youngest children, trying to assess the impact of death on their children. They were forced to suspend aspects of their own grief to contend with their children's grief. Although they could not avoid dealing with the reality of their loss, the presence and demands of needy children had the effect of distracting them from their own suffering.

> Beth's son, Mark, was only a year old when his father died in the plane crash. Although Beth thought "he was too young to know what's going on," he did exhibit heightened distress and some sleep disturbance during the week that followed the crash. Beth attributed these responses to the unusual amount of activity in their home. Although Beth was very concerned about him, she did not see any evidence of problems. She wanted him to have a sense of his father and showed Mark his pictures and talked about him regularly. When Mark was three, other children began to ask him about his father, but "he just shrugs it off." He identified a picture of his father as his father. Around that time he began asking Beth "Is Daddy still a pilot?" and many other

questions about death and his father. However, Beth was reassured that he was growing up healthy and developing well.

Perry's worries about Jason were focused on the reality that he may have missed an important phase of bonding with his mother when he was an infant. June was already quite sick at the time her brain tumor was discovered during her sixth month of pregnancy. After Jason's birth June was relatively unavailable to him, and Perry relied on himself and outside help for Jason's primary caretaking. Perry could not point to any specific signs of distress. However, at age four Jason did not appear to be learning as quickly as Perry thought he should, considering how otherwise bright he appeared to be. After Perry remarried, Jason quickly "adopted" his new mother and was developing well.

These two examples demonstrate the difficulties in assessing the impact of a parent's death on very young children, who do not have the cognitive ability to understand what has happened and yet have formed an attachment to the parent who has died. Certainly, the consequences for these two children were lessened by the fact that the dead parent was not their primary caretaker, a circumstance that would likely lead to much more profound results, both in the child and in the surviving parent.

Since children do not have the broad repertoire of coping skills that most adults have acquired, their grief reactions may appear quite different from their parents' reactions. Probably the ability most lacking in small children through latency age and even into adolescence is the capacity to tolerate the raw emotions of grief; as a result, they may display forms of regressive behaviors and disguised grief. Many of the surviving parents would have felt much more capable of dealing with their children's grief if they could see it and confront it directly. To parents the most disconcerting of all responses on the part of their children was no response: no distress, no change of behavior, no expression of feelings or thoughts about their dead parent.

> After Dick's death Sharon's two-and-a-half-year-old daughter clung to her mother almost continuously. She would not let her out of her sight and was unable to play by herself for any length of time. Sharon understood her daughter's fears that Sharon, too, would disappear but could not allay them for weeks.

> Daphne's twelve-year-old daughter, Tami, seemed to cling to her often. "She will come up to me and hug me. I guess she's probably worried about losing me, too." Also, despite Daphne's efforts to talk to her daughter about Ray, Tami was unable to talk about her father.

> Ralph's son, Stuart, was fourteen when his mother died from alcohol poisoning. Stuart had been very close to his mother and also had been a well-adjusted teenager. After the death Stuart went through a brief period of fearfulness about sleeping alone and began sleeping with his father.

> Agnes's eleven-year-old-son, Don, felt responsible for his father's death. He felt that if he had prayed hard enough his dad would not have died. He had let his dad down.

Don's experience exemplifies some of the problems encountered by children. Because of their limited experience in life and understanding of people and causality, there is a self-centeredness in children, which often remains fixed in the face of tragedy. They tend to regard all that happens around them as a product of their feelings, fears, and wishes. Their security systems are more easily undermined than those of adults. Finally, their ability to comprehend death is very limited. As a result, grief in children may be overrepresented by primitive fears, irrational guilt, and attempts at avoidance of all feeling. Such experiences will put a great strain on the relationship between parent and child as the parent attempts to lead the child down the correct path between appropriate regression and continuing progress in his development.

At the same time, there is an opportunity for growth, especially in older children, that can contribute to the relationships with parents in very positive and productive ways.

> Ralph was pleased by his children's handling of their grief. "I think we kind of drew on each other's strength. I felt that I have really been lucky. My kids—I've never had any problem with their school-work or anything, so I could come home and if I had some work to do I could do that or if I wanted to read while they were sitting there doing homework. They've become very self-sufficient. They can wash their clothes, they can cook meals, they can clean, they can do just about anything. Before, their mother would always do everything for them. Now they're able to do it. I know I'm more sensitive to their feelings, and I think they are more considerate to me than they—you know how kids when they're growing up, sometimes they're not really that considerate. [Mine are] considerate."

> Shirley could see the development of her sons' sensitivity when she took them to the fair and they reflected, "Mom doesn't have anybody to walk with."

This intensification of their children's needs makes the role of parenting more difficult for the bereaved, not only by demanding more of them but also by heightening any conflicts they may have experienced because of their own perceived needs.

> Shirley struggled constantly with the dilemma she faced over spending enough time with her teenage sons and the demands of her newfound niche in life—racing autos. On the one hand, she perceived her sons as doing well and not having great needs

from her. Yet her life had been oriented around her caretaking role, and she was nagged by guilt whenever she took time for herself, even though she recognized how important this "selfish" time was for her own survival and well-being.

The loss of a spouse and parent creates a void in the family and forces a shifting of roles, often with the surviving parent assuming most of the old responsibilities. Where there is no shift or other form of compensation in this structure, there may be a disruption in the family's functioning.

The family meal seemed to die with Art. Shirley fixed meals for her children but only nibbled herself. For a year after Art's death, they did not sit down at the table for dinner as they had when he was alive. The children took their meals into their rooms. It seemed to Shirley that "without a father, a family dinner would be silly."

Daphne felt that Ray's illness brought the family close together. Her four teenage children and older daughter all contributed to his care. "We were living on a treadmill just keeping up with the demands of his illness and trying to keep up a façade when things weren't going well, you know, trying to be hopeful for him. When he died, it was hard to break away from all the feelings you have to go through. In a way there was a feeling of relief, but yet it was hard to get used to the idea that you didn't have all these demands to meet. You didn't have the commitment that we felt as a family to take care of him. That was gone. It wasn't very many months after he died that I got the feeling that my family was falling apart. My children all seemed to be going their own separate ways. I realize each one of us had to deal with his own grief, and we couldn't seem really to help each other deal with it. It was just too tough, so it was like we all became fragmented. It was like the binding force of his personality that was there before he was ill and then the binding force of the commitment of dealing with his illness—they weren't there anymore."

The role of single parent is universally experienced as very demanding.

Perry: "She underwent surgery late in the pregnancy, but she never really related with [the baby] very well. I understand that to be a result of the surgery more than anything else. He was my baby, literally, physically, and every other way. So he and I have always had a special relationship ever since he was born. I've always tried to give him two parents' worth of attention." Perry found that he had to develop the nurturing and patient side of his personality, since he had always been cerebral and driven. The results were very rewarding to him as he perceived himself becoming a more sensitive, responsive person.

Daphne learned that the task of being two parents was not possible for her. "I think I've done a pretty good job of dealing with what I've had to deal with. It took me a long time to get over the fact that I could not be two parents. I could only be me. I could only be their mother. I tried to be their father, too, and I finally gave that up. I felt very sorry for them that they had been deprived of a parent and a wonderful influence on their lives. But I just finally decided that they'd have to accommodate themselves to that. I can't do it for them. I can't be their father, I can only be their mother. We were two different personalities and we sort of complemented each other, but I couldn't be him."

Even where single parents feel adequate to the demands, they are aware that their spouses had provided valuable support, which they now missed.

Beth: "Most of the anxiety I have is in regards to my son. Nobody to discuss what to do and what's right for him. I worry about raising him alone."

Ross: "I'm sure I took on a few new roles with my son, though I'd be hard put to actually pinpoint them because they'd really be just extensions of roles that I already had. For me, single parenting is difficult. Parenting, something I've always taken very seriously, requires a sounding board. Even if you know that what you're doing is right, it makes you feel a lot better to talk to somebody else who thinks you're right, too, or if you think you're wrong, to have that verified. Or if you're uncertain, maybe they have feelings there."

Single parents have to confront their sense of inadequacy or failure at a time when many other aspects of life seem to be disintegrating around them or within themselves. The greatest sense of futility seems to focus on the inability of parents to help their children who are in trouble.

Diane experienced a pervasive sense of inadequacy because of her youngest daughter's withdrawal. Tina, seventeen, had been very close to her father. After his death Diane could see "a complete personality change" in her. Tina withdrew from all her activities and, according to an older sister, would not communicate with her mother because of her fear of getting too close. She was afraid that Diane would also die. Diane's reaction was "I feel guilty, like I've failed as a mother." Six months later Tina remained closed off from her mother, and Diane continued to take responsibility. "I'm the one who should have died. Dad would have the answers."

Daphne had also been frustrated and disheartened by her efforts to help her children. She too had felt totally responsible for the family's difficulty in coping with her husband's death, and so she consulted a psychiatrist. "Well, in some ways I tried talking to my children, not only for my relief, but I also thought if I could draw them out it would help them. But they just were not able to do that. In fact, I was really concerned about them, especially my daughter. I work at the hospital and I talked to a psychiatrist there when I was really upset about my daughter. I found out she was having a sexual relationship, and I guess that really blew my mind because I'm pretty old-fashioned. Anyway, when I talked to him, he said this might be part of my daughter's reaction to her grief, that she was looking for something to fill her emptiness. He said we all probably needed grief counseling." The family went for a few sessions, but the children remained unable to talk about their feelings. "He was really a wonderful father. He was very strict and required a lot of them, but he had a real good sense of humor and he was a lot of fun. I know they miss him probably a lot still."

As Diane stated and Daphne implied, the surviving parent often believes that the other parent would have been more capable of dealing with the children's problems, or at least would have known what to do in specific situations.

Amalia's son got into a fight at school and was threatened with suspension. That night the distress hit both children, and they began to cry because they missed their father. Amalia also began to cry, missing Ted and wishing that he could come home to straighten out all the problems. "He always knew what to do."

Bill's eighteen-year-old son squandered a sizable inheritance from his grandparents while Bill looked on in utter frustration. "He's broke and he's never messed with dope or drank, but he has tried to buy friends and tried to have money give him self-confidence. . . . Then to watch him go through his struggles without being able to do anything for him. I know his mother could have. She wouldn't have let him have the money, number one. The lawyer told him, 'This is yours when you're eighteen, yours to do what you want, that's the law.' If he hadn't said that, I could have held the money for him, made money with it, and given it to him when he was twenty-one and a little more mature. He would have had a great start in life. But he blew it all, and I stood by and watched it going and him making a fool of himself. Boy, it hurt. I know what his mother would have done. She would have said, 'Damn the laws, he's not going to do that to himself.' But I didn't. I wasn't wise enough to believe that he would really go ahead and do what he did. She could have been so far ahead of him and known what he would do. It just never would have happened. She was always that way with the boys. They couldn't lie to her and they couldn't con her into a thing. She was just ahead of them all the time."

Most widowed parents believe that they would be able to contend with their children's difficulties if they had their spouses back. Sometimes children will try to take things into their own hands to solve the problem of having only one parent.

Agnes's children were seven, nine, and eleven when their father died. For months her youngest repeated, "I want a new daddy." Whenever the children were around another adult male, they would jump on him. Agnes felt the pressure of her children's needs and wanted to provide them with another father. "I can do without a husband but would like one for the kids' sake."

In addition to solving the parent's problems by getting a replacement from the outside, young children may attempt to step into the void left by their dead parent or through "role reversal" assume a caretaking role in relation to the surviving parent. These children appear to relinquish their own needs for nurturance or to obtain them through identification with either the nurtured parent or the deceased one. Although such children may seem unusually mature and poised on the surface, they harbor the same needs and pain as other children who are not coping with their loss in this manner. This means of coping with grief offers the child an opportunity to exert a sense of control and mastery over a situation that is otherwise frightening and disorganizing. At times a very needy parent may collude with this reversal, believing that it will benefit both. The most frequent forms of such adaptation are not blatant but appear as concern for and protectiveness toward the parent.

During the second year after his father died, Shirley's older son (sixteen years old) became increasingly solicitous toward her. He had a dream in which his mother committed suicide because of her loss. He expressed his concern that she was not dating. Shirley thought he might have been worried that he would always have to remain at home to care for his widowed mother.

Daphne: "My oldest son [seventeen years old] wanted to be his father. . . . You know, he missed him a lot. This son really was able to talk about his grief more than any of the other kids. He used to follow his dad around and do everything he did whenever my husband was working on anything. He learned a lot

of things from my husband. Still now he wanted to
do everything my husband did, including being the
disciplinarian for the other kids, telling them what to
do. That did not work. He tried to tell his older sister
what to do and tried to do all the chores around the
house and besides keep up his schoolwork. It got to
the point where I finally had to convince him that it
was more than he could carry and more than anyone
could expect of him. I had to make him see that he
couldn't be his father, although I didn't tell him that
outright."

Daphne's son was able to gain mastery of his situation, not only by
becoming a caretaker and protector but also, through his identification with his father, by keeping his father alive as a part of
himself.

The relationships of the bereaved with their young children
are not simply a burden, a drain on what few depleted resources
the surviving parent may have. These children can also provide
great satisfaction for their parents—primarily by fulfilling the
surviving parent's need for purpose and direction. As we shall
explore in Chapter Seven, for the first one to two years, a great
many widows and widowers flounder in their efforts to determine
the meaning of their "new" lives without a mate. They may not
know who they are, where they are going, what they should be
doing. Growing children, at least temporarily, solve this problem
by their needs, and the continuing demands for attention and
response from the parent serve as a major distraction from the pain
of bereavement. They also are a product and a legacy of their dead
parent.

Beth describes the evolution of her feelings toward
her son, Mark. "I just didn't really enjoy him before
Barry died. He just was sort of this little body that
was there, interfering with the calm life that I had
before. He wasn't a planned child, just sort of
happened. I think that I really never accepted his
being before the accident. I've been eternally grateful

to him afterwards. I never could really understand why we had Mark, you know, at the beginning. And the day of the accident, I realized why he was there. After I found out that Barry had been on the plane— Mark was having a nap at that time, and I went up and woke him up to get out of bed. I picked him up, and it was just then that I realized why I had Mark— because I had lost Barry. He was there, not to take his place, but he was certainly an important part. It was just like a little light bulb lit up, and suddenly I knew why Mark was there."

The bonds between parent and child are probably the closest available compensation for the wrenched bonds of marital intimacy, especially when the children are young. Studies have demonstrated that grief for a young child is even more intense than that for a spouse (Levav, 1982; Raphael, 1983). As a result of such bonds, surviving parents of developing children do reap the benefits of these relationships.

Ross and his sixteen-year-old son, Pat, had always had a good relationship. After Pamela's death they became even closer. They traveled together to spread her ashes in the mountains and shared their grief with each other. With the help of his son, Ross was able to stave off some of his loneliness. "My son stayed very very close, and we kind of clung to each other through that summer."

Ralph: "I would have had a very difficult time adjusting to widowhood if I had not had the kids." His teenagers were helpful around the house, did well in school, and showed concern about his feelings. They became a very tight-knit unit. Ralph and his son were especially close companions, spending a lot of time together, attending different sporting events. "He's my best friend."

After Phil died, Susan's sense of freedom from the tyranny of Phil's illness and the accompanying personality changes was shared by her teenage sons. The relationships among the three of them became much more open and free-flowing. *Susan:* "We get along really well. If there's something that bugs them about me, they'll tell me. They'll say, 'I want to talk to you.' I'll say, 'Okay,' and then we'll sit and talk. If I'm angry with them, we get it out and that's it. We don't stay mad at each other." The new freedom and openness in their home led to a greater sense of communication and intimacy. "They're really cute when I go out on a date. Before the guy will get there, they'll say, 'What time will you be in, young lady?' And then I'll crack up and I'll say, 'Oh, late, and I'm not a young lady anymore. Well, you have the girls out by the time I come in, and when I come in, I'll leave the guy there.'" Susan would solicit her sons' opinions and advice, and in the same bantering style they would reveal their thoughts and feelings about the many issues in their lives. Susan relished both the sharing and the "lightness" that had been absent from her marriage for many years.

Grown Children. The expectations of the bereaved are usually substantially different for their grown children than for their growing ones. There is a general assumption that adult children will provide emotional and practical support for their surviving parent. This does not always occur, not only because of the unavailability of children due to physical dislocation but also because of their competing needs. For the first time, in many families there may be a genuine conflict of roles because of this tragedy and its upheaval among different family members.

Regardless of the relationships among family members prior to the death of a parent, an inevitable shift occurs in the relationships of the remaining members. At times such shifts are subtle and unnoticeable. More often there is a conspicuous need that requires attention, a void that needs filling, or a conflict that is either produced or relieved by the death.

> *Daniel:* "The relationship I have with the children is different than it was then. My children are not the same to me as they were. At least I see it that way. They were affected by her death in that they expected me to take over where she left off. She was more sociable with them, visited with them more, took more interest in the grandchildren. I haven't changed in that respect. I never was that close socially. I never took that much of an interest outwardly in the grandchildren or them. I think they've learned to accept that I am what I am and that I don't take her place. They resented me for a while, I think, for that. I believe that they have come to realize that they can't make me what they want me to be."

> Bobbi and her youngest daughter had always engaged in competition over Nathan. While his death was difficult for both of them, his absence removed a barrier between them and brought them closer.

In three families in the study, there had been considerable conflict between the fathers who died and their sons (one stepson) who were young adults. In each instance the death removed the ongoing, day-to-day conflicts.

> Merle reported that she and her son were able to talk about his father seven months after his death. For the first time that she could recall, her son was able to express a sense of appreciation for his father despite the fact that "they did not get along very well." As a result, Merle was very pleased and felt closer to her son.

> Linda's son, David, demonstrated an even more dramatic "turnaround." "A lot of bickering was always going on between them. Not that they didn't have the love for each other, but they just had

different ideas and different views on things. David wasn't around as much when his father was there. He was out doing different things, working longer hours and things that way. He sort of took on a protective attitude toward me after Paul passed away. The things that him and his dad would differ on, he has just sort of come over and taken over his dad's viewpoints." David's identification with his father changed Linda's relationship with him.

In Viola's home there had been constant tension between her husband, Lyle, and his mother-in-law and stepson. "It's been much more relaxing for all three of us now because the tension was practically unbearable before. My son would come home from somewhere, and Lyle would head for the bedroom and shut the door. It was an obvious disappearing act. We have a relaxed home life now. We have problems, but everyone has problems. But that tension is gone. I could never want that back."

The great majority of widowed men and women with grown children found that these children were able to provide them with understanding, comfort, and emotional support.

Carol's first recognition that her children really were adults grew out of her experience with them after David's death. "In some ways I think we're closer, because we've shared something. We lost something that, I don't know, I guess people never think they're going to lose. One of the things that I noticed about my children is, of course, they're grown. I see them for the first time as grown. I always looked at them—I was always a parent. David and I were always parents. We never needed them. We always said we needed them, but really we never needed them. I needed them, and they were very strong. I see them as adults and I never saw them that way. I really wish David could have had that feeling."

Phyllis's daughter was helpful to her after Bradley's death. "She was very supportive. In fact, she was the one that would call me up and take me out to dinner. None of my friends did. But my kid remembered me. I felt she was doing more than she would have done if life had gone along okay, because she was very busy and had her own life. I felt tremendously supported and a lot of love coming from my kid, that she was really there."

While Carolyn's daughters were supportive of her when Sam died, after six months she began feeling somewhat smothered by their concern. "I had to get them to give me some air and some room. They were being too protective."

Marie's son was successfully encouraging in his efforts to get his mother out of the house, though his methods of persuasion were rather strong. "He says to me, 'Mom, why don't you go out? You need to get out. You work all week and don't you think you ought to get out on your night off?' I said, 'I don't think I feel right without your father going with us.' And he turned around and he looked at me and he said, 'What are you trying to do, follow him? Look at the Sloans up the street. Six months after her husband died, she died too. And look at Mrs. Forster: her husband dies after fifty-five years, and she's still alive and going strong. She's not a young woman by a long shot but she does volunteer work. She didn't follow her husband because she got out and got herself busy. Are you going to be like her or like Mrs. Sloan?' Well, it worked. I never felt that way again."

At times emotional support may include practical help with things that the bereaved may feel unable to do because of their general state of mind. The family will often offer this help—with chores around the house, transportation, or decision making—in the same way that a parent will "pamper" a sick child: as a tangible sign of emotional support for one who is momentarily "helpless."

> *Doris:* "This time last year I wouldn't have thought I could have coped like I am now. I realize I was very demanding of my children the first year after my husband died, and I'm sort of sorry that I was, but I don't think that I could have gotten over it if I hadn't been. I'm not saying I was demanding all the time, but it was just that I had been so used to talking things over with my husband that I felt the necessity to still have to talk things over. I was afraid to make a decision. I didn't feel I was capable of making a decision on my own." For many months Doris would talk with one of her children about every minor or major decision. Her son and daughter proved to be very understanding and patient.

Some children, for reasons that often go beyond altruism, may try to assume the role of their deceased parent in relationship to the surviving members of the family, including the widowed parent. Such children may need to relate to the surviving parent in a way other than as his child, or to effect some mastery and control where none has existed, or to identify with the dead parent as a means of perpetuation and self-enhancement, or to avoid their own grief over the loss. Consequently, they will devote themselves to the widowed parent and effectively deny their own needs.

> Carl and his daughter, Lena, became close after Faith died, leading eventually to difficulties when Carl became involved with someone else. "My daughter and I always do things together. If I'm going somewhere, I always ask, 'Honey, I'm going here. Do you want to go along?' She's more or less been my companion for the last couple of years. I take her

with me. She's twenty-three years old and I have a good time." When Carl became engaged to a woman with whom he worked, his fiancée was reluctant to spend time in Carl's home. "She would say, 'Carl, I can't go down there. That's your daughter's house.' And I'd say, 'You mean I work my whole damn life for a house and now the house is not mine anymore?'" It became clear to Carl that Lena was jealous, and he later learned from his mother about his daughter's plans. "My mother told my fiancée the best thing to do was to get me out of this area and away from my daughter for a while. Lena had told her that she's not going to get married, that she's going to stay single and take care of me."

When Jonesy died, Donald was twenty-one years old and living at home with his mother. Merle quickly became aware of Donald's need to "take care of me." She found his presence reassuring and comforting but also understood that he was fulfilling his own needs. "Sometimes I allow him to take over for the simple reason I feel that it builds up his ego. I think many is the time I did that for my husband. I felt it was an ego trip. However, I do remind Donald sometimes, 'You are my son, not my husband.'" As time went on, Merle became concerned that Donald's dependency on her was becoming a problem. She made concerted efforts to demonstrate her self-sufficiency in order to undermine his conscious concerns, while giving him a moving date three years after Jonesy's death. Eventually, two years later, they achieved a compromise wherein Donald was building a separate apartment on her property.

Sometimes, because of their own limitations or problems, grown children are not able to give support to their parents. In such instances the surviving parent usually assumes the continuing role as caretaker, despite the disappointment of not having her own needs met.

> Bobbi had some difficulties with one of her daughters. "Her grief was competing with my grief. I felt like if I wanted to talk about him I might say, 'I dreamed about Nathan last night.' She would say, 'I dreamed twice about him.' I felt that I could not talk to her about him because she was asking support from me that I was not able to give at that time."

> Six months after her husband's death, Louise became extremely depressed when her daughter was hospitalized with an undiagnosed ailment that had many symptoms in common with her husband's brain tumor. Louise thought that she might kill both herself and her daughter if this was a brain tumor. "I could not go through watching my daughter die as my husband had." When it was discovered that her daughter had two deteriorating discs, Louise was greatly relieved. Surgical repair was successful, and Louise helped care for her daughter during her recovery. "We have a lot to be grateful for."

One of the areas of greatest difficulty among family as well as friends involves the limited capacities of those around the grieving spouse to tolerate the emotional upheavals that accompany death. This intolerance of emotional pain prevents the person from being empathic and emotionally supportive. At the same time, such a person may try to prevent the bereaved person from expressing his or her grief. The grieving spouse will often recognize the criticism and control and will assume the responsibility and guilt for "unacceptable" behavior, while the offending party expresses righteous indignation or appeals to "rationality" in rejecting the widowed person's emotionalism. The bereaved spouse soon learns to suppress his or her feelings around such a person, in order to avoid being rejected. Further discussion and examples of these phenomena are presented later in this chapter (see "Old Friends").

Parents. Given the ages of the widows and widowers in our study, a significant proportion had no living parents, and those who were alive were frequently quite elderly. In instances where the parent or parents were managing to live autonomously, however, parental support and empathy were available to the bereaved persons in our study.

> Paul died of pancreatic cancer after a year-long illness during which Linda felt that she had largely come to terms with the inevitable. Death came easily to Paul with his whole family around him. "It was a beautiful experience." Linda could accept his death but could not tolerate the loneliness. Her family was generally very supportive of her. Her son helped her fix up her house and redecorate and frequently checked in with her. Her daughter-in-law encouraged Linda to take her two-year-old granddaughter for weekends. Most important, to help her stave off her loneliness, Linda's mother came to stay with her six weeks after Paul's death and remained there for the next six months. They spent much time together, with Linda helping her mother physically and her mother supporting her emotionally. Linda recognized the importance of her support. "When she left, I had to grow up again."

> *Agnes:* "My parents are both still alive. My husband's illness and death had a terrible impact on my mother, who is the world's number-one worrier anyway. But my mother, well she's seventy-eight now—when my husband got sick, she started losing weight and she just hasn't stopped [two years later]. She worried so much about me, you know, mostly about me and not so much about my husband, but how I was going to cope and what was going to happen to me. At the

time I guess she weighed 140 and she's down to about
95. Now she may have something else, some other
physical ailment, but she always remarks she started
losing weight when my husband got sick and she just
has never stopped. So it had a tremendous impact on
her. And, of course, if I do remarry, that will stop my
mother from worrying about me. My dad took it in
his stride, but that's his nature."

The relationship between a parent and a widowed child is
likely to become more intense—for good or ill—than it was before
the spouse's death.

Susan: "I think that I'm much closer with my parents
than I was. It was a difficult time for them. They felt
that I was going through a very hard time trying to
take care of him. I know that they didn't, they
couldn't understand it, because they are both well,
knock on wood. They would say to me, 'How about
if we come down for a couple days?' And I would say,
'Fine.' And I would immediately get very tense
because I knew that they didn't understand what he
was going through on so much medication. They
wanted to see the children and see what was going on
with him. He was very critical of them and they were
very critical of him. I think they resented him for
what he was doing to me. He resented their—I don't
want to say butting in but maybe their concern. I
think they're very relieved at this point that I'm able
to go about my business. My parents are absolutely
ecstatic that I'm dating. They can't seem to do
enough for me. They just seem so elated when I go
up there that it makes me feel so good. And it's been
a long time since that happened. There was always a
barrier there when Phil was alive. They knew that he
came first, and it was difficult for them to accept."

Sharon: "My relationship with my mother has changed. She's more a part of my life than she was before, and not because she's a comfort to me; actually, I'm a comfort to her. I don't have Dick yelling at me not to do so much for her."

Removing a barrier that existed between parent and child through the child's marriage can exacerbate long-dormant conflicts or intensify ongoing ones. The child or parent may be confronted by feelings that were "under wraps" before the spouse's death.

Throughout her life Daphne had struggled with her resentment toward her mother, always trying to push it out of her mind in an effort to maintain some semblance of balance in their relationship. Throughout her childhood her nagging mother and her alcoholic father fought constantly. When she was seven, her mother was spanking her and accidentally hit her in the eye with a cord. Daphne lost sight in her eye, which was treated surgically but never straightened. She was teased in school because of her appearance, but she managed to rise above this and excel. "I was the model child." She was able to maintain a good relationship with her mother "mainly because I kept my feelings to myself. But I always did resent her." Her resentment intensified when she went out into the world and found that people discriminated against her because of her unusual appearance. After her marriage to Ray, she resented the way that her mother treated him, exploiting his abilities but showing him little appreciation or respect. Ray's illness and death were the final injury. "Is it a punishment? In all of my life I've had struggles; all the way through, I've had fights." Despite her rational awareness of reality, each of these injuries seemed to tap into the childhood fantasy that she was somehow to blame for her own misfortune, while at the same time she harbored anger and blame toward her mother. Despite all this she still clung to the hope for a good relationship. "After he got sick, she would call a lot and was worried, really worried. She really worried about him a lot, and she worried about me and my children a lot. So I appreciated that."

Fran and Boris had moved to San Diego to retire. Fran's elderly mother had lived alone in her own mobile home, but Fran felt that she would have to move with them. Therefore, for the two years before Boris died, the three of them shared a house. Boris served as a barrier to the mother's dependency demands, which limited any direct confrontation between the two women. "I think, if he had lived and things had gone on, there would have been some friction because she was extremely jealous of my taking off with him. You know, we'd go on little short cruises and things, and she didn't like it at all. Even to this day, if I'm going somewhere and I say 'Do you want to go?' she's the first one in the car. You know what I mean? It's just that she wants to go and she wants to be with you. Now that he's gone, I don't mind. It really doesn't bother me that much. I still don't take her on the boat, though. You can't have an eighty-one-year-old woman on a sailboat." Despite her mother's demands for time, Fran utilized her involvement with sailing to establish her own autonomy, the boat then serving as the barrier.

When Lyle died, Viola's mother was eighty-one and in compromised health. While he was alive, Lyle was openly hostile to and contemptuous of Viola's mother and son, leading to a great deal of isolation on everyone's part within the house. His death lowered the tension level for all but intensified problems between Viola and her mother. While Viola struggled to become more independent and start a new life through work and volunteer efforts, her mother focused all her energies on Viola, constantly encouraging Viola to stay at home and be financially supported by her mother. Viola fought valiantly against this regression and tried to ignore her feelings of guilt. "We're trying to get enough money coming in through my own effort, through jobs, and, of course, I have a dish-washing job once a week. And now I have these shopping jobs for shut-ins. Every now and then my mother will say, 'If you don't want to do that, you don't have to, and I'll give you that much money.' And I tell her, 'Well, that's just you taking care of your child. That isn't the way I want to do it.' She would just prefer that she give me enough money to live on and let me be with her all the time. I cannot allow that. That would really be crippling for me. So I tell her, 'No, I don't mind going and washing the dishes,' because I'm making $10 a week. I'd rather bring in as much as I can with my own labors. Otherwise, I'd just feel so much her child instead of a grown-up. I wish I could eliminate that, but as long as she's with me, I can't."

For the newly bereaved who must take care of an aging parent, the parent's needs serve as a distraction from the pain of grief, and the company of another person helps the grieving spouse avoid loneliness. As time goes on and the wound starts to heal, however, the widowed person may find the burdens of this caretaking stifling to personal development and autonomy. Still, many adults, both widowed and still married, cannot in good conscience shift this responsibility to anyone else. It remains their "cross to bear," an act of humanity that is necessary and hard. One of the more profound effects of spousal death in these circumstances can be the loss of one's support system in shouldering this burden.

Carol: "I'm finding that being a parent to an eighty-five-year-old has got a lot of problems, too. David and I were beginning to find that out. One of the things that I miss terribly is being able to discuss my mother with him, especially at night. There are a lot of things happening during the day that mother just drives me wild about. You know, living with an eighty-five-year-old is not the most desirable, even though it's been a blessing that I was not alone—there was not that loneliness in the house. I've always had somebody in the house. And she really is delightful. She's not cranky, but she's not that much entertainment or comfort either. And she is a chore sometimes. She's a real problem, but she was with David and me too. We always—at night we could discuss some things, and a lot of times we could find a sense of humor, we could laugh about it. Then I could take it. I can't do that now."

In-Laws. A spouse's death can place a major stress on the relationship between the surviving spouse and the dead spouse's parents. Any differences that existed between the surviving spouse and the in-laws before their child's death will usually be expanded, exposing conflicts more blatantly. Possibly the parents, in their grief over the death, must assess some responsibility, often unconsciously, and usually toward the spouse; at least they may resent the survivor, feeling that it should have been the spouse who died rather than their child. This underlying dynamic affects both the parents and the surviving spouse, who may sense their antagonism.

What is being said here is neither an indictment of all in-law relationships nor even a statement that this aspect of these relationships is invariably present. Many people are able to develop primary attachments to their in-laws that transcend the earlier attachments and loyalties of the parent-child relation. In such circumstances the relationships between the bereaved spouse and the parents of the deceased can take on any of the characteristics of a parent-child relationship or a friendship. In this study many of the newly bereaved took on primarily supportive roles in relation to their in-laws, at times being aware that the in-laws' grief equaled or surpassed their own. As parents themselves, they understood and accepted this situation. Where conflicts do exist, their manifestations can appear in a variety of ways, with perceptions ranging from nonsupport to malice.

> Perry was disappointed and angered when he saw June's family gradually become less involved with her as her illness progressed. While he was struggling to keep his head above water, her family contributed little of the time, effort, or financial support that would have made his task easier. After her death the family made little attempt to support him or his son. Eventually, after repeated disappointments he tried to write them off psychologically.

> *Bill:* "My wife's mother was a pain. She was a total jerk. My father-in-law was a great guy, but she was an endless irritation—not only to me but generally to my wife. My wife kept as much as she could from me because she knew that I was unhappy [about] the way [her mother would] treat her. She was an insensitive person to the point of—the day my wife was buried, she walks over and just starts picking flowers off the casket because she wanted to go put some on Daddy's grave and other friends' graves. Just like her daughter wasn't even in that casket. No concern. She had no fears, nothing. Finally, one of my sons walked over and said, 'Grandma, don't you have any respect at all for your daughter? Those are her flowers. We bought them for her.' So she stopped. She was like that. She thought only of herself."

> Gretchen remained furious with her mother-in-law, who refused to comply with her son's request that she tell him she loved him before he died.

Even where the relationship between the surviving spouse and the bereaved parents may have started off well, changes are likely to occur as the spouse's bereavement evolves.

Six months after Faith's death, her mother had a stroke. She became partially paralyzed, and many aspects of her illness reminded Carl of the multiple sclerosis with which Faith suffered. Although his mother-in-law was married, he began to brood about the possibility that he would be called on to be more responsible for her care. Every time he saw her, he was reminded of his wife. Soon this became too difficult for him to tolerate, and he withdrew from the situation.

While she and Dick were married, Sharon had had a very good relationship with Dick's parents. They were quite supportive of her despite their own grief when Dick died. However, a significant breach in their relationship occurred when Sharon became involved with and subsequently married Andy. When they first were involved, Sharon had long talks with her in-laws regularly, and things went well, although every time Dick's mother came over she cried and seemed not to be adjusting well. "She couldn't believe that I could think about Dick without crying [sixteen months after his death]." After the wedding Dick's parents had no contact with her for six months. His mother requested that Sharon bring the children to their grandmother's house rather than have the grandparents see them in their new home. At that point Sharon felt that she was letting the children see their grandparents mainly out of respect for Dick, since his parents seemed to provide little for the children and they disliked Andy. She began to fear that her in-laws might meet their needs at the expense of the children. Their relationship became more strained when Sharon and Andy had a child two years after their marriage, and Andy proceeded to adopt Dick's two children. Sharon was aware of her in-laws' feelings of "betrayal" and experienced these herself in a transient way. Despite their initially good relationship and her sensitive efforts to deal with their hurt, the relationship showed signs of deterioration that seemed inevitable in the situation.

Other Family Relationships. Many other family relationships—with siblings, grandparents, and other in-laws—have the potential for providing important support or disruptive conflicts. A few of these are illustrated here.

> *Daphne:* "I have one sister who is very close to me. In fact, she lost a little girl with leukemia. She was sick from almost the same time that my husband was sick. So we shared a lot. But she's the only one that I feel that I can really talk to and I really feel understands, you know."

> *Carol:* "If I tried to express it [my feelings] with my kids, they kind of went all to pieces. So I saw right away that I couldn't use my children. I have a sister-in-law that lost her husband. She lost him three years before. He had a brain tumor and he lived three years, and we shared all this with her. So she was a great deal of help to me. She'd just come right out a lot of times and said, 'Carol, I know how you're feeling and things are going to be all right.' I didn't have to say a lot. She said a lot of it for me. So I just used her. She would just come over and she said, 'I think you ought to get out of the house for a while.' So she just sort of took my hand and led me around."

> Joanne was greatly distressed by her ninety-five-year-old grandmother's "mean attitude toward me after I met Jerry [her new husband]. She was very hateful. I thought she would be happy that I had someone and it wasn't that I was seeing her and my mother any

less, but she just developed a very miserable attitude toward me." Joanne tried to talk with her, but she was quiet. Finally, she revealed her disapproval of Joanne's living with Jerry without being married. They had a big argument, ending with mutual bad feelings. After Joanne and Jerry got married, her grandmother's antagonism disappeared. "I saw her two days later and she said, 'Oh, Joanne, I'm so happy. It's so much better than the way you were living.'"

Sharon: "My relationship with my brother has changed. My brother thought that after Dick died he would step in and be the man. I don't think he's ever really accepted the fact that he never could be or that I never wanted him to be. That bothered him, so there's always been a little something between us now."

Friends

Old Friends. In addition to family, old friends provide a major network of support for the newly bereaved. The continuity and stability of these relationships form a kind of "holding state," in which the bereaved can carry on their day-to-day routines, reaching out for company, compassion, distraction, or practical help as needs arise. This network allows the grieving spouse to continue feeling appreciated, needed, and loved by people who are valued. In the initial weeks of mourning, good friends can understand and accept the widowed person's withdrawal and isolation, not be put off or hurt, and still be prepared to make themselves available when the time is right. At other times friends will move in and offer encouragement and direction where the bereaved feel more or less paralyzed. Friends can share some of the pain of grief and allow for its free expression. The memories of the deceased that they share with the bereaved can help initiate the process of symbolic retrieval of what has been lost.

Marie: "Several women friends have been especially good to me. They allowed me to be depressed when I was, and they let me talk whenever I needed them for that. I couldn't have recovered without them."

June's husband, Jack, had many business acquaintances but few friends, so that when he died June was on her own except for a sorority in which she had been active. "I belong to a sorority and I have some very close friends there. They're the only ones that I really have been in close contact with. Some of them have called me every day for a long time, even though we meet only twice a month. Otherwise, I was not in contact with very many people. I don't have any relatives here. No one to go visit."

After George's death Gloria's friends moved in to care for her, spend time with her, and keep her busy in ways that were extremely beneficial until she could stand by herself. "I remember one day thinking, 'Enough already, enough! I'm going to survive. You don't have to do all this.' Not that they really overdid it that much, but there was a point about two or three weeks later that I thought, 'Gosh, I wish they'd treat me like a normal human being again.'"

Neighbors are an important part of the widowed person's social network of friends, often providing valuable help by virtue of their proximity. They can be readily available to talk or listen, and they also can "watch over" the comings and goings of the newly bereaved. Some people were surprised by kinds of services that were volunteered.

Ross: "But the support from all these people was—I wasn't prepared for that. I must have gotten enough food after my wife's death to last the three of us for, God, I don't know how long."

Louis: "I've got the sweetest neighbors in the country. They watch out for me and watch over me like I
was a brother. And they do. If somebody comes
around my place, my neighbors call me. As a matter
of fact, their daughter is in my house right now
cooking something that she found out I liked."

Louise found the support of her friends doubly
helpful: both for its intrinsic worth and for the
reassurance of her own worth. "I always felt that
Doug was probably liked better than myself because
of his gentler nature. I wondered if after I was alone
if people would like me for myself alone or if they
used to like me because I was part of 'Doug and
Louise.' It was very gratifying to find out they like
Louise."

As described earlier in this chapter, some family members or
friends are unable to tolerate the emotionality of the bereaved;
cannot empathize with them because of the threat to themselves of
such feelings; and either avoid them, or do not know how to listen
to them or what to say to them, or push them to relinquish their
grief. As a result of such reactions by others, the bereaved may
experience alienation, isolation, rejection, and anger.

Three months after Larry's death, Joanne went to a
seminar with a group of people whom she had
known for years. "It was one of the worst weekends
of my life. I felt like a fifth wheel. People didn't
know how to talk to me. They didn't know how I
felt. In return, I did not know how to talk to them.
And I had spent years talking to these people. All of
a sudden a definite wall. Nobody mentioned anything. One person said how sorry he was, but everyone else skirted the issue. People do not know how to
talk, and people do not realize that you need to talk."

Ross: "I was embarrassed because I felt after a point in time, when I wanted to talk to people, they were embarrassed to listen and I was embarrassed because I wanted to talk and they didn't want to talk about Pamela. . . . It was okay for them to talk about her for a couple of weeks, but four or five months later they didn't want to hear about it. That bothered me."

Daphne: "There are very few people you can talk about it with because it makes them very uncomfortable. And they don't really want to hear it. They may say they do, you know, they may sympathize, and, you know, they're trying to, but you can tell after you talk to them that it makes them really uncomfortable and they really don't want to."

Beth: "I think my friends treat me differently. They're real cautious about things that they say. I think not so much anymore, but in the beginning they certainly are, just very, very careful, and I find that I even have to be cautious about things that I say around them, maybe even more so than they are around me. They're real uncomfortable talking about anything to do with the accident or about Barry or referring to the past. I just don't do that because I can tell it makes them uncomfortable." She and some friends were reading a book on widowhood. Beth, who owned the book, had underlined sections that seemed to express her own feelings. "So they were reading the book and they came trotting right over and said, 'Is this the way you really feel? That you can't mention anything about it around us?' And I said, 'Yes, it's really true because it makes you feel uncomfortable.' They said, 'Oh, we don't want you to feel that way. You can say anything you want.' I know that they really believe that, but they're still uncomfortable, so I couldn't." Beth felt that there were certain limitations in her friends that could not be transcended despite their most sincere wishes and efforts.

Beth's reaction is a fairly common one: when they sense that others cannot or will not listen to what they are saying or feeling, the bereaved will begin to avoid expressing their feelings or talking about their spouse. Occasionally they will avoid these friends. More often, however, since they still have needs for companionship and activity, the bereaved will find ways to make their friends more at ease.

> After Sam died, Carolyn continued her subscription to the theater, in order to invite someone to go with her and to avoid having her friends feel that they had to call her and invite her to go out with them. She did not want her friends to feel obligated to call her or to think of her as "poor Carolyn"; so she tried to maintain an upbeat stance, reserving her pain for times when she was alone.

Rather than confront their own discomfort or limitations, old friends may deal with the bereaved by avoiding them. They may recognize what is "correct," or even feel a strong internal sense of obligation, and yet remain unable to face the situation. The grieving spouse, who is already experiencing a markedly impaired sense of self-esteem, is left feeling abandoned, rejected, and isolated and may respond to such feelings by becoming angry or by assuming responsibility for these further losses.

> *Perry:* "Certain people have yet to express their condolences [two years later]. Just never have said anything, just weren't in evidence. And these are people we were fairly friendly with, or thought we were. That tended to cool me very dramatically toward them. I tend to look at friendship as a fairly serious thing, and with people with whom I felt we had a deeper relationship, but proved to me that we didn't, I guess I backed up some. I guess I'm not

going to give them a second shot at me—just being more protective of myself. Their absence hurt. It was more than a small void. I mean, there were a number of people who performed that way. It disappointed me."

Bill: "One of the things that's been a little difficult to understand is people that you were pretty close with as friends and often visited them after she died—there are some that absolutely drop you completely. They don't call. There's nothing. It's like you were poison. I don't know whether it's that they don't know how to cope with this thing or whether it's because you don't have a wife and you're a threat to their marriage. I don't understand it at all. One couple in particular, hardly a day went by that they weren't in contact with us and me especially right up until the day my wife died. In two years and three months, they have never called me one time. Not one time. That hurt and leaves me with a total lack of understanding. There's no way I can justify it. I couldn't do that to someone, and I don't understand why they've done that to me."

Jonathan's experience was the opposite of Bill's. Friends who had avoided him while Sandra was sick and dying contacted him after her death. Their avoidance seemed to reflect their inability to deal with the dying, whereas apparently they were able to handle Jonathan's grief.

Other widows and widowers find that some friends are too acutely bereaved themselves to be able to confront a grieving spouse. Such friends can make renewed contact only after their own wounds have begun to heal. Learning *why* people have disappeared can have very therapeutic effects for the bereaved, both because it usually attenuates some of that sense of rejection and because it helps the bereaved understand that they were not responsible for the earlier avoidance.

> *Doris:* "I wanted things to continue with regards to
> friends, relatives, and neighbors as they did when my
> husband was alive. I felt really concerned because I
> thought I was going to lose this one couple that we
> knew. I had been concerned about those particular
> people for a long time. Everyone else has remained
> friends except this one couple, and it's bothered me
> because I thought maybe when I was mourning I said
> something or did something that upset them. But I
> found out two weeks ago that all our other friends
> felt the same way about them. It turns out they're
> having marital problems. . . . I did feel reassured
> because I really thought it was my fault."

Many other cultures sanction periods of "official" mourning, during which time the mourner is supposed to be in isolation.
In these cultures the question of how others might respond does
not arise.

> Marie's husband, Oscar, was of Guamanian descent.
> Guamanian custom was to leave a widow to mourn
> during her first year of bereavement. Marie did not
> have to face any possible sense of rejection or resent-
> ment because of this ritual social avoidance. "It's
> okay. It's just the way it's done."

In our culture, however, friends who cannot empathize with the
bereaved and who cannot tolerate expressions of grief may try to
curtail the mourning period. Such friends are almost always
oblivious to the underlying issues that make the emotionality of
grief unacceptable and intolerable to them. Their means of coping
with these internal conflicts is to externalize the issues and turn
them into "rational" and even moral problems of the bereaved,
who may be "accused" of being weak, irresponsible, or "unbal-
anced" because of their grief. Fortunately, this reaction to the
bereaved is unusual in its most strident form, but subtle manifestations of it can be seen in friends whose wish to believe that the

bereaved person is not suffering leads them to act as though this were actually the case.

> *Blanche:* "There is no way to describe to someone else what being widowed is like. Most people do not want to accept the fact that being widowed equals suffering. One does not believe that the pain will ever leave, and time passes so slowly. Friends want you to 'move on' and leave it behind you even when you are still in pain."

> *Phyllis:* "I was abandoned almost immediately by all of my friends. After about two or three weeks of calling people up on the telephone, my experience is they say, 'Oh, you should go out and date and you should do this.' They'll tell you this three weeks after somebody dies. And, of course, it's unreal. And pretty soon after you try to find somebody to talk to but you can't get anybody that's on your wavelength, you shut up and you just don't talk to them. They didn't want to talk about death, and I don't blame them, you know. They've got to face up to their own mortality, and nobody wants to look at that. That's tough to handle."

Avoidance of the bereaved by friends is not always a product of the inability of others to deal with grief. It can also result from biases against the bereaved. Historically, the prevailing stigma attached to the widower or widow is that such a person is a dangerous, lonely, predatory creature who will either devour you with his or her neediness or steal your spouse. While this portrayal of the bereaved carries with it a certain truth about the loneliness and neediness, the notion of a widowed person's dangerousness usually reflects the personal or marital insecurities of the perceiver. Yet this perception is the source of a great deal of pain, especially in the newly bereaved.

Pamela noticed that her married friends did not call her as much as they had before her husband's death. A male friend of hers and her husband's was in San Diego for a meeting. Pamela looked forward to this visit with an important connection to her past and to Tom but learned that the man's wife forbade him to see Pamela. She was very disappointed but said that she "understood."

Fay's efforts to get away from the past led her to become active with new friends, buy new clothes, and get a new job within three months of Gilbert's death. Her neighbors seemed to expect that she would remain in mourning for a longer time. One day, when she had a plumber come to her home to work, a neighbor asked her whether she was "having men in for coffee." These attitudes led to her selling her home and moving.

Daphne: "People view you differently, too, you know. Some husbands think, 'Oh, that's the poor lonely widow,' and they're going to give her a big thrill by being a little flirtatious. And some wives look at you. I was really surprised. I had this couple that were very good friends. The man was a good friend of my husband's in the Navy, and we knew each other for several years. They both came over often. One time my water heater gave out, and water was running all over my garage. I had to do some-thing and I thought, 'I'll just call him and see what he thinks, if it needs replacement or what,' because I didn't know. And she took offence at that, like I was trying to promote something with her husband."

Shirley's presence in car races "didn't please the wives." She thought that she might have to give up racing because of the wives' jealousies. "A widow is a social outcast. We're treated the same as gays or blacks. Because I'm single, my friends all think I'm loose."

Independent of the reactions that the bereaved may encounter among their friends, the bereaved themselves may begin to behave differently toward their friends—as a result of efforts at secondary gain, internal distortions, role changes precipitated by the loss, a heightened sense of vulnerability, or painful responses to triggers created by the relationship.

Early in his grief, Jonathan became aware that he was using his wife's death to get a reaction of sympathy and concern from the people around him. At times he even questioned the legitimacy of his suffering, failing to recognize that he might be operating on multiple psychological levels at once; that is, having both primary pain and secondary gain.

Carol's periods of depression resulted in distortions of her relationships to friends. "I went into a shell and couldn't express how I felt. I would be with the same people, and I was lonely. Then I saw that my distress began to show on them. They really didn't know what to do with me. My nerves were on edge. I became very offended by a lot of things they said. But I didn't voice it, you see; I kept it all inside. So I really became very warped."

Ross felt uncomfortable engaging in what social life he had with friends. He became quite sensitive to the motivations of his friends and distressed by the idea that he was being invited out on the basis of his weakness or vulnerability rather than the positive features of his personality. "It's not that I think they're pitying me or anything, but I have this feeling that if I were not by myself—the reason that they're inviting me for dinner is because they know I'm by myself. It's not for my company. It's to help me with my loneliness. It's not that it's so distasteful—I like these people. But it just doesn't feel right."

Almost a year and a half after Edwin's death, Doris lost a very good friend to death and subsequently spent a good deal of time with the friend's widow. This woman was partially paralyzed and in a wheelchair from a prior stroke and had no family to help her. Therefore, Doris tried to help her in whatever ways she could. The two women had long talks together. Each time Doris went to see her, she would leave feeling depressed and ambivalent about returning. Because she realized that such contact was important for the widow, she continued to visit her, tolerating the painful feelings that their talks precipitated. While the sense of obligation kept Doris going, eventually she felt that this contact, though painful, was also helpful to her.

A particularly strong bond often develops between people who have lost their spouses through death, a "kinship" that sustains them when other relationships may fail. At the same time, because of the inevitable pain that they feel when they encounter others who are grieving, some grieving spouses may avoid people in this "condition."

Beth: "I don't know why it is, but there's a gal who lives across the street from me, and her husband has cancer. He's terminal and he's at home. He's been at home for I don't even know how long—several months. I have not been able to go over there, and it bothers me. You know, I feel I should do something. I mean, there's nothing I can do but just . . . I don't know if I'd do her harm or good to go over there and talk to her. I don't know what to do. I hate ignoring the situation. It's not something that should be ignored. It could be that I just don't want to face it."

Beth clearly anticipated that such an interaction would be painful both for her neighbor and for her and could not face it despite her obvious sense that she "should." Such dilemmas are commonplace for the bereaved and are not easily resolved, often leaving the person feeling guilt or shame because of an inability to act "properly" and despite what others almost always understand as mitigating circumstances.

New Friendships. The bereaved quickly learn which people in their environment are sympathetic to their suffering and capable of accepting their grief. When family and friends prove to be limited in their capacity to offer the comfort and relief that occur only with catharsis and understanding, the widowed person may look elsewhere for sympathy and acceptance. Sometimes a person who also has experienced grief following the loss of a spouse, a child, or a friend will reach out to the grieving spouse and provide important links to the suffering and to life beyond grief. These relationships can provide valuable assistance to the newly bereaved and lead to the deepest of bonds.

Phyllis: "I was lucky inasmuch as there were two widows at my school. I think I would have been in pretty bad shape if it hadn't been for Dinah. Any time of the day or night I knew I could call her, and me being me I had to be in awfully bad shape before I would. Then one month I had a telephone bill of $90, and that was for talking four hours to Ocean-side, where she lives. I kept feeling like she's so much further along than I am and I hate to dump it on her all over again and make her go through this all over again. She kept insisting it didn't bother her and I know where she was at now because I could do that for somebody else now. And it would not bother me at all to offer somebody to just call me any time of the day or night. 'If you need to talk to me, wake me up at three o'clock in the morning.' Who else is up at three o'clock in the morning?"

In addition to individuals who may give support and assistance, coalitions of bereaved men and women have evolved for the specific purpose of providing support in many ways. These support groups exist in many large cities as self-help widow-to-widow organizations, as extensions of hospice programs, as aftercare from large hospitals, or as small groups affiliated with local churches. They have been developed as an extension of the principle "It takes one to know one" (see Chapter Eight). The relationships that develop from such groups can be among the most meaningful and helpful in the lives of the newly bereaved.

> *Carol:* "The friends that I've made in these two years are probably closer friends than the ones I've ever had in the past. I think we're closer with our inner feelings with those people who were strangers, and so it's really hard to describe, because really they're very, very close. There's just nothing I can't talk to them about."

> There were nine pilots on the airplane that crashed, killing Barry and everyone else on board. Six months after his death, Beth became friendly with one of the other pilot's wives, and together they organized their own support group, made up of all nine widows. They felt that they had unique problems of adjustment because of their ages, the suddenness of death, and the widespread and recurrent publicity that occurred long after the crash. "With my other friends, it is hard because I like to be able to remember and say, 'Oh, I remember when this or that happened.' I just don't because it makes everybody uncomfortable. So that's one nice thing about the new friendships that I have: the people are in the same situation that I am, my little group of friends, because we all feel free to say or talk about anything we want. It doesn't bother anybody."

While the relationships with other bereaved people may provide a unique sanctuary in which to open up one's deepest feelings and share in another's tragedies, these relationships can become stultifying when they are unidimensional and lack a broad base of activities and feeling tones; that is, when they become limited to the sharing of grief experiences.

> *Carol:* "I don't know whether these relationships will last or not, or how long. I'm beginning to be like my old self, and these relationships that we have formed are with people who really didn't have anything in common except our grief. . . . When the closeness is intense and the feelings are intense, one is aware of the intimacy. When things back away a little bit, you become aware of annoyances. I'm also in a different place. I feel myself growing away from some of them. Sometimes I see that I'm getting a lot better, whereas I feel that they're not. Either that or some of their needs are beginning to depress me. I'm a runner, I back away from some of these things. I really hate to because I love some of those relationships. I'm longing for a close relationship anyhow, kind of like what my husband and I had. I think the group was a substitute for a while."

> Ann was frustrated with all of her exposure to suffering and felt the need to deal with the healthy side of life. "The biggest adjustment I had to make was getting back to the living because I was involved with death and dying for four months—every day. It just became a way of life." She relied on her widowed friends to deal with her suffering, yet she knew that she must reorient herself toward health. "Finally, I . . . joined an exercise class and I started identifying with health."

Besides seeking acceptance and support for their grief, bereaved persons often yearn for new relationships to replace what they have lost. Although people usually prefer retrieval to replacement, especially in regard to the loss of a spouse, they ultimately do "the best that they can."

> Lucille was painfully aware of the vacuum left by Arthur's death. "In fact, I wanted people. I wanted people more than when I was married. Married I was more aloof. Now I'm more open to people, open in the sense that I'm more available to people. When I was married, my privacy was very important to me. I didn't care if I saw people or if I didn't. I didn't mind being alone, and I could stay home all day without even leaving the house, just reading all day, and it didn't bother me. I can't do it today. Now I need people where before I didn't."

In this search for new relationships, the widowed person embarks on a voyage into the world with a different orientation. No longer part of a couple, he or she must deal with new encounters alone, with the potential advantages and disadvantages that accompany this altered state: the trepidations, limited experience, and newness as well as the freedom and adventure that develop with time.

> *Fran:* "The first time I went out, I was terrified because I had been married for thirty-five years and I'd never been anywhere without him, you know, out alone looking for friends or at a club or anything. I'd never been anywhere. And so the first couple of times that I went to this sailing club I was devastated because there weren't too many people who paid any attention to me and I thought, 'I'm not going back there.' But then when I'd get home I'd say, 'I've got to go back there because I've got to have some friends and they have something in common with me.' After that when I'd go back, I'd just go up to people and start talking and come to find out most of those people were in my position. Maybe not widowed, but

by divorce or some reason, they're all single. And so
now I have a lot of friends and I'm an officer in that
club and it's enjoyable. I really enjoy all these people.
But it was just very awkward and difficult for me at
first. I think maybe that would be a hard thing for
anyone to do."

Doris slowly became aware of a great sense of freedom in dealing with people that she met. "I don't
feel as awkward now as I did when I first became a
widow." As her wounds healed, it became easier to be
with people, including couples. "I think I must be
getting used to it." She could exercise her independence as never before. She had been invited to stay over
at some friend's home and would never have considered this while married, but agreed to do so.

Unlike old friends, new friends will relate to the bereaved
person as a single individual rather than as someone who was once
part of a couple.

One of Shirley's early pleasures in racing was making
friends with other participants. She wanted to be
treated as an individual, but her old friends still
related to her as "Art's widow." The race drivers,
however, just knew her as "Shirley." She liked that.

Fran saw a dramatic contrast between being with her
old friends and new ones. "One thing that bothers
me occasionally is that we lived up north in Sacra-
mento, and whenever I go home I feel like I'm 'Mrs.
Thomas' because all our friends are there. But I'm
here and I have different friends and I'm just plain
'Fran.' So when I go up home it is a little more
difficult with the memories because of the things we
did together with friends there. When we moved here,
we were only here a short time when he passed away,
and we didn't have time to make friends. So all the
friends that I have now he never knew."

Romance and Remarriage

Although it may be a struggle for some, most widows and widowers welcome the attention, affection, and companionship of their family and friends while they begin to adjust to the loss of their spouse. The conflicts and problems that arise are the inevitable consequences of being in relationships, but there are very few conflicts about *having* the relationships in the first place. The same cannot be said about the subsequent development of romantic heterosexual relationships.

The bereaved are in a quandary, a dilemma created by the needs that brought them to marry in the first place and the reality of their continuing relationship with the spouse who has died. In addition, the pain of loss, the changes evolving within themselves, and reality considerations all play a role in determining the bereaved person's ultimate "readiness" to become involved again in an intimate, romantic relationship.

At the beginning of one's grief, romance and remarriage may seem unthinkable, impossible, unacceptable. Most newly widowed men and women still feel married to their spouses, and such considerations would be met with guilt, abhorrence, or contempt. Yet, as months and years pass, questions about involvement and remarriage invariably arise for the widowed person, either from within or from family or friends. Given the right circumstances or sometimes even the wrong circumstances, the bereaved are likely to make actual decisions about reinvolvement and remarriage that they might not have predicted they would make.

Needs for Reinvolvement. The forces pushing the bereaved toward reinvolvement are usually the same ones that drew them toward marriage in the first place: the need for intimacy, companionship, security, support, and sexuality. While some of these needs (for example, sexuality) may diminish during the more acute stages of grief, others have certainly intensified. Over time, the former will usually reemerge and the intensity of the latter subside. Still, in the absence of the person who had helped to satisfy these needs, they will continue, attenuated only to the extent that the bereaved person has been able to provide for their satisfaction through internal growth and outside resources—friends and family.

> *Linda* [eighteen months after her husband's death]: "When I see happy couples, I have a fleeting feeling, 'I've lost my partner.' I get a pent-up feeling. I tell my friends, 'I wasn't born to be a widow,' yet I have no desire to go and look for someone else. Our life was so private. I couldn't accept someone else. I'm afraid I would make comparisons. I don't want to give up my thoughts about our marriage. But it's a lonesome life, and I'm not ready to give up the way we lived before." She recognized that her needs for such a relationship were still there, even though she wasn't yet "ready" to get involved with someone else because her husband and their relationship were still too active a part of her life.

> *Ross:* "I am not meant to live alone. I don't like living alone. I don't intend to continue living alone, and I like having someone dependent on me and being dependent on someone, a mutual dependency."

Those men and women who did become romantically involved within several months after their spouses died felt a sense of relief from their intense loneliness, even though they continued to grieve for their dead spouses. Usually there was support from friends and families—an understanding of the intensity of such needs—that helped the bereaved accept this involvement. Except in rare instances, any reservations about romantic involvements and remarriage came from the bereaved themselves, rather than their families or friends.

Another important impetus, or at least sanction, for reinvolvement was the stated wish by the dead spouse that the survivor find happiness with someone else. Such wishes cannot provide a positive desire for involvement with anyone else, nor can they override the initial feelings of intense avoidance experienced by the bereaved. However, as time goes on, these wishes can help grieving spouses overcome some of the resistance and enhance their receptivity to the development of a new relationship.

> When Joanne started dating three months after Larry died, her grandmother was shocked. Joanne told her, "It's not the same as when you were widowed." She felt that she was ready to meet someone. "I know that Larry wanted me to do this."

> When Glenn began seeing Martha, an old friend of the family, his whole family and all his friends were accepting of their relationship and seemed to welcome her even though it had been only three months since Eileen died. While Glenn shed some tears over the reminders of Eileen, he had no regrets or guilt about his involvement with Martha. "I know Eileen would be happy."

Preferences for Remaining Alone or Single. There is a commonly held view that eventually all widows and widowers would like to remarry. Furthermore, many people believe that remarriage is the only "healthy" form of adjustment for someone who has lost his or her spouse. At the same time, eligible women outnumber eligible men during the years of middle age and beyond. Can these views and realities be reconciled, or do they conspire to guarantee a continual supply of unhappy and frustrated widows? First of all, the reality of numbers does not and will not go away. There are, in fact, and will be for the foreseeable future, many more women than men who are bereaved. At the same time, men and women are capable of making excellent adaptations to being single. Most surprising, though, is the fact that many people who have lost their spouses to death *prefer* being single and are, therefore, not only not frustrated by the lack of suitable or available partners but even relieved by that fact. There are many reasons why the bereaved prefer to be alone—reasons that reflect on their growth, fears, loyalty, values, and sense of reality.

Bereavement offers many the opportunity for profound growth and development (see Chapter Seven)—for developing new experiences and values and restructuring priorities. Accompanying the growing awareness of their strengths and capacities to manage by themselves is often a newfound sense of freedom, one that they most likely would not have sought but are now reluctant to relinquish. These sentiments are much more prevalent among women than men, presumably as a reflection of the greater sense of autonomy, control, and freedom that men have traditionally experienced in their lives and marriages.

> *Pamela:* "As far as getting married again, I don't think I would ever want to. No particular reason other than the last few years I've learned to do things on my own, learned to be my own boss, and I don't know if I want somebody now telling me what to do. Now that I know I can do things and handle things, I don't know that I'd want somebody to step in and tell me what to do. I find that I enjoy having my time to do what I want . . . and, like I said, it's getting easier all the time."

> Bobbi felt great relief from the constant fear that Nathan would have another heart attack. "Once that fear was gone, it was a good feeling . . . not to be afraid. This feeling of independence that I have—I think if I met him now, where I am now, I don't think I would marry him. I don't think right now I want to marry anyone. A relationship, yes. But I don't think I'd want to give up my control for a relationship."

> *Beatrice:* "I don't think I'd ever go into another marriage. It's too tight a relationship. Even if I met a man, I'd proceed with extreme caution. I don't want another man in control of my life. There are advantages to controlling my own life even if it is scary."

For these women the notion of control emerged powerfully—as a reflection not only of their experience of their marital relationships but also of their bereavement, a time when much of one's experience seems out of control. Since these were not unhappy marriages, these views clearly reflected only a single dimension of the relationships; but this dimension assumed greater significance with time and experience.

Issues of freedom were not limited to women. Men also experienced certain kinds of freedom that seemed desirable.

> Early in the course of his grief, Bill assumed that he would get married again, if only to escape from his pain and loneliness. As time went on, he realized that he could be reasonably comfortable without marrying. "Since being widowed, I've grown a bit more independent than I ever was. I'm no longer afraid of being alone. I know I can get dates if I want to."

> Ralph was enjoying being single. He started dating in the middle of the second year of bereavement but wasn't interested in getting serious. He particularly enjoyed being alone, with no one to tell him what to do. "If I want to read, I can read, or go to any movie I want. Maybe this is selfish, but it feels good."

Men and women whose spouses had died after a prolonged illness were especially hesitant about getting involved with someone else. They could not bear the thought of reexperiencing the pain and suffering in which both they and their spouses had been submerged. The effects of the "death imprint" were the development of avoidance as well as the intellectual conviction that marriage was not for them.

> *Susan:* "People say, 'Well, you'll get married again,' but I don't want to get married again. I don't—again it sounds selfish—but I don't want to take care of a man again. You know, the thought that maybe I would die first didn't occur to me, but I feel almost

like I've paid my dues and I just want to do what I want to do."

Three years after Doug's death, Louise was dating Ron regularly. "I won't marry him as I've become accustomed to living my own life." She laughs when she sees the similarities between Doug and Ron: gentle, lazy men who want mothers. "Apparently this is the kind of man I like. I don't want to nurse and bury another man, though. Taking care of Doug was a long, hard row."

Ann: "When it comes down to it, I run, I run away from it. And I don't know if I run away from it because I feel like I'm being unfaithful to Billy or if I'm just afraid, 'Gee, if I fall in love with this person and he gets sick, he might die. I don't know why I run, but I know I am very apprehensive."

Blanche: "I need a handyman, but I don't want a husband. I don't want to go through a sickness again."

Another obstacle to the formation of new romantic relationships is the bereaved person's tendency to compare a new acquaintance—unfavorably—with the dead spouse.

Harold: "A great many friends have advised me, 'Don't use her as the yardstick by which to measure anyone else you become involved with.' I don't think anyone will be like Rose. I never met anyone remotely like her before I met her and all during the years we were married. I expect she was a very unusual person."

Pamela: "It's like I told my brother, as far as dating, at this point [two years later] it wouldn't be fair to the man because I'd be comparing, and nobody at this point could measure up to him. I just don't

think it would work out. It's not fair to compare
people, and I would."

Although Earl was dating a woman regularly, he
didn't think it would be fair to marry her, because he
would be constantly comparing her to Rita. "I don't
think I could find anyone to replace her. She looked
after me like I was the Hope Diamond."

Five years after Edwin's death, Doris was aware that
she wanted primarily to hold on to her memories of
him and their relationship. "A lot of people say,
'You should get out and meet somebody and start
dating,' and stuff like that. I wouldn't mind going
out on an occasional date, but I don't think I want to
go with anyone steady because I feel in the back of
my mind [that] everything would change, and maybe
it would be good to change, but I don't know if I
want to. I want to keep all those memories. I'd hate
to have to sell my home and move in with someone
else and put all these memories away. A lot of people
that are widowed think I'm crazy because I keep
pictures of my husband around. That's the way I like
it. You know, some of them seem to think you've got
to put all these things away in a drawer and get rid of
them and go ahead, and I guess, in a way, that's right
for some people. But I just don't feel that way. Maybe
I'm weird."

The people in our study had been married for an average of
more than twenty years. Experience had taught them how much
pain, effort, and energy are necessary to make a relationship work.
Many people, even those who had good marriages, were reluctant
to get married again because they anticipated the hardship and the
chances for failure. Others recognized their own personal liabilities, which also increased the risks of failure.

Bill remembered how difficult it had been for him to
adjust to marriage when he was twenty-six years old.

During his thirty-three years of marriage, the relationship worked out well. After two years of adjusting to being alone, he felt that he was doing well and wondered whether he could readjust to marriage. "I've seen people my age remarry and the marriage falls apart. If I could be reasonably sure that I could have a marriage which would be as good as my first, I'd do it. But I don't want to buy any heartaches."

Shirley felt that, if she found herself getting "ready" for remarriage, "I would fight it, because I don't want to go through that. It's work. I worked hard and I don't want the pain. How many acquaintances are you going to have to have relationships with before you find the man you want to marry? Okay, there's a lot of pain involved there. Even when you find a good one and you're happy with him, there's still pain and I don't want that. Why take the chance of it working? Divorce. No. No. Or take the chance of him dying again? No thank you." Shirley found the process of making herself available a difficult one. "I was so mad because I learned in one evening you cannot smile at a man, you cannot dance with him, and you don't let him buy you a drink because he thinks he owns you for the whole evening. I don't want to do it again. I don't have to go through that mess." Finally, she was aware of her tendency to fall for men with whom there is no future—"strays." As a result, she was reluctant to make herself available or to get involved with anyone. It just seemed too much trouble at every turn.

June also felt that she would only pick a man who would make her unhappy. "I don't feel that I will ever get married again. I've been married twice. I think that I have a—I always say, 'I have no charisma.' Everybody treats me the same. The more I do, the more they expect me to do and I find myself doing more than I can do." Her solution was to

> remain single, so that she would not have to feel exploited.
>
> Bobbi expressed another common concern: how another person would react to or accept her. She was afraid that she might be inadequate in a new relationship and that "I might not be good enough in bed."

Certainly, any area of interpersonal conflict or prior experience of difficulty can serve as a focus for concern and reluctance to enter into a new relationship. People in successful marriages sometimes learn about their worth and capacity to make a relationship work and can carry this knowledge with confidence into another relationship. Others experience the valuable aspects of their relationship as tied up with a specific person and feel that they can only reproduce their happiness with exactly the right person; clearly, these people will anticipate remarriage with much greater hesitance, reluctance, and skepticism.

Certain reality considerations also make the question of remarriage a difficult one for many bereaved, particularly for widows. There are many forms of entitlement from pensions, Social Security, and other insurance benefits that accrue only to an unmarried person. Remarriage for such people would mean a loss of income, substantial in many instances. Other people are cautious about considering remarriage because they do not want somebody else controlling their financial resources and are, in any event, suspicious of the motives of prospective marital candidates. The other side of this coin represents those widows or widowers who seek out marriage as a means of establishing greater financial security.

> *Fran:* "If I found somebody and I thought I would have to develop the relationship as far as getting married again, it worries me because my husband left me a nice pension. If I remarry I will lose that, and if this fellow would die in the next two weeks, where am I financially?"

John began dating Cathy, a widow, about a year after his wife died. They developed an excellent and intimate relationship over the next few months. They ate together, had much contact by phone, played golf regularly, and began to travel. They considered getting married but decided against it when it became clear that they would lose about $1,000 a month in pension and Social Security benefits. Four years later they still maintained separate homes but provided regular companionship for each other.

Joanne and Jerry decided to live together but not marry because, if they married, her pension would be stopped and he would lose some Social Security. This situation worked well for both of them until Joanne's grandmother protested their immorality. Therefore, they had a nonlegal ceremony performed for the woman's benefit.

Bill was very suspicious of the women he met and dated. "I suppose I shouldn't say it, but I think lots of women are very great actresses. I guess I can say that because I've seen other men that thought they had found *the* thing and then not too many months after they had gotten married it wasn't at all like they thought it was going to be. . . . I'm not wealthy, but I'm not poor. Some don't make any bones about wanting to know what you have and how you live and how much you've got to live on pretty quick, and you can tell they'd like to move into a nice home and share whatever you have right off." Bill was afraid of what might happen to the resources he had accumulated for his sons. "I have seen some that almost as soon as the wedding ceremony was over, boy, they start boring in on that new husband to get him to change his will. Someone comes in from nowhere and gets all the accumulation that Dad and Mom put together that really should have been the

children's. So I think of things like that. They're sad
thoughts to put into a romance.''

Dating. For people who have been married twenty or thirty
years, the prospect of dating can be exciting. At the same time,
they usually feel nervous, awkward, and worried about what to
expect, how they will be received, who might be available, and
how to act. Times have changed, and even the well prepared
invariably encounter a certain amount of "culture shock." Well-
meaning friends try to be matchmakers, with occasional successes
but more frequent failures. The widows and widowers who begin
dating expose themselves to the injuries of rejection and the
discomfort of being treated as a sexual object or prize, for good or
ill. Many widows and widowers are able to accommodate to the
early surprises and awkwardness of dating and enjoy this "new"
experience, both as an end in itself and as a means to an end,
matrimony. Others recoil and look for different avenues—such as
church groups or singles clubs—to fill their social lives. Because of
the preponderance of middle-aged and older eligible women
compared to men, dating is easier for men from the standpoint of
"supply and demand." There seems to be a greater degree of
freedom and choice for men who are widowed, but problems
accompany this statistical advantage.

> Ross found himself besieged by women to the point
> where he was becoming suspicious of all women.
> "The married ones want to fix you up, and the
> unmarried ones want to come and live with you." He
> was particularly shocked by the extent of the sexual
> overtures he encountered. "The number of women
> that decided I really shouldn't be sleeping alone
> didn't shock me, but it was the fact that they felt that
> way and they were quite willing to hop in bed. These
> are single people, married people, widowed people,
> the age group from about twenty-five through about
> fifty."

Carl's transition from isolation to dating occurred abruptly and with its own form of culture shock. "For the first year, I didn't want companionship. I didn't want to date. For one thing, I think I considered myself being forty-two years old as being out of the mainstream, over the hill for a while. I'd been married since I was eighteen years old. Married life was a way of life to me, and I never thought about dating or anything. I think the hardest thing was when I had my first date after twenty-six years of not dating at all. I think it's one of the toughest moments I've ever had in my life." Carl had been on a charter boat when a young woman he had been talking with approached him. "She leaned against me and I didn't know how to handle it. I just said to myself, 'Oh, my God.' I didn't know what to do."

Bill: "I guess I didn't even know how to act on the first date. The lady called me up and asked me to go to a concert with her. I had known her for quite a while. I took her out a couple of times after that to dinner. Her husband had been a very successful contractor. She talked about him continually, what a great man he was and so forth, and by the time I had gone with her the third time, I said to myself, 'You're wasting your time, brother. This woman is so deep into her husband there's no way you can ever compete with that. Why waste your time and money?' So I never asked her for another date. And I tried to put it in my mind as something I should not do—burden any girl that I went with, any date, with the greatness of my wife, carry on and on endlessly about how wonderful she was and everything she did for me. I thought that that's unfair competition." Bill was also taken aback by the dating scene. "It's a different ball game out there now than it was. The women are much more aggressive now than they were when I was young and dating. Most of them won't hesitate

to ask you for a date, or they will set something up.
They will be the first one to call sometimes if they
can find your number."

Women in particular expressed distress and reluctance
about many of the forums for single people's activities and dating.

Carolyn: "I don't think I'd ever go to a singles dance
or go to a bar, or do some of the things that some of
my acquaintances have done. I just can't envision
myself doing that. I just don't do things well alone. It
would be too difficult."

A bereaved person's children can be highly ambivalent
about their parent's dating. On the one hand, younger children
may have continuing needs for a second parent and may support
and encourage dating and remarriage; and older children, both at
home and on their own, may perceive their parent's dating as a
means of attaining happiness or of relieving themselves of
responsibilities. On the other hand, there is often a sense of loyalty
to the deceased and a feeling of betrayal when the survivor begins
looking for another mate. The tension between these two conflicting aspects of the parent's dating may be dealt with through the
use of humor and teasing by the children.

Carolyn had a terrible time on her first date with a
man who tried to convince her that she was in bad
shape and could really use a husband, him, to help
her deal with her life—which was actually in very
good shape. Her daughter decided to help her out.
"Jane embarrassed me. She and her head nurse
decided that since both their moms were widows,
they've got to go find guys for them at the local
Mexican restaurant up near the VA Hospital. And
they indeed did start talking with five men in their
fifties. They were telling them that they had moms
that were widows and needed to go out. She brought
me home this man's card and said, "Mom, he's really

kind of a nice man. Would you give him a call?' I said, 'Absolutely not. No way,' and she said, 'Oh, come on.' And it was bantering sort of on that level, kidding around. Two or three days later, Jane says again, 'Mom, here's that guy's card.' I said 'There's no way I could call that man.' " Carolyn's daughters kidded her regularly about her dating and yet were her warmest supporters.

Romantic Relationships. If one considers dating the preliminaries to the development of romantic and intimate relationships, than these relationships are the preliminaries to remarriage. They offer the bereaved a time to encounter and contend with their reactions to this new intimacy, to face the internal and external conflicts created by such involvement, and to resolve their ongoing relationship with the deceased sufficiently to consider a commitment to another person.

Getting involved in a new relationship can be very complicated for the bereaved. Usually the impetus comes from within—the powerful emotional forces that appear as longing, yearning, and loneliness. These are counteracted by fears of the unknown as well as the feelings of continuing loyalty and love toward the deceased spouse. Whatever would act to diminish these opposing forces would also enhance the receptivity and availability of the bereaved to new involvements. Such barriers can be lowered when the new romantic interest is someone whom the bereaved person already knows. During the early months of grief, survivors are particularly vulnerable to the rekindling of old flames. They want desperately to recapture the past with their spouses but will often settle for the memories of prior romances.

Bobbi began corresponding with a man whom she had dated briefly thirty-five years earlier. Through her aunt—who lived in Phoenix, where he also lived—he had learned of her being widowed and had been sending her tapes and love poems. Although it seemed strange to her that he would send love poems to someone he had not seen in many years, this contact was very seductive; and Bobbi let him know that she would be visiting her aunt in Phoenix. When she met him after months of correspondence, she became aware of how intensely she wanted intimacy. However, he turned out to be homosexual, and Bobbi's hopes were disappointed.

Gloria was contacted by a man who had proposed to her thirty years before. Very quickly "the relationship is getting out of hand." Cal was married but began calling continually from Washington, D.C., telling Gloria that she was the only woman he had ever loved and asking her to come to Washington to visit him. Gloria's initial concerns were that Cal was "so impulsive that if I don't put the brakes on it he will get a divorce. Our backgrounds are so dissimilar. He is too free wheeling. We'd mix like oil and water. I want out of this. Yet it is tempting. I don't know what I'm gong to do with it. His attention has done wonderful things for my self-esteem. It is all a widow needs." Concurrently, at home, Gloria became increasingly aware of her loneliness and wishes for intimacy. "I want to be half of a set." Her contact with Cal initiated her thoughts of being in a new relationship. "I'm still alive and I have a lot of life left. Maybe I don't want to be alone." Shortly after this point, she vacationed with Cal in San Francisco and they fell "madly in love." Within weeks he told his wife, began to get a divorce, and planned for Gloria to move east to be married. "If I were any happier I'd burst." They pursued these plans and were subsequently married, despite Gloria's reservations about Cal's impetuousness, the upheaval, and his possible heart condition.

During the depths of her grief, Agnes frequently thought about her first serious romance. The breakup of this romance had also resulted in a strong grief reaction with prolonged depression. She was very drawn to this boyfriend and fantasized about the feelings of falling in love again. She often wondered what it would have been like to have made love with him. In the context of these feelings, Agnes became involved with Mike. "He's fifty-three years old but acts like a teenager. He reminds me of Lars, my first love."

The widowed person may also be receptive to relationships that provide a clear connection to the deceased or evidence that the deceased would encourage or approve of the relationship, again allowing for the continuity of their ties. Two widows in the study became romantically involved with colleagues of their husbands within weeks of their spouses' deaths, receiving comfort from the illusion of continuing contact with someone close to their spouses. Others were supported in their new relationships by the knowledge that their spouses would have been happy for them.

Joanne felt that she and Jerry, a widower, were "destined to meet." They met nine months after Larry died, introduced to each other by friends. From the first, "We've seemed to know each other all our lives." There were striking similarities in their lives with their former spouses. Larry and Jerry's names were similar, they both worked for the Post Office, Larry had a twin named Jerry, Jerry had a cousin named Larry. Both previous couples had December anniversaries and had met in roller rinks. Both had good marriages. All these similarities led them to believe that their relationship was predestined, and they flowed into it very easily without any reservations.

Melinda developed a romantic relationship on the rebound, feeling almost as though she were continuing her relationship with her husband, Jim. She met Ira through a friend. "It was just one of those weird things. And I thought, 'It's such an interesting way of meeting someone, I wonder if there's something more to it than this.' It was like Jim was saying, 'Well, you need some kind of preoccupation, you know, so this guy is going to come into your life.' And it was at the perfect time because it sparked me up a little bit because he was just like Jim. It's like they say, you try to replace someone if you really care about them. He was tall, he was good-looking, he was outgoing, he was intelligent, he was all the things I admire in people and, of course, really, really loved about Jim. But the idea of getting close to this guy was just totally out of the question. So we went out, and I didn't want to stop. We had such a good time, it was one of those things. We did one thing after another. I was just full of energy. It was somebody that I was enjoying sharing the company of. And what I was doing in my head—I was thinking it was Jim. I was just making him into Jim. I said, 'Okay, what the heck.' For a little while I allowed that to happen. I allowed myself to open romantically with him. But it was my connection to Jim. I felt so strongly because there were so many similarities. It was incredible. I said to myself that Jim was coming back in a different form. . . . It always bothered Jim that there was twenty years between us. He'd say, 'I wish I were twenty years younger,' and Ira would be exactly that age, I mean almost to the day. It was really weird. And we met on the fifteenth, the same day Jim and I used to celebrate year after year, month after month. All those things told me, 'This is what I was looking for obviously. This is somebody for some reason I'm supposed to be connected to in some form.' So we became very close. Sometimes I'd be driving and I would just burst into tears of pain, of missing Jim, because I suddenly realized that it was not Jim with me. It was his substitute and I wanted Jim there. I'd start thinking about the pain and then I'd think, 'Okay, it's okay,

because I have someone to take his place and I can
put my emotions toward him. Well, then I put more
and more emotion toward him as I would have to
Jim. Then all of a sudden he said that it's not going
to work, and the whole world crashed in. I was
heartbroken, absolutely heartbroken."

The widowed person who has begun to expose his or her
vulnerability and opens up to someone else carries a whole set of
emotional responses that have been associated with being in love,
making falling in love easy once the barriers are down.

A few months after Frank's death, Annette fell in
love. "A man came into my life who happened to be
a naval officer. We met, he said hello, he asked me to
dance, and all the world was trembling and shaking.
The fireworks went off. The chemistry was there
when we just said hello, and he felt the same way. A
handsome, wonderful, everything man. There is the
guy I'll say, 'Yes, I'll marry you' if he walked in the
door and said, 'Will you marry me?' I'd find out
about him later because I found him exciting,
stimulating, loving, and just about everything that I
would have liked. He disturbed me. I mean I fell in
love with him. But he was married."

While the development of a new romantic relationship may
alleviate many feelings associated with loss, aspects of this
relationship also may initiate strong feelings of loss. Reminders of
loss can be stimulated by the similarity of feelings toward the
former spouse and the new love interest; by the appearance,
mannerisms, tastes, or interests of this person; or by the experiences of the new couple.

Once Carl started dating, he began having disturbing
feelings of his dead wife's presence. "I had offers to
go camping with Gina, but I won't go. It will bring

back memories of Faith, and that wouldn't be fair to others."

Harold became involved with a widow who was often preoccupied with and discussing her husband's illness and death. "I'm continually recollecting all the difficulties in the last stage of [Rose's] terminal illness, the problems that she had with getting what I felt was adequate treatment. . . . It's not good for me emotionally to get into a close personal involvement with someone who's still in grief because we don't do each other any good."

When Perry first became involved with the woman he would subsequently marry, he felt very ambivalent toward her. "She lessens my loneliness and really interests me, but she makes me remember my wife's ways."

As new relationships develop, widowed persons inevitably make comparisons between their dead spouses and their new romantic interests and prospective marriage partners. These comparisons reflect not only the continuing relationship with the deceased but also the widowed person's reactions to different (or similar) qualities in another person. Because of the years of living together in a committed relationship, bereaved persons accept many aspects of their former marriages as givens, and the development of new relationships will often require an adjustment to different sets of values from those that prevailed.

Harold was involved with a woman for several months but could not reconcile himself to the differences between this woman and Rose. Most important, Rose had provided "unqualified acceptance," whereas this woman did not. He was critical of her using sex as a weapon by not going to bed with him when she was angry. He assumed that she operated emotionally in the same way that Rose had and that the fact that they were going steadily and exclusively with each other ought to mean that she would always be available to him sexually. "Rose and I had agreed to be always on speaking terms before going to bed. Disagreements should stop at the bedroom door."

The differences between one's spouse and a new relationship can often be gratifying and appealing. In any new relationship that is enjoyable, some characteristics about the new person invariably represent a change for the better, even if those same characteristics are limiting or a problem in other ways.

When Glenn began seeing Martha, he found himself adjusting to a very different way of relating. He had been used to taking care of Eileen, attending to her needs. Now Martha was always catering to his needs, fixing him many kinds of foods and mowing the lawn when he was tired. He was flexible in being able to accept this giving on her part. At the same time, he felt that he was becoming too passive and was eating too much and gaining weight.

The differences between former and prospective spouses can also become the focus of deliberations about remarriage when there are reservations on the part of the bereaved.

To help resolve her conflict over the decision to marry Mike, Agnes almost resorted to a "checklist" of characteristics comparing Mike with Jeff. While she had fallen in love with Mike easily enough and he appeared to be a solution to her children's need for a new father, Agnes had great reservations about his stability because he had problems with alcohol and at times became verbally abusive when drinking. He also demonstrated strong mood shifts and had never been married. On the other hand, she could communicate much better with Mike than with Jeff. Mike was more emotional and more empathic. Jeff had never said, "I love you." He felt that there was no need to do so, that it was understood. Mike was outgoing and considerate and loved animals and children. Jeff was introverted, disliked animals, and was cool toward the children. Agnes and Mike were both Catholic; Jeff was Protestant. All these things were in Mike's favor. On the negative side, Mike's drinking and verbal abuse were in contrast to Jeff's sobriety and peacefulness. Mike was flamboyant and made up stories, whereas Jeff was "honesty personi- fied." Jeff's mood was stable; Mike's fluctuated. Mike was jealous of Agnes's outside activities, whereas Jeff had basically left her free to pursue her interests. Eventually Mike became involved in Alcoholics Anonymous and got treatment for his mood changes. With her fingers crossed, Agnes decided to take the risk, and they were married. Two years later the marriage was a stable and happy one for both.

Remarriage. Among the group of widows and widowers in our study, one fourth of those interviewed between four and five years after their spouses' deaths had remarried. This represented half of the men and only one tenth of the women. Given the preponderance of eligible women in the forty-to-sixty age group, it is difficult to draw conclusions about the different rates of remarriage between men and women other than to say that the opportunities are statistically greater for men. Most of the men and women who did remarry did so within two years of their spouses' deaths. The period around two years is the time when the great majority of widows and widowers have achieved a modicum of stability: have made significant adjustments to their loss, living on their own, contending with their loneliness, establishing a new identity, and finding a direction in their lives. The comments of those who had the opportunity to marry but chose not to do so suggest that, as adjustment to widowhood occurs over time, the need for remarriage may subside. Conversely, those who did remarry certainly were able to identify their needs: to help them contend with the loss, their loneliness, their children's needs. Yet it is still difficult to know for certain what factors determined whether or not a person chose to remarry, because almost two thirds of the people in the study did develop some form of heterosexual relationship of varying degrees of closeness and intimacy. These relationships were able to provide many of the essential needs for those who did not marry: support, companionship, emotional closeness, and intimacy and sexuality.

Some people were able to identify certain internal or external pressures to marry. These included concerns about moral values and the needs of children, family, and spouse-to-be.

> Agnes's kids were crazy about Mike and wanted desperately to have a father around again. This weighed heavily on Agnes's decision to marry after three years of widowhood. After the marriage took place, she sighed, "It's a normal family life again; everything is back into one place." Her mother had been quite ill since Jeff's death, and Agnes believed that the illness was related to her mother's worries about her and her children. "If I do remarry, that will stop my mother from worrying."

> Morrie and April were married six months after Pauline died. He would have wanted to wait a full year but was in love with April and worried that he might lose her. "I couldn't expect her to dangle and wait."

> After more than a year of living together, Glenn and Martha got married. They had never had any particular reservations about marriage or felt any external pressure to get married. However, they had "old-fashioned" views about living together, and once they were married, "We no longer have complexes about it."

Remarriage does not mark the end of grief. In fact, the marriage itself often initiates strong, though usually short-lived, emotional reactions in the grieving person. Just as many other landmark events and dates serve as triggers for the bereaved, this symbol of recommitment triggers emotions—such as guilt, regret, and feelings of loss—pertinent to their prior commitment. The dead may return in memories and dreams or as a physical presence.

> As her wedding approached, Sharon was aware of suppressing her thoughts about Dick to avoid putting a damper on the occasion. She felt as if she were divorcing him and became critical of him and their marriage and guilty about having such thoughts.

> At the time of his remarriage to Martha, Glenn had a number of vivid and intense memories and dreams about Eileen. She was on his mind more than at any time in the year and a half since her death. He was reminded of how much he missed her, but he did not allow himself to dwell on these thoughts and feelings.

Elements of grief continue to have their impact on the bereaved, and potentially on the new spouse, after they are married.

> Martha had been a friend to both Glenn and Eileen. After she and Glenn were married, Glenn found that her presence made his grieving for Eileen an easier task. They would often bring up her name and reminisce about times when they had all been together. Martha herself had been widowed years before and appreciated what Glenn was going through.

> Morrie felt lucky to have found April. "I wasn't prepared to live alone. She has made a tremendous difference in my adjustment. If she has had a problem dealing with Pauline's memory, she has not shown it. Pictures of Pauline and her parents are still on display."

Comparisons between the former and present spouses become a part of the new relationship as the bereaved continue to struggle with their loss.

Morrie felt very good about the differences between Pauline and April. "It's nice to have a wife who has her own pursuits. Pauline never worked. Her outlets were through my outlets. I like April's independence because it gives me more freedom. I used to feel guilty leaving Pauline alone when I had business engagements. Also, having a healthy wife is refreshing, and her large salary doesn't hurt."

After his remarriage Van felt easier going and more relaxed than he had been in the past. He could not talk to his first wife as openly and easily as to his current wife. Their sex life was "the best ever."

Sharon's remarriage to Andy was very beneficial to her self-esteem. "Ever since I knew him, Dick always harped on two things: smoking and eating. Every time I would eat, he would look at me, glare at me. The more he told me to stop, the more I was angry and the more I kept doing it. But Andy never said anything like that, and Andy always thought of me as being very beautiful. So the reverse happened. I stopped eating for a long time to try and look better. I also got the feeling that he thought I was very feminine. I had never thought I was feminine. I always felt very masculine. That feeling of feminity started in with wearing makeup. I had never worn makeup very much before unless we went out. Wearing makeup, putting on dresses more than I wore pants, not dressing in jeans all the time. It just was a gradual overhaul. Taking dancing lessons. These things were not in the plans when I was married to Dick, and I don't know why, it just wasn't there. Those things weren't important to him. Andy is not as critical and not as selfish."

Perry was struck with how similar Rene was to June. "It's uncanny." Both were oriented toward family life and had similar value systems. "They would have

been dear friends had they known one another."
Perry even noted that both of them "oriented"
themselves to the same building when they drove
from San Diego to Los Angeles.

During the time in which these remarriages were followed,
only one did not work out well. Furthermore, our subjects
expressed very little criticism of their new spouses—possibly
because, first of all, these marriages were relatively new, still in the
"honeymoon" phases, and had not been given the test of time.
Moreover, if they had had significant complaints, or if their new
relationships paled in comparison to their prior marriages, they
probably would have avoided such a commitment; in fact, many
people did just that. Finally, the longevity of their first marriages
should attest to their capacities to select for compatibility or to
accommodate to differences by focusing on the positive elements in
their relationships and minimizing the areas of difficulty.

When either or both of the new spouses have young
children, remarriage naturally becomes more complicated. Blended
families are faced with the difficult tasks of sorting out and
resolving competing loyalties, the distribution of limited real and
emotional resources, and the practical problems of deciding whose
house, furnishings, dishes, tastes, and goals shall take precedence.
Even where such tasks are undertaken with the greatest commitment, love, abundant resources, and best intentions, there are
details, decisions, hurt feelings, and unpredictables that have to be
confronted and resolved.

When Perry and Rene married, they decided to live in
his home. They had some initial difficulties in
strategy: where to put all the possessions from two
households. Perry worked hard to build a good
relationship with Rene's ten- and seven-year-old
daughters, and they seemed to accept him. However,
they were "cranky" because of having to move to a
new neighborhood and a different school. Perry had
to give up his study for a needed bedroom. The house
was noisier. While his son continued to orient toward

him, within a year the boy considered Rene's family as his own and with the completion of his adoption, Rene became his mother. Perry felt that they had attained cohesion as a family.

Sexuality

Sexual functions are subservient to higher survival mechanisms and are sensitive to such threats as the illness or death of a spouse. Furthermore, since sexuality is a "luxury" item among human biological functions, it can tolerate being shut down for long periods of time without any irreversible damages to the system. Most men and women experience a decline or absence of sexual feelings during the acute phases of illness and in the period immediately following the deaths of their spouses. There are many exceptions to this principle, including those who may respond to duress with an intensified sexuality as a part of an overall state of heightened physiological arousal and psychological preparedness to contend with danger.

For couples who live through an extended illness prior to death, their sexual lives can be affected by the illness itself, the treatment, or their personal reactions to the situation. Many of those in the study had been without sex lives for prolonged periods before the death occurred.

Merle and Jonesy had gone for several years without sexual relations because of the medication Jonesy took for his hypertension. Up to that point, they had had a very satisfying sex life. While Merle was initially distressed by Jonesy's impotence, she adjusted to it. Two years after his death, "I have lost interest in sex completely."

Viola's husband had bone cancer and then leukemia. He was ill for six years before his death and was impotent for this entire period. Viola did not regard his impotence as a great problem. "We were able to be more affectionate than those who had intercourse." Even two years after his death, she experienced almost no sexual feelings. "I had sexual desires for him, but I just learned to squelch them because there was no complete satisfaction. That probably is deep rooted now. I've learned to just roll it up and put it in a drawer."

Bill: "I never touched my wife sexually after I found out that she was sick with cancer. She forced me to talk to the doctor in a conference, and the doctor insisted that there would be nothing wrong with it. However, my thoughts toward her were of love, but not from a sexual standpoint. I could not have loved her any more than I did for the last year and nine months that she lived, but I had no desire for sex with her at all. I knew she was going to die and I just could not, I just couldn't have thoughts of . . . my sex life died, that's all. I couldn't do it. It had been more than three years since I had any sex at all when I had sex the first time."

After Frank's heart attack, he and Annette stopped having sex. Frank withdrew from her because of his fears. Annette was initially depressed over this; then she began having sexual fantasies about other men. After his death she felt "horny as a toad" but also felt guilty and hesitant about her sexual feelings. However, she succumbed to these feelings because of "an insatiable desire to be cuddled, fondled, and loved."

Even where sexuality has not been stifled by illness, the death of a spouse is most often responded to by the inhibition of sexual feelings, usually for a period of months or longer. At times these feelings reemerge spontaneously; at other times they are stimulated by another person of significance.

Beth: "They were gone in the beginning. There was a total absence. They just sort of slowly came back."

Susan: "I felt nothing. I thought, 'What's going on? What's happening?' So I was glad that the feelings did come back."

Gloria: "They were absolutely gone for a while, absolutely gone. I thought it had died forever. But about a year and a half after my husband died, a man that I knew years ago, who asked me to marry him years ago, reappeared and so did my sex urges. I was very happy about that."

Ralph lost his interest in sex when Darlene died. He first became aware of any stirrings about three months later. As his sexual drive increased, he found himself more sexually aware and looking more for other women.

Emerging Sexual Feelings. When sexual feelings emerge again, the widowed person must deal with them, both psychologically and physically. The initial psychological responses of the bereaved to their sexual feelings usually consist of some combination of surprise, reassurance, frustration, and guilt, together with any pangs of loss that are triggered by sexual feelings and memories.

Daphne: "I tell myself I don't have any sexual feelings, but I think sometimes at night when I wake up, you know, I'll be half dreaming and I think that's part of it, and I feel strange about it. So I do have more sexual feelings that have kind of emerged that I don't answer to in daylight. Maybe I feel a little bit guilty that I have them when I don't have my husband anymore."

When Ralph was bereaved for three months, his sexual feelings returned, and he was "a little concerned. Maybe it was too soon. As I look back on it now, that seems kind of silly, but at the time . . ."

Susan: "I felt guilt at first and then relief. There's no guilt anymore."

Prior to the development of ongoing sexual relationships, the bereaved are left to contend with their sexual feelings in a limited number of ways. These include suppression, distraction, sublimation into other activities, or direct discharge through masturbation. The choice of a coping mechanism is highly dependent on the individual's personality and value system, and, as in many other situations, more than one mechanism may be employed concurrently.

Carol: "After a year I began to be aware, 'Yes, I have some longings.' I felt they were sexual drives, I really did have some real sexual drives. And I figured that was normal. It didn't really bother me. I just figured that was the way it was supposed to be. There were times that I really felt, you know, that I would like to have gotten relief sexually. I don't know how it is with men, but with women—I'd just get up and I'd begin to find that exercise would help if I couldn't sleep at night. If I just got up and walked around the room and did some exercises, they would go away."

Linda tried to deal with sexual feelings by distraction. "I just try to forget them, or I get up and do something else. What do you do? You either go to bed with somebody—and I can't do that, I would feel too guilty. Most of it is at night when you go to bed and you're there by yourself. There is nobody for your comforting and your love. Sometimes I get up and go read a book or something, or go turn on the TV. That's it. When it happens I just say, 'Well, what are you going to do? You're not going to do anything and put it out of your mind.' And that's hard, too. That's a normal part of your life, and now you don't have that. So it's not easy. And I would feel guilty if I masturbated."

Six months after Jack's death, June had lost a good deal of weight and found herself experiencing sexual desires, which were frustrating both because she was alone and because she had not felt this way during the later stages of her marriage. "Well, it comes and goes, and I don't know whether it's because of my cycle or whatever, but sometimes it's worse than others. I don't know how to masturbate. I have a spa. I get in there, and I let the heat soothe me."

Harold was very active physically, which kept his sexual feelings to a minimum. "Maybe every four or five weeks I'd masturbate just to see if I'd work. I was starting to wonder what the hell's the matter with me."

Carolyn: "I've masturbated a few times. Usually that's happened if I've been reading one of those romantic novels or something that has had sex in it. I haven't had any problems. Our sex life was not as good as most married couples because of Sam's illness, and I was sort of used to it. I don't have any qualms if I would meet somebody."

Sexual Relationships. Half of the widows and widowers in the study eventually developed some form of sexual relationship, encountering few significant difficulties and many gratifying experiences. Their early sexual experiences, however, were occasionally disappointing.

Ralph's first sexual experience was dampened by the circumstances. "I don't think they were as fulfilling in the beginning. Maybe that was because it was a relationship where I wasn't married and where the one particular girl was married—kind of a cheating arrangement. I didn't care much for that. I felt guilty, too, like a year should go by."

Bill was distressed by the lack of meaningful relationships while he was dating and the sexual
aggressiveness of the women he dated. After three
years without sex, his first opportunity to sleep with
a woman left him feeling confused by the lack of
sexual excitement he encountered in the woman,
something that had never occurred with his wife.

Louis found himself somewhat overwhelmed by his
girlfriend's sexuality and her exclusive interests in
marriage. "After about three months I realized that
she was just looking for somebody to marry. And her
sex, too, because she was sex from the word go. She'd
come in the house and drop her drawers as soon as
she got in the house. One of those things. She really
loved it. I did too, but I didn't get the enjoyment that
I wanted out of it."

These early sexual experiences were important sources of
reassurance for those who had concerns about their sexuality.

Gloria: "When George died, I thought that my sex
life was over. I couldn't imagine a sex life with
anyone else. When I became involved with Cal, I was
very glad to know that I'm still alive sexually. I can
still do a lot of living and be very happy."

Eighteen months after Arthur's death, Lucille went
to bed with a friend of theirs who had been very
supportive during her bereavement. She had an
indescribable feeling of "strangeness" about this.
While in bed, she kept thinking, "What am I doing
with someone strange?" At the same time, her
experience "was a great help in making me feel like
a woman again." Even more important, this experience was an important form of "therapy" for her
deepest fears. After Arthur's death in her arms, "I was
left with a terrible fear that every time I have any

sexual relations with a man, he was going to die. So that would inhibit my sexual functioning whether I did or not. The fear was there, and it bothered me terribly because [even] if I didn't want to get involved with anybody sexually, I felt at least I wanted to be in control of that situation. But I didn't want to feel this way because of the fear, and so what this did to me was that it took that fear away from me. I found out that no, the man isn't going to die if I go to bed with him, you see. Now, because I am right back without fear, sex is on just a 'take it or leave it' basis. I mean, if I find it, fine. If not, I'm not desperate. I don't go out and run the streets looking for men."

After Annette's prolonged sexual deprivation during Frank's illness, she had a number of affairs, particularly with younger men. After overcoming some initial guilt, she felt great about herself—her desirability and lovability.

For many people who had been in marriages that were sexually unfulfilling or limited by the inhibitions or illnesses of their spouses, their new sexual experiences in the context of intimate relationships—both married and unmarried—provided a new meaning to their own sexuality.

Daniel: "In the area of sexual relationships, I think there was something that I wanted to learn in the marriage but either didn't know how to approach it or didn't get the cooperation that I needed—by exploring and learning new things and finding greater satisfaction. Now sex is something that is significant in my life, where I don't think that I really felt that I had found the complete satisfaction even though I was married twenty-five years."

Bobbi was delighted about her newfound sexuality with Joe. "He is fantastic in bed. It's never been so good." Nathan had had a heart attack six months after their marriage. "Now I see that I was holding back with him sexually because of my fears about his health."

Susan: "I think I'm much more sexually aware now than I ever was. My husband, I think, always felt very inadequate sexually. A lot of it had to do with medication. And it was a difficult time for me. I've been told, 'I can't believe that you never had an affair when your husband was ill. I can't believe that you have the sexual feelings that you do and yet you never strayed.' And to which I replied, 'I never even thought about it.' It was the furthest thing from my mind. I wouldn't have hurt him like that."

Agnes's marriage to Mike brought her great sexual fulfillment. Throughout her marriage to Jeff, she could "take it or leave it," always wondering what she was missing. "Our sexual relationship was not ideal. It was a satisfactory relationship, but I would not call it ideal or extraordinary. Mike has reawakened sexual feelings in me. I have better communication with him than I had with my husband. My husband was kind of an introvert, and it was very difficult for him to express himself in an intimate relationship. It inhibited me and, well, he was already inhibited."

Sexual Dysfunction. In a sense, most widows and widowers experience sexual dysfunction in that the predictable response to bereavement is the decline of sexual impulses and desire. The other common forms of sexual dysfunction—erectile and ejaculatory problems in men and anorgasmia in women—are also encountered regularly, though these are usually transient phenomena in healthy widows and widowers without prior sexual difficulties.

During the six months after Bradley's death, when Phyllis was totally constricted emotionally, this constriction appeared in the sexual area as well. "I was frigid until the spring. Elliot and I started going to dances. He was very affectionate, and we happened to wind up in bed a couple of times, and in the beginning I was frigid. It was just like it died. When I found out I was frigid, that worried me. It was after everything came out, some months after the shit hit the fan, and I let it all out. Then I had an orgasm, and I was no longer frigid."

During Glenn's first attempt at sexual intercourse with Martha, he was so nervous that he could not get an erection. He became scared and embarrassed, but Martha was very understanding and accepting. Later that night he "performed" adequately and had no further problems.

After three years without sex, Bill had a few episodes of premature ejaculation: "I was like a rabbit for a while."

Louis was subject to episodes of retarded ejaculation when confronted by his "oversexed" girlfriend. "I've had sexual relations with this gal a number of times. As a matter of fact she was sort of a nymphomaniac. I'd get on that gal getting a piece of nooky, and I'd work and work and work and couldn't get my discharge. Just keep working at it and working at it and couldn't do it."

A year after his first wife's death and six months after his remarriage, Morrie was concerned that "my sex drive is not as strong as it was." He was afraid that his younger wife's sexual aggressiveness may have been "turning him off," resulting in his losing erections. He felt uneasy about this because he did not want to jeopardize the marriage but chose not to talk with his wife about it. He rationalized that his mind was on business more than sex and that success in business often increased as a man's interest in sex diminished. Within a few months, he stopped worry-

ing about his performance and it improved. After two
years of marriage, their sex life was very good, "an
exciting affair." April was less inhibited than Pauline had been, and they were having forms of sex that
he had never experienced before.

Joe's history of sexual impotence created considerable
anxiety about any sexual involvement and consequent avoidance of possible close relationships. He
had had a heart attack many years earlier and was on
"heavy medication," which caused impotence for
several months. His sexual function returned, but he
and his wife had had little sexual activity. "She
wasn't the kind of gal that, you know, was ready to
jump into bed the minute I got in at night and
wanted some before I left in the morning, you know.
And me, I'm so goddam busy with habeas corpus and
all this crap down at my job, sex wasn't involved."
After Loretta's death Joe's sexual feelings returned,
but he was still fearful of being sexually inadequate.
"I've had desire. Now when I worked, there was a
lady there who I used to take to lunch once in a
while. And I had, let's say, designs on her, you know.
But it was a little frustrating there because if she ever
said 'yes,' I wouldn't know what to do with her, you
know what I mean, because of my built-in problem."

 Chapter 7

The Evolution of Identity

Some of the most profound changes that occur in the bereaved are those that reflect their personal identity: those characteristics by which one establishes the sense of who one is, self-perceptions about one's transient states and enduring qualities. The ordeal of losing one's spouse places the grieving person under greater duress than most people ever experience in their lives. Every aspect of one's capacity to cope is tested. Under these cicumstances—a harsh reality that must be faced and from which there is limited opportunity to escape—the bereaved often find themselves thinking, feeling, and behaving in ways that may previously have been foreign to them. These new experiences can permanently alter their self-perceptions. The survivor's social identity also changes after the death of a spouse. The bereaved develop a sense of their position in society as a product of their new social status and the reactions of others to them. Further, their functional roles are often changed by the absence of their spouses and their need to continue living and providing for the demands of reality. These social and functional self-perceptions are also incorporated into a total identity by the bereaved person.

Being "Widowed"

In all societies losing one's spouse to death has certain implications for the survivor. The status conferred on the widowed person depends on the social structure of a given culture (Lopata, 1973). In many cultures a widow is considered useless. She may be expected to throw herself on the funeral pyre; or a family member—often her husband's brother—is designated to take responsibility for her care and the care of her children. In other cultures the widow may be incorporated into an existing family structure, continuing to carry out her previous responsibilities. In our society the continuing responsibility and usually the couple's financial resources shift entirely to the bereaved spouse, whether widow or widower.

The social position of the bereaved is generally considered an "honorable" one. They are usually held in greater esteem than other single people who have been divorced (viewed as a failure) or never married (viewed as a limitation), yet not in as great esteem as those who are married. The social status of women in particular has traditionally been based, largely or in part, on the status of their spouses; and the loss of their spouses can have a marked effect on their own sense of themselves. As the late Zero Mostel, playing an unsuccessful theatrical producer in Mel Brooks's movie *The Producers*, queried, "Don't you know who I used to be?" The woman whose identity was intimately tied to her husband's accomplishments and status is diminished by his death in just this way. She has then lost an important part of herself, of her identity.

> Muriel came to several meetings of the widowhood group when she moved to San Diego from the East Coast. She had lived alone for many years in a large home in a small community where her husband had been a highly respected physician. Muriel had difficulty making friends among the group members because she spoke constantly about her life back "home," her high social status, and the importance of her husband. While the other members of the group could appreciate how unimportant and alone she must have been feeling, her inability to acknowledge her vulnerability and her persistent pretentions kept anyone else from getting to know or appreciate *her*. She had apparently never recovered from the loss of her husband and the part of her "importance" that he took with him.

The "widowed" label is also an attempt on the part of society to identify a group of people who have special problems and needs, and therefore special entitlements. In addition to the financial entitlements of Social Security and other insurance benefits provided to assist the bereaved in their efforts to deal with practical realities, the designation of widowhood announces, "Here is a person who is injured, damaged, in need of special considerations." The bereaved, depending on their personalities and attitudes, may accept or reject this designation as a reflection of their identity.

> Jonathan became very self-conscious about his new status as a widower. On the one hand, he used the fact of Sandra's death as a means of obtaining sympathy from others. On the other hand, he found himself becoming more and more concerned about how others saw him and his own reactions: was he doing too well either to warrant empathy or to demonstrate that he loved her?

> *Daphne:* "I hate the word 'widow.'" For her it denoted pain, solitariness, and loneliness, all of which she felt and even accepted. Yet it was difficult for her to incorporate this concept as a continuing statement of her own identity.

> Bobbi felt that she had recovered from her grief after almost a year and a half. "Life is good. I'm glad I'm alive. I never think of myself as a widow. A widow is an object of pity. I don't feel helpless or that I'm in a victim's role as a widow. Victims give others power, and I don't feel it is necessary to be protected now."

Being Single

The effects of being single, by themselves, precipitate many changes in the identity of the bereaved: the incorporation of "singleness" into one's identity and the reorientation to being single, the effects of changing roles that accompany loss of one's spouse, and the change of those aspects of identity that required or utilized the reinforcement of one's spouse.

Self-Perceptions of Being Single. There is often a significant lag time of months and even one to two years between the
reality of being single and the incorporation of this fact into
the bereaved person's identity. Being part of a couple has been the
reality for long enough that it is usually a stable part of one's self-
concept. Consequently, the idea of "singleness" requires a change
that most married couples would not choose and do not easily
accept. Besides the change in self-perception, there is also the loss
of the "old" part of one's identity, the part attached to one's
spouse.

> Carol: "I really didn't feel there was much left of me.
> I really didn't know what I was or who I was or what
> kind of being I was. It seemed it always revolved
> around the two of us all the time. Your total self,
> your thinking processes, how you handle each day,
> how you cope—it seems like it always just revolves
> around two people. Even just thinking about some-
> thing, I would say to myself, 'Well, I know that
> David would think the other way.' He was such a
> part of everything I did that it was a total aloneness.
> . . . I'm beginning to find myself now, and I'm
> beginning to feel good about this, because what I'm
> finding out is really neat."
>
> *Merle* [nineteen months later]: "I still feel completely
> married. After thirty years you don't change your
> feelings."
>
> Lucille was able to make the transition back to single
> life fairly easily. She had not married until age
> twenty-six and had already traveled alone extensively
> and was very independent. "Twenty-eight years of
> married life had set my life into sharing, but I had
> had good training as a single." Still, after two years
> she continued to feel married. "I'm still Arthur's
> wife. I still feel that I am half of something."

Susan: "I just feel like a person. I lived so much for my husband when he was so sick that I forgot that I had my own personality and I was a person. It seemed like day or night my thoughts were always on him. And I feel now that it's time for me."

Reorientation to a Single Self. Going on concurrently with the adoption of the self-image as a single is the change from thinking and acting as part of a couple to operating as an individual. People who have adopted lifestyles with spouses and children are often other-oriented in their motivations. Even where they may not have been at the outset of their marriage, they have probably developed such an orientation in order to sustain a marriage and family. Some widowed people make the transition fairly easily and find it gratifying, a refreshing change. Others encounter initial resistances, which are fairly easily overcome once they learn the advantages of this enlightened form of "selfishness." Still others seem unable to tolerate this "selfishness" and become involved in relationships where they can again be selfless or, in more extreme circumstances, "martyrs."

Ann: "I'm taking a course in personal growth and I took a course in interpersonal communication last fall, and that helped me a lot because I feel like I'm getting acquainted with me, just me as an individual. Always before, I had a little identity crisis. I was either someone's wife or I was someone's mother, and now I'm just learning that I'm me. I feel really good that I'm doing things for me. Always before, I couldn't do so-and-so because I had to do something for someone else. Now if it isn't compatible with my schedule, I've learned to say, 'No, I can't do that.' You know, I'm important, too. So I feel that my life has definitely turned around, completely around."

Susan: "I guess it just goes back to thinking about myself again, which I hadn't done in so long. Eating the right food and getting more exercise, and I realize how important it is to be with people because, when my husband was sick, we weren't with anyone. We weren't friends with anyone. Everyone that I knew was healthy and was out, and we couldn't plan from one day to the next. If I feel like getting in the car and going up to see my parents for a weekend, I do. Nothing stops me anymore. . . . I never begrudged him. It's just that I don't think I realized how much time I was devoting to him, and I wouldn't have had it any other way. He needed to be taken care of. It was like a child, I suppose."

Viola had spent thirty-seven years of her adult life catering to the demands of her husband, son, and mother. After her husband's death, she felt a strong sense of "obligation to myself"; she wanted to concentrate on herself and develop a career. Although she still was obliged to care for her mother, she also volunteered to take in a teenage runaway and spent time counseling an elderly woman. Her self-image demanded that she be in the role of helper even as she pursued other self-oriented goals. Her long-term career goal was, quite understandably, to do what she did most easily—that is, to work as a counselor.

June had to care for her two disabled sons, and she despaired of ever being in a relationship where anyone would be interested in her needs. She saw herself as an exploited martyr. "I don't ask people to do things for me. It's like the organization I belong to. I can take on all kinds of jobs and do them, and they're grateful and all that. But whenever I want someone to do something for me, I can't get them to do it. And that's the way it is with everybody. So I figure it's me, it's my fault."

Changing Roles. The death of one's spouse often forces the survivor to take on new roles that had been selected by or delegated to the deceased. These new roles may be functions of daily living or aspects of personality that the survivor assumes in order to compensate for their absence, created by the death. For example, a widower may take on the role of nurturing his children to a far greater extent than he would have done if his wife were still alive, thereby developing this aspect of his personality. This role or personality trait will then be incorporated into the person's self-image. Many such characteristics are subject to change throughout the grief process.

Loss of Mirror. The fact that "beauty is in the eye of the beholder" has sustained many relationships. The attractiveness of one's partner—in physical appearance and in personality characteristics—is often highly idiosyncratic. The continuation of a loving relationship over time further enhances such perceptions and reinforces the positive self-image of a marriage partner. A wife, for instance, comes to see herself in a mirror that often reflects more favorably than the reality she might choose to interpret if left alone. With the death of her spouse, she loses this mirror and, with it, these positive self-images—the sense of being important, beautiful, or loved, even lovable.

> *Phyllis:* "I had the wonderful sense of how marvelous it was to be so loved and to love somebody, and we were a good mirror for each other. We had a lot of respect for ourselves and good feelings and a good image. And it died when Bradley died, and then there was nobody to do that for me. I hated him for taking that away, for not being there for me to love and for him to love me. All that wonderful stuff was gone when he died."

> Annette basked in Frank's love, appreciation, and admiration of her beauty. After he died, she felt that no one would say "I love you" or "You light up my life."

Many of the bereaved feel that they have lost their physical attractiveness to others and go about reshaping their appearance by trying to lose weight and get into better physical shape.

> Merle and a friend were discussing Merle's date: "I said, 'The day I'm interested, you'll know it.' And she asked, 'How?' And I said, 'For the simple reason I'll go and have a face lift.' And that is really how I feel. I mean, there's nothing wrong with being old, but you have to take away some of the ugly and wrinkles, you know."

There are other reasons why the bereaved try to change their images through altering their physical appearances.

> Shirley had been self-conscious about her small breasts throughout her adult life. Eighteen months after Art died, she had an augmentation mammo-plasty done in order to feel better about herself. She had felt that her body was disproportioned, and she had been dubbed "bones" by her racing friends. In the event of remarriage, she did not want to go through another marriage feeling sorry for her husband because of her small breasts.

> A year after Rose's death, Harold was still tortured by the ubiquitous triggers in his environment that set him off emotionally. He began thinking about orthodontia as part of his wish to "remake Harold." He wanted the "old Harold" to disappear when Rose died. His "rebirth" included weight loss, orthodontia, ice skating, and efforts to change his social attitudes.

Changes in Personal Qualities

Negative Self-Images. The early stages of grief are usually accompanied by changes in self-images that are regressive and largely negative in nature (Horowitz, Wilner, Marmar, and Krupnick, 1980). Many of these changes were examined in Chapter Two as dimensions of such early emotional states as heightened dependence, fearfulness, helplessness, inadequacy, failure, and loss of control. These feelings recall early life experiences when such self-images may have been predominant ones. They can be extremely painful states, which seem to "rule" over grieving spouses and color all or most of their self-perceptions.

> *Phyllis:* "I had terrible, terrible feelings of inadequacy to cope with what was happening to me."

> *Melinda:* "A failure feeling. I felt, 'You horrible person, you. How could you let him die? You failed him. How could you let this happen?' There was an anger at myself, a failure feeling, a complete disregard for myself. I was blaming myself for everything that had ever happened."

> *Carol:* "The thing that bothered me the most was that I was completely shocked that I was so dependent upon one person, because I'd always considered myself pretty independent even though I was married, but I wasn't. I really was very dependent upon one person and that has bothered me—to be so dependent upon anybody."

Fortunately, these negative self-images gradually dissipate as the bereaved perceive that they are capable of dealing with their grief. This process usually consolidates during the second year of bereavement.

> *Carol:* "I heard a new song the other day that said, 'I see a new morning, I see a new light.' I mean, I'm beginning to see that there are . . . I'm coming out of it. I feel good about everything, and I'm feeling good about myself again. I'm feeling that I'm not so alone. Some of the decisions that I have made in the past two years have not been real bad. So I'm beginning to

step forward again to being independent like I always
thought I used to be.''

Most widows and widowers who have lost their self-esteem
through the early onslaught of grief experiences find that they are
able to recapture or even surpass this prior image. However, for
those who, for whatever reason, are unable to recover emotionally
and functionally, the negative self-image remains and may even be
worsened by such failure—particularly where there is evidence of
continuing depression.

> Ronald's wife and small child both were killed when
> an airplane crashed into their home. After five years
> he remained mildly depressed, bored, lonely, and
> withdrawn and was unable to think about his wife or
> child without becoming acutely upset and depressed.
> "If anything, the pain has become worse." The fact
> that his feelings had stayed the same for such an
> extended period of time made the situation even
> worse. "I probably have a more negative self-image
> now than ever."

Positive Self-Images and Growth. By the end of two years of
bereavement, the majority of widows and widowers are able to
regard their grief as a growth-promoting experience, and their self-
images as primarily positive. This process usually does not occur
until the most painful elements of their acute wounds have begun
to heal. The healing process seems to proceed almost independently of the changes in identity once the survivors have sufficient
insulation from pain to be able to reflect on their accomplishments
during this period of greatest suffering. During the earliest and
most acutely painful periods, the bereaved are usually utilizing all
their resources simply to keep their heads, and hearts, above water.
The intrapsychic forces that operate throughout the grieving
process are very powerful: losses of such proportion and importance provide the impetus and inescapable motivation for personality changes that may not be seen anywhere else in human adult
experience. Regardless of whatever suffering has occurred and may

still be occurring on an ongoing basis, it is the exceptional widow
or widower who does not experience some sense of growth and
enhancement of self-image as a result of coping with and surviving
the grief process.

The changes that the bereaved describe in themselves are
many and varied. They mention, for example, self-perceptions of
developing strength and confidence, a sense of heightened
autonomy and freedom, and greater assertiveness and openness;
many of them also believe that they have become more realistic,
spiritual, patient, sensitive, and compassionate. They almost
always see themselves as being better people for their experience
and are also aware that their suffering has brought about these
changes.

> *Daniel* [1 year later]: "I feel more growth in the past
> six months than in the prior ten years."

> *Phyllis:* "Bradley delayed my growing up, but then
> he died and the marvelous gift he gave me was the
> grief. Riding on the grief train from point A, where
> I wanted to drop dead, to point B, where I am now,
> has been one of the greatest learning experiences of
> my life, and, of course, it was very painful. I learned
> a lot about myself and more about my relationship
> with him after he was gone than I had while he was
> alive. It was great; it was tremendous."

People derive strength through suffering. The collective
wisdom of the ages has endorsed this view, and it is reinforced in
religions, classical literature, and the various gurus of our times. It
is a view that has been utilized as a rationalization for the
inevitable suffering that has always been a part of the human
experience. Few enlightened minds would suggest that suffering is
a particularly desirable event. Furthermore, there seems little doubt
that the majority of children who are subject to great poverty and
hunger, deprivation, and abuse are ill equipped to cope with such
suffering and succumb through maldevelopment or death. However, there is still a niche for such wisdom among those adults who

have reached their maturity and encounter the tragedy of losing their spouses. Under these circumstances the bereaved demonstrate an amazing amount of durability, flexibility, and capacity to sustain such losses and not only survive but become stronger and flourish as a result.

Perry: "One thing that I think came out of this whole thing was a tremendous amount of strength in a certain way. I had gone through this thing and persevered and had come out in one piece basically. I think it's true that I did a pretty remarkable job of holding everything together. I had a tremendous amount of responsibility at work, a tremendous amount of responsibility at home, and at a pretty tender age really, and held all that together. Despite everything I just said about the negatives of it, the experience, I think I tend to like myself a little better. I feel okay, you know, in a sense better for it."

Joanne: "I always felt that I would be the kind of person to fall apart. We never know how we are going to react until we are in the situation. I was surprised that I was able to handle all matters and make all decisions. I found an inner strength that other people knew I had but I didn't know. I really feel that it made a stronger person of me."

Sharon: "I feel more strength in me than I had before. And yet I always felt that I was a strong person. I don't think the philosophy has changed drastically other than it's made me more sure of it. The loneliness, the anxiety, and everything else—it's made me stronger, more experienced. I see myself as more valuable, more capable than I thought of myself before. I know I can raise two children by myself. I know I can work and I can support everyone if I had to. I would never be afraid. I wouldn't want to be alone, but I would never be afraid again."

Viola: "I've seen myself as strong. I'm finding that I can do things that I didn't try before. I guess I always knew that I could do about everything anyone else can do. It's just getting out there and giving it a try. I've had more opportunity for trying now, instead of wishful thinking. It's always been sort of like not knowing how to drive a car when everyone else knows how. It bothers you that there's something you aren't doing that everyone else can do."

Ann: "I believe I could face just about anything because I think I've been through the worst. Anything else, hey, it's a piece of cake after this."

Widowed persons gain strength not only from surviving and coping with the pain of loss but also from acquiring independence and autonomy.

Bobbi: "I see myself as independent and in control, self-confident, able to accomplish what I want to. I could have had that when we were married. My husband tried very hard to get me to be more confident, be more aware of my potential. He never tried to put me down or hold me back. But for some reason I couldn't. There were feelings of inadequacy that were there. I still have them but not like they were. There was something in my response to his being there, a security of some sort, I suppose. I deferred to him in a lot of things, in most things, and I was comfortable with that. Now I don't know if I would."

Ann: "I relied on Billy so much, you know. I let him make the decisions and take care of things, and I just sort of stayed in the background because I thought that this gave him a feeling of being in the driver's seat. Now I'm learning that I should learn to take care of my own affairs—my business affairs or personal life or whatever. I learned to put gas in my car. That was a big thing. I always thought, 'Ooh, I'd get that smelly stuff on my hands.' I had to change a tire on my girlfriend's car and I said, 'I don't know how.' I'd watched people change tires before and I just never thought I could, but I did. I felt kind of proud of myself that I could do that. You know, I didn't have to call on someone to come and rescue us, and that was an enlightening experience. I find that I can handle things pretty well.''

Bill: "I expect I'm probably a bit more independent now than I've ever been in my life. I feel like I'll be very self-sufficient from here on. Maybe that's one of the reasons that I don't find myself having a great desire for marriage.''

Doris: "Now I have a sense of myself as being capable. I proved this to myself. I've been getting things done. I'm more independent now. I say to myself, 'I can do it,' especially about things around the house. I'm more confident about my decisions. I'm not bothered by problems with insurance, and I've taken up mowing, gardening, taking out the garbage. I've accomplished quite a bit this year: my trip, I painted the house, got a new roof.''

Accompanying the sense of being single and the developing sense of personal autonomy is the awareness of one's freedom, a self-perception that is often new to the widowed person's experience, and an appreciation of the value of such freedom, since it has come at such a high price.

Susan: "I was never this happy or free when Phil was alive. I think I really feel good about myself for the first time in a long time. I feel younger. I feel like if I wanted to do something, I'm just going to do it. I'm not going to worry about how it's going to look, because nobody is really paying attention anyway. If

it's a nice afternoon, I'm just going to leave everything and go to the ocean and spend two or three
hours, and then when I come back, it's there, waiting
for me. After so many years of being tied down by
Phil's illness, I like the fact that I have no one to
report to or explain to."

Doris: "I'm enjoying my sense of freedom. I don't
have to prepare a hot meal at 5 o'clock."

Daniel: "I have the feeling of freedom now if I want
it. I'm not obligated to take care of anyone but
myself."

Bereaved persons also may become more outgoing, outspoken, and assertive than they formerly were.

Gloria: "I feel much more confident socially. My
husband was more gregarious than I was. He loved
people and he loved to talk, and everybody loved
him. He was the more outgoing. It was easier a lot of
the time to just sit there and be amused than to do a
whole lot myself. Now I find that I do very nicely by
myself, and I enjoy it, and I like myself more."

Beth: "I think I'm a little more outgoing than I used
to be. Not much, because I never have been a real
outgoing person. I'm certainly anxious to meet new
people, much more so than I was before. I went
pretty much with Barry and the friends we had, and
I didn't have much need for new people in our life at
that time, and now I certainly do. I need everybody
that's available, interesting. That's just great."

Daniel felt much more confident and free, no longer
dependent on his wife or vulnerable to the demands
of his children. He had learned to be more open and
expressive. In his work be became more honest and
abrupt with his superiors, feeling free from his old
fears and inhibitions.

As Susan observed herself learning to be more expressive and assertive, she became angry at the way she had handled her marriage. "I should have spoken up, but I was always afraid I'd create tension. I was afraid Phil would have another heart attack and I'd have it on my conscience. So I kept things bottled up inside. I can now talk to dates for hours, but I wouldn't ever talk to Phil."

Having suffered through the death of a spouse, the bereaved often lose the inhibitions that keep people from being assertive.

Merle became much more assertive. She was not afraid to speak her mind and openly disagree with people. "As a matter of fact, I think I'm being a little belligerent about it. Every time someone tells me that I should do something, I say, 'I don't have to do anything I don't want to.' It's a childish rebellion probably."

Sharon found herself unwilling to be as totally compliant as she had been. "I'm more assertive. I can't be manipulated." When she would "lay down the law" with her mother, she was accused of being "cold."

Carl: "I've become more outspoken. A friend of mine said I've become hard. I'm not hard. I just feel that I don't reserve my judgment as I used to. I say what I think."

Along with their new assertiveness, the bereaved also learn to accept limitations in themselves and others. They may soften their criticism or demands, becoming more flexible and tolerant of things that had previously bothered them, experiencing a greater degree of humility. Their loss taught them that people are never strong enough to be unaffected by suffering, that they and others are vulnerable.

Ralph began to notice the good things in people more than he had before he was bereaved. He became less critical of people, especially his two children, whom he now—for the first time in his life—had to depend on for support.

Ann: "I think I have great humility now. Maybe I was overly confident that I can handle anything and I was strong, and especially I thought I was emotionally strong, you know. I found out I wasn't. This experience definitely made me see that I wasn't as strong as I thought I was, that I did have to be dependent on others, I couldn't come back by myself. I needed help and I had to rely on my friends and family, which I had not done before."

Perry: "The most critical difference probably is I think I have lost a certain degree of confidence. We were like 'golden children' in the sense that both of us had gone through life easily. Suddenly this halcyon situation ended up kind of on the rocks in a very meaningful sort of a way. And I sense in myself the feeling that things are not going to automatically happen right. So I guess that is vulnerability."

Beth: "I think I'm certainly more willing to accept help from anybody that offers anything, where I never would have. I was sort of an 'I can do it myself' person. But now anybody that offers to help with anything, 'Great, come on and do it.' I just thought I could always do everything myself. Now I realize that maybe I can't."

Bereaved persons also may develop a more cautious, serious, and "realistic" view of themselves, again reflecting their sense of vulnerability. Whereas many of the early emotional states experienced by the bereaved are transient, these traits become relatively permanent and stable and are incorporated into the changing configuration of the person's new identity.

Two years after June's death, Perry was feeling back in control of his own destiny. He was again happily married but in a different way. "June and I were younger, more carefree. I am a quieter person now. I've been through a scarring process."

Blanche: "Widowhood has been the most difficult experience of my life. I used to be outgoing. I'm probably more introspective now. I realize that nothing lasts forever."

Sharon: "I used to be a Pollyanna, a dreamer. Now I'm more realistic."

Joe: "I'm originally one of the fighters. I've been fighting the system. I got lumps to prove it. Now some of the fight is gone. I don't feel the urge to jump in where angels fear to tread anymore."

Glenn stopped drinking alcohol and getting drunk as he had when Eileen was alive. Alcohol did not affect him in the same way. "I used to have a ball. Now it just dulls me, gives me a headache. I'm more serious than I was."

The experience of losing one's spouse creates many circumstances that are conducive to developing characteristics of nurturance: patience, sensitivity, and compassion. New roles, for instance, may thrust otherwise nonnurturing people, usually men, into "maternal" relationships with their children. The role of caretaker for a spouse with a long-standing illness may also initiate this transformation. Finally, the experience of great personal suffering enhances the awareness of and sensitivity to such feelings among all who have lost a spouse.

Carl: "I think being with her when she was sick that way taught me patience. Always before then, if there was something to get done, I'd go do it. I got to the point where I couldn't just up and go do it. I had to stay with her."

Perry: "I think I've worked through being mother to both my wife and my son in a lot of ways. I'm a much more sensitive individual than I would have been, much more sensitive to people, and I sense very subtle nuances in people's behavior and conversation. It's been helpful to some degree in my work, I think. It's made me a little more responsive to people's needs in a direct sort of way."

Ralph: "I think I've become a more caring father now. . . . When you're a man . . . you do the work and you come home, and any problems the mother usually handles. And now, if the kids have any problems, they come to me. I think you really have to be more sensitive to the children, and maybe that's made me a better person."

Susan: "You become very conscious of other people's needs and their feelings. Sometimes people go through a whole lifetime and they don't feel that. I feel like I've got more compassion now than I ever did for other people. . . . I have more of an understanding of my feelings for the first time in a long time."

While his wife was sick, Jonathan, a helping professional, frequently felt "out of sympathy" with his patients. After her death he found himself becoming more empathic in his work, much less calloused, than he had been.

Bill: "I'm sure I've grown. I came in today [for his interview] because I'd like to help someone else if I can that is going to go through this or is going through it. I don't believe that anyone can grasp the hurt that this thing can give you until they have gone through it. Three months ago a friend died. I went by his widow's house last Saturday, and she was up on a ladder picking oranges with tears streaming down

her face. She just cried and cried. She says, 'This is
something my husband would have been doing. I
have to do it. It's good that I have to do it, but I can't
do it without thinking of him doing it all the time.'
Well, I ran off a copy of your article, and I'm going
to take it by this lady's house. There may be something in there that she'll see that is what's happening
to her. It might help her a bit. She needs help. She is
really hurting something fierce. Probably I wouldn't
have been very concerned before. I would have been
like a lot of my friends. 'What would I say? I don't
know what you say to a person like that. I'm sorry.'
You know. Or the silly thing, 'Well, they're probably
better off.' Or 'They're going to be with the Lord.' A
lot of these clichés, you know, that they throw you,
they don't do any good. I'm sure I have more compassion and patience with people than I've ever had
in my life. I think I would tend to reach out to
people more than I ever did."

The effects of grief experiences have a particular effect on
people with traits of drivenness, compulsivity, and intensity. These
people often change their dispositions and become more even-
tempered, easy-going, and relaxed, taking life in stride. Their
experiences have enabled them to put things in perspective, to
appreciate the "important" things in life without being distressed
or driven by more trivial things.

Bill: "I think I have time to smell the flowers a bit
more than I ever did, to admire and enjoy the beauty
around me—not only of what I live in and what God
gave me to enjoy here on earth, but to enjoy the
beautiful people that are on this earth."

Perry found that he was not "digging in" at work as
much as he always had in the past. He had been very
perfectionistic and driven, ambitious to make good in
his career, until June's tumor was discovered and his

life became disrupted. After her death Perry felt that his work, although still important, ran a distant second to his family life. His ambition had been dampened. "I think it's taken some of the toughness and drive out of me."

Daniel: "I don't feel quite as anxious as I did. I very rarely flare up in temper anymore. I don't understand that. I had a lot of anxiety and resentment, discomfort with where I was with myself. For a long time after she died, I waited to see when I would react to certain situations with anger, that I did react to that way before. And it doesn't happen. And it's been more than two years that it hasn't happened. It's puzzling to me why I don't react that way."

Changes in World View

People conduct their lives on the basis of sets of beliefs about how the world and the people in it, including themselves, operate. These beliefs have been tailored by their life experiences. They have been influenced by the modeling of their parents and family, the belief systems of their peers and culture, the formal education of their society, and the indoctrination by religions or institutions. These beliefs, combined with the individual's goals and aspirations, make up a world view. An individual's world view evolves and changes throughout life, affected by the influences cited above; but its major components remain fairly stable. The emotional, psychological, physical, and social upheavals created by the death of a spouse often have a significant impact on the person's world view. Beliefs are undermined and changed, directions are lost, and new goals are forced on the bereaved.

Loss of Direction. During the early weeks and months following the death of a spouse, the surviving spouse may experience an acute loss of meaning, direction, and goals in his or her life. The belief systems underlying such meaning and direction are often shaken by the enormity of the event and those characteristics that run contrary to many of these belief systems. The tragedy challenges one's beliefs in the goodness of God, the predictability and control of life and one's self, the limitlessness of life, the value of one's efforts or of "saving for a rainy day," or the optimism one has felt throughout life. When such beliefs are first challenged, there is usually nothing to replace them immediately, and the bereaved experience a void, an absence of belief. They have no sense of direction or of a future purpose—especially since their purpose in life and their plans for the future had relied heavily on a relationship that no longer exists.

> *Daniel:* "Maybe the most intense thing could be described as having a feeling where I have no real direction."

> *Marie* [four months later]: "I have no reason to live. No one really needs me. I don't work, and I can't find employment."

> After six months Merle experienced great pessimism. "What I feel is that I don't have much of a future." Her son was still living at home, and "he still needs me." However, as time went on, it became clear that he was capable of managing his own affairs. At two years: "I don't have a sense of purpose in life. Donald can take care of himself. I was important to my husband, but I don't think I could ever be that important to someone else."

> *Shirley:* "What am I here for? Because I was raised, you know, you grow up and you raise a family. That's your mission, that's your purpose on this earth. Okay, I did that and I was doing that, and now my kids are almost raised. A couple more years and then I don't know what's going to happen when they turn eighteen—if they'll stay home or go on their own. But the other part of it, you know, being a wife, it's gone. What are you here for?"

Harold: "Probably the biggest single thing is the lack of well-defined ambitions, goals, desires. Self-satisfaction is not a sufficient motivation. My values have changed. I used to feel that [people] should always try to better themselves financially because it assured a greater degree of personal independence. I would be continually striving for that if my wife were still alive. Now I figure, 'What the hell!'"

Unable to identify any guiding principles, the bereaved often enter a "holding pattern," operating on a day-to-day basis without being quite sure why they are doing things. Of course, they are proceeding under the influence of whatever other beliefs sustain them, even without their knowledge. At the very least, they operate, as we all do, on the basis of their primitive survival instincts.

Blanche: "I feel like my life is at an end. I'm just taking up space, not making a contribution. I'm just marking time. I often wonder, 'Where am I going?' I don't have any future expectations. I feel like a fool."

Beth did not know what would happen to her or what she wanted to happen. She approached the future in a passive way. "I see myself living a day-to-day existence."

Viola: "I don't think I see any purpose to life now, except just accepting. The pressure of just getting through the month and getting the bills paid and the food on the table and the car kept up. I'm just living in the present. I'm not thinking much about the future, where I am going. I'm just getting through right now."

Evolution of New Beliefs. One of the highly adaptive traits of human beings as thinking creatures is our continued drive throughout life to comprehend our own universe: what is inside us and around us. The primary motivation for such activity lies in our deepest security needs. Adopting the "correct" belief systems and principles of living will make us feel safe, secure, protected, invulnerable, blessed, worthy of salvation. This drive to know and believe (or its most common form among people: the belief that they know) has led mankind to the greatest scientific discoveries and the most irrational fanaticism. It leads us all to grasp onto belief systems, which then guide our lives.

Over time, the impact of death on the survivor leads to a gradual incorporation of the various components of his or her new reality into a revised system of beliefs. As mentioned, the survivor learns that people cannot have complete personal control over themselves and the environment. The resulting sense of vulnerability and appreciation of the vulnerability of others become incorporated into this revised system. Although some people lose their faith or trust in God, more frequently those with religious beliefs now seek more help from God or intensify their faith as a means of finding answers, even when there do not seem to be any answers.

> Linda felt cheated by Paul's premature illness and death. She wondered why this had happened and turned to her religion for answers, reading the Bible regularly. When some of her questions did not seem to have answers, she felt that "there are mysteries in life that one cannot figure out, and it is not useful to try to figure them out."

> Even after five years, Joe still had questions. "How do you explain the mystery of why it happened? Why was she chosen to go first? Am I a better survivor?"

Concurrent with the loss of a sense of personal control, fatalistic beliefs may emerge. Such beliefs sometimes relieve one's sense of responsibility for what happened.

> *Lucille:* "I have learned that this is part of life. There was nothing I could do about it. Whether I felt guilty

or not, that has nothing to do with it. It was out of my hands really to do anything. In a way, you can say I have assumed a fatalistic attitude, which I never used to have. I've never been a very fatalistic person. I believed you can do something about a problem, there's always a solution to every problem. What happens to us is mainly because we are responsible for what happens to us, not because it was willed that way, but now this. Because death is such a final thing, I have through the past two years decided that, well, with respect to death you have to be fatalistic in order to survive."

Perry: "My outlook has been almost an existential sort of perspective. Qué será será—that sort of thing. What's going to happen is going to happen, and it's not really within our grasp to change it or to affect it very much. Somewhat fatalistic. I'm just more deeply convinced that that's the case."

Beth was not able to look toward the future at first. Once she was healing and able to begin, she chose not to do so: "For a while it wasn't okay [to avoid planning]. It bothered me, but I think that it's okay now. You know, whatever will be will be." Beth adopted the position that she would take life as it comes and make the most of it. She no longer wanted a highly developed plan as she had in the past.

Instead of "Work before pleasure" and "Save for a rainy day," the bereaved—forced to recognize the fragility and finiteness of life—often adopt new principles of "Do it now" and "You can't take it with you."

Doris: "Well, I don't like to look too far ahead—not like I used to. At one time we used to save for a rainy day, and I believed it. I felt like not going out and using everything today. But my outlook in that respect has changed. I'm not saying you should blow everything today, but I'm a firm believer if anybody says, 'We'd like to go [somewhere],' I'll say, 'Well, do it, don't wait,' you know. Now we say, 'Live for today; you don't know what tomorrow will bring.'"

Daphne: "My philosophy of life has changed quite a bit since my husband died. Before, we always looked forward to the future, what was going to be in the future. I don't feel that way anymore. I feel you should take advantage of right now because, you know, you may not have a future. That's my experience. It didn't happen with him, he didn't have any future. We didn't have one. So when an opportunity comes up that I can do something with my children—if it costs money, if it can do something to tighten our relationship, I'll do it. Like I paid for all of us to fly up to Seattle for my son's wedding. It did cost a lot of money, but I don't care. I'm so glad we went."

Susan: "I think there is a definite need to live for today and a definite need to do the things that you want to do and not put it off. I think I'm angry that we put off so many things. He was always so close with his money. So when he died, he did leave a nice savings for the children and me, which is great, except it would have been nicer to have enjoyed some of that savings while he was alive."

As noted, the evolving self-concepts of many of the bereaved are frequently in the direction of greater strength, autonomy, assertiveness, and confidence—all of which would lend themselves to a more optimistic view of the future. At the same time, pessimism can persist and prevail in the form of lost hopes for the future, a negative cast to the present, and preoccupation with dying rather than living. While the great majority of widows and widowers see their world view returning to the previous prevalent stance of optimism, significant elements of pessimism may be retained.

After a year of bereavement, Merle had "a sense of marking time" until her son finished school and she could be sure that he would be able to take better care of himself. She began to get her affairs in order, preparing for her own death. "I should go to the doctor, but I keep putting it off. I can't visualize living long enough to be able to see a grandchild."

Joe [two years later]: "I make plans every day and never carry them out, you know. One of the things I think every day, 'I better go up there and see the mortician and make arrangements to bury me,' you know what I mean? That comes to my mind. I have a cemetery plot that's all paid for."

Sharon experienced the day-to-day shadow of death in her relationships with her family. "I feel that I have to hold on to everybody much more tightly. Anything could happen at any time, and therefore it's a tenuous thing. I told you before that I would never use the world 'never' again. I think I can now, but I don't know how much I believe it."

Because of their deep awareness of the fragility of life, the bereaved usually develop a keen appreciation for the beauty, richness, and importance of their lives and their families and friends. There is a growing sense of gratefulness, a reexamination of priorities, and an effort to extract all the goodness from life while it is available.

Sharon: "I guess I realized the fragileness of life and of relationships and that nothing lasts forever, and, therefore, you have to take advantage of what's there when it's there. Be happy with it when it's there."

Daniel: "I'm grateful for where I am and who I am and what I am. I'm thankful for the fact that I'm not

crippled or blind or unhealthy, and I think life has a
lot to offer. It's good for me, it's good to be alive."

Phyllis had experienced great physical pain from her
TMJ (temporo-mandibular joint) dislocation, but her
attitude was still positive: "No matter how bad the
pain gets now on the TMJ thing, I know they can fix
the appliance and pull me out of it. And no matter
how low I feel now about things, or [how] depressed
I feel, I'm alive and Bradley isn't. And I'm going to
appreciate the fact that I am [alive] until I'm not, you
know. And it's okay to feel low or whatever. Whatever comes up, you know, if you're feeling bad, feel
bad. If you're feeling good, feel good. Just be one
with whatever it is. That's my Zen practice. That's
what they tell you to do—that that's the way to
handle life."

Louise: "You become more aware of what friends
and family mean and how they affect you and how
grateful you are if you have a good family."

Joanne: "Life is very precious. I feel very blessed.
God has been very good to me to give me two good
men in my life."

What was important before the death of one's spouse may
take on increasing value following the loss. However, many things
that once seemed important may become trivial—small or petty
when viewed in the larger perspective that is evolving.

Beth: "I view life differently now than I did before
and I tend to—I know things don't bother me that
would have bothered me before. I've really just
realized how fragile life is, how quickly things can
change. I think I value some things more than I did
before, certainly my friendships."

After forty years of being together, Glenn and Eileen
bickered over trivial things. Glenn and his second

wife, Martha, never argue. "When you've lost someone, little things don't mean much. Other people
don't realize how lucky they are, how the 'big' things
outweigh the 'little' ones."

Perry's priorities in life changed dramatically after
June's death. His outlook became much more focused on the importance of his family life and
personal relationships. "I define achievement differently. Money does not mean as much to me now."

Along with the newfound or intensified appreciation of the
richness of life and its consequences in a more intense and
different kind of living, there is a heightened empathic appreciation for the suffering of others. As a result, survivors often adopt a
more humanitarian view of the world and feel a greater investment
in meeting with the needs of others.

Agnes had found her lapidary and other interests very
therapeutic means of distraction, involvement, and
purpose during the early months of her grief. After
two years she began to wonder, "In the end what's
the purpose of it, you know, what am I achieving?
Except my own self-satisfaction or my own pleasure.
It seems to me that there probably is some higher
goal like 'How can I be helpful to other people?' I
guess I became more aware of this when I was
involved with all these hospitals when Jeff died,
seeing all these old people sitting around in these
convalescent homes. They're all so sad, and nobody
visits them, you know. I feel like the most important
thing you can do in life is somehow to help other
people. I haven't resolved in my mind how I can do
that. I just became more aware of how much real
suffering there is."

Gloria: "What is important is to do enough good to
make life worthwhile, on any level you can. Just
being nice to someone during the day, or helping

someone who needs it, to become the best person I
can in every area."

Many widows and widowers become particularly empathic
about the plight of others in the same situation and make
themselves available to befriend, counsel, and otherwise support
others who are bereaved.

Future Goals and Directions. During the early stages of
grief, planning for the future is almost impossible. The newly
bereaved are so involved in managing the present, particularly
their emotional states and the turmoil of day-to-day living, that it
is hard even to consider the future. Whatever sense of direction
there is seems to derive from situations of demand, particularly
work or family needs, and to a lesser extent from ongoing internal
personal obligations: to self, spouse, God. Finally, direction may
have to arise from one's survival instincts. Aside from the
obligations of life, it often takes between one and two years for the
bereaved to achieve some sense of direction and purpose in their
lives. The incorporation of new beliefs and the consolidation of an
evolving identity and world view take time. This process will
continue beyond two years, but two years seems to be the period at
which most widows and widowers are able to formulate a reasoned
view of the future with a direction and specific goals.

Goals are by their very nature concrete, definable, and
observable. The kinds of goals arrived at by those men and women
in the study revolved around people-oriented activities and the
development of personal interests.

By the end of two years, many men and women had already
remarried, so that for them what would otherwise have been one of
the most prevalent goals had already been achieved—another
intimate relationship. For those who had not become involved
again, this did remain an important goal.

> *Lucille:* "One thing I always think about is that I am
> not going to spend the rest of my life alone. If I can
> meet someone of the opposite sex in the future,
> somebody that I would be interested in, that I would

feel that I could care for, and if I can find someone who will fulfill me in a way that I would be happy with life, fine. If not, I would later on just make arrangements to live with a friend or a relative. I mean I just can't be alone. This is my goal for the future in that I don't plan to become a recluse, one person living alone in an apartment locked up alone, or as I grow older to live in a building with lots of other widows who live alone. That's not what I want for myself in the future."

Linda: "I think there's still a lot out there for me. But I just haven't been at the right place to meet the right people, or even the right person. I still feel like there might be somebody else out there that I can learn to love and continue my good life."

Despite her concerns about the cross she had to bear in caring for her mother, and the deterrent that might create for her chances, Viola maintained a steadfast hope: "to find that one man in my life."

For those people who had not become seriously involved or remarried, continuing involvement in their relationships with their children and families were often seen as important goals.

After two years Beth's family and friends continually inquired about her future plans, feeling that she should begin some kind of career outside the home. However, she decided that she wanted to be home with her son, Mark, then three. She realized that it would probably not be particularly harmful to him if she worked, but she did not think that an outside job would satisfy her as much as spending her time with Mark did. "If I had something I wanted to do, it would be different."

Joe gave a lot of thought to the idea of remarriage but had too many self-doubts to pursue that as a goal. He felt that he was in a position to help out his children financially and become more involved in their lives through his support.

In addition to goals of developing new romantic relationships or improving relationships with their families, the bereaved may pursue involvement with others for altruistic and humanitarian reasons. Through their contributions to church and civic organizations, they may develop new relationships as well as enhance their own sense of purpose and meaning.

> *Viola:* "Well, someday I will face the Judgment Day, and the big question will be 'What did you do for me while you were living your life?' So I'm trying to do for others. I want to have something to be proud of when I do go. I just want to take care of others while I still can, while I'm still physically able to do it." Viola also wanted to prepare for her distant future, by making arrangements with a retirement home, so that she would not be a burden on her daughter the way Viola's mother has been for her.

A new job and career can provide important directions for the healing widow or widower. At the same time, work can become a financial necessity with which many widows and widowers must contend, especially if they are still relatively young or have been provided with little security.

> Two years after Frank's death, Annette began looking for jobs and was frustrated by the responses of many employers, who she felt were rejecting her partially because she appeared to be overqualified. While these rejections were difficult blows to her self-esteem, they were also of great concern because of her financial situation. Still in her early fifties, she realized that while she had considerable equity in her home, it would eventually be worth far more to her when she retired and that for her own financial security she

needed to support herself. This all made "finding a direction" much easier.

Daphne [two years later]: "When I look back, I think what happened changed my life in some ways. I think it forced me to do something more with my life. I had always been content, you know. I had a happy marriage, and I was satisfied to be a mother and to be a wife, you know, and to work. I had a fairly good job, and I was satisfied and I did well in my job. But I'd often thought, 'I wish I had gone to college. I wish I had done some of the things . . .' When my husband died, the only thing I could settle on that I wanted to do was to go to school. I had put that off for so many years and probably never would have gone back except it was the only thing I could think of. I had to do something. I felt like I had to do something to get some kind of an interest in my life where I could have just sunk into the depression, and I needed a kind of therapy for me—something that would work for me. And that was the only thing I could think of. So I did that, and, believe me, it was a hard thing for me to do at my age, fifty years old. I changed my job. That wasn't so difficult. An opportunity came up in something I was interested in, and some people helped me that were interested in me. But then going to school was the real difficult thing for me to do. I really had to force myself to do it. . . . Going to school has helped me very much. It was something I could put my time at and gear my thinking toward to help me through a rough time. . . . Now I've got a very difficult and really challenging job." For Daphne, what started as both a means of protection from acute pain and a long-term direction gradually evolved into the latter as time went on and her grief subsided.

Carl had retired from the Navy and returned to school to begin a second career in accounting while he was still quite young. He had been out of the work force for four years when Faith died. "I enjoyed going to school and I enjoyed the challenge of it. But I just don't want to be locked up in an office, and I didn't know exactly what I was going to do. And I think I was really just wandering around, I'd say lost, didn't know what I was going to do." Carl puttered around for over a year doing household projects, fishing, looking at job possibilities. After a year and a half, he got a supervisory job at a nuclear plant, which quickly became the focus of his life: working long hours, developing an esprit de corps in his unit, feeling mentally challenged. He felt confident, optimistic about the future, and subsequently married a woman he met at work.

Shirley began her new racing career after a year of bereavement. She felt that it provided a "niche" for her and gave her future some goals—the challenge of developing her skills and mastery in a new arena.

Another frequent type of goal setting for the bereaved is the pursuit of enjoyment through a great variety of leisure-time or otherwise pleasurable activities. These are easier to pursue when there is adequate financial security to preclude the need for employment, but many working people also developed such goals.

Merle decided to retire two years after Jonesy's death. Although her work had helped her cope with her grief, late in the second year she began to feel that she was not only ready for a change but looking forward to it, anticipating that she would be able to spend more time in her garden. She looked forward to her free time and began to toy with ideas of joining a begonia society, the historical society, or the Gray Panthers.

Shortly after Boris's death, Fran became involved in boating. At first it was for him. "That's what we were going to do was cruise. In fact, just before he got sick, we were looking at a bigger boat. That's why he retired. So I kind of feel like, if I get to do those things, I'm doing it for him." After a while it had become the central focus of her life, providing her with purpose, pleasure, friendships, and great self-esteem from her mastery of boating.

Lucille: "I wouldn't mind going back to school, but I don't have anything in particular that I would want to do in the way of studies. There are areas that I'm interested in, but if I did, it would be just for the joy of studying, going back to that atmosphere."

Ralph: "I've got a lot of things to look forward to. I enjoy my work. I do enjoy times when I'm off. I enjoy my family. I enjoy books. I just enjoy daily situations. I'm not looking for something that's off in the distance, you know, the brass ring so to speak."

As Ralph suggests, the bereaved are usually fully capable of attaining full, rich, meaningful lives, even though they are no longer with their partners and the impact of their loss lives on in many ways.

Chapter 8

Working Therapeutically with the Bereaved: Implications for Practice

As the previous chapters have demonstrated, spousal bereavement brings with it a myriad of potential problems that can cause great emotional distress, inhibited or maladaptive behavioral dysfunction, disruption of relationships, or demoralization of many kinds. It is not enough to say that a person is having a "pathological grief reaction," both because the parameters of "pathological" have not been validly defined and because the term in no way defines the nature of the problems. A major purpose of this book has been to develop a perspective for examining spousal bereavement. The most important therapeutic implication of this model is that clinical problems encountered by a professional working with the bereaved can be defined by thorough assessment of each of the dimensions described here. In order to consider what is likely to be therapeutic, one must have some definitions of "healthy" outcomes toward which the bereaved and their therapists might aspire.

The Tasks of Grief

Out of this work has evolved a series of "tasks" associated with each of the dimensions of grief—tasks that must be accomplished if one is to make a successful adjustment to loss. The term "adjustment" is used here in preference to "recovery" or "resolution" because of the difficulties inherent in those two expressions. "Recovery" usually implies a return to a former state and is most often used to describe a return to health after an illness. While the illness model has been applied to bereavement, recovery from bereavement can only be partial, never complete: many things are lost; many things are changed for both better and worse; they are *never* the same. "Resolution," as it applies to grief or other conflicts and crises in life, suggests that the matter is completed or determined. This idea is antithetical to the process as it unfolds. A more literal interpretation of the term "re-solved" would be more appropriate to a process of continual evolution of many issues on many fronts. Bereavement affects almost every aspect of one's life; and, accordingly, definitions of improvement must take into account all these dimensions and the great variation within each.

The tasks discussed in this chapter represent a synthesis of such variations in the context of a multidimensional view of "recovery" and "resolution." These tasks are required of the bereaved for the attainment of "optimal" though never complete resolution. It is toward these goals that therapists would direct their efforts.

Tasks 1 and 2: Learning to Experience, Express, and Integrate Painful Affects; Finding the Most Adaptive Means of Modulating Painful Affects. The first and second tasks are considered together because of the inevitable interactions between the two dimensions that they represent. The bereaved must, first of all, confront the reality of their loss and learn to cope successfully with the onslaught of feelings that naturally accompany such loss. "Successful" coping with all the potentially painful emotions of grief does not necessarily imply simply warding off these feelings for the protection of the individual from suffering, nor does it mean that the bereaved must be completely stripped of their defenses in order to "face reality." Instead, the bereaved must achieve some balance that allows them to experience their pain, sense of loss, loneliness, fear, anger, guilt, and sadness; to let in their anguish and let out their expressions of such anguish; to know and feel in the very core of their souls what has happened to them; and yet to do all this in doses, so that they will not be overwhelmed by such feelings. The human body and psyche are more or less built to provide such a balance between the emerging feelings, the coping mechanisms that modulate them when necessary, and the wisdom to understand when the emotions can be tolerated and dealt with more directly.

In addition to the appropriately balanced (and, from what has been written, one can see that "appropriateness" is highly individualized) modulation of emotions, success in this task also involves the development or use of relatively adaptive coping mechanisms. While coping mechanisms are all, by definition, primarily adaptive in their protective capacities, some are more likely than others to serve the individual's other day-to-day needs and are thus relatively more adaptive. For example, both distraction in one's work and involvement with others can be effective means of warding off one's difficult or painful emotions. These coping mechanisms are both more likely to be productive than compulsive eating, drinking, or spending—all of which may be equally as effective in protecting the individual from the pain of grief.

The conscious experience and expression of thoughts and feelings emerging after the death of a spouse are generally considered desirable, despite their frequently painful nature, because the survivor must contend with the reality of his situation. Does the same hold true for "understanding"—and thereby integrating—these experiences? There is no substantiation in any of the scientific literature that understanding is a necessary precondition for psychological well-being. However, most mental health professionals do hold such beliefs, and we feel obligated to subscribe to its inclusion among the tasks of grief. As we look at the specific affects with which the bereaved contend, the value of "understanding" becomes clearer. For example, when bereaved persons feel that they are "out of control," understanding can help them reassert a modicum of order.

Task 3: Integrating the Continuing Relationship with the Dead Spouse. The process of integrating the loss of one's spouse psychologically involves a series of internal events, beginning with the realization of the loss (achieved through recurrent painful encounters with the bereaved person's new reality) and culminating in an acceptance of a physical and psychological reality.

While the concept of "acceptance" seems necessary to any definition of resolution or recovery, the question of what is being accepted becomes crucial. During the early weeks of one's grief, where the realization of loss has occurred with its accompanying painful emotions, the bereaved are usually in such a state of mental and emotional upheaval that questions of acceptance rarely occur to them. The loss seems raw; they feel unprotected and overwhelmed much of the time. But what is acceptance? How does one accept the death of one's spouse? Is acceptance a resignation to live with something tragic, to embrace a disdainful reality, to agree that the death has happened? If that is the case, then, in fact, almost all the bereaved can be said to have "accepted" their loss. But if "acceptance" means that the bereaved truly believe that the relationship with their spouse is *over, finished, completed* and that they are emotionally prepared to live with that, then it is the extraordinary person who achieves this kind of acceptance. Perhaps, then, we need a different definition of "acceptance."

Freud (1917) described the work of grief as enabling the bereaved to "decathect" the lost object. Bowlby (1969), Parkes (1972), and others have suggested that the grief reaction represents a specific, evolutionarily adaptive response whose primary purpose is to reunite the bereaved with the lost object. This latter view is consistent with the observations of Glick, Parkes, and Weiss (1975) that continuing ties to the dead spouse appear consistently through the first year of bereavement. Data presented in this book and the work of others confirm the extension of such ties indefinitely over time. It is our contention that partial mitigation of the loss of a spouse through the continued emotional connection is both universal and essential, and that the task of the therapist is not to help the bereaved "let go" or "give up" the relationship but to help them find an appropriate place for the dead in their emotional lives—a place that enables them both to grieve and to continue living effectively in the world.

Psychologically, we are incapable of relinquishing all the bonds, connections, and ties that are a part of our most intimate relationships. As a result, a revised definition of "acceptance" must include the notion that the bereaved person is emotionally prepared to live with an altered relationship with the dead spouse, sustained by ongoing contact and communication, dreams, memories, and living legacies. It is a mistake to expect that the death of a spouse means that the relationship is over. Instead, a healthy adaptation to the death includes the evolution of a new form of this relationship and its integration into the changing life and personality of the bereaved.

Task 4: Maintaining Health and Continued Functioning. It seems self-evident that health and good functioning in one's work and relationships would be considered goals to be achieved in contending with bereavement—or almost any other condition, for that matter. The forces that interfere with health and functioning are frequently involuntary biological phenomena, such as insomnia and agitation, altered immune systems, depression, and confusional states (see Chapter Five).

Task 5: Adapting Successfully to Altered Relationships. While many of the bereaved continue their relationships with family and friends in much the same way after their spouses' deaths, it is difficult to imagine a situation where no change occurs. At times these changes are abrupt and dramatic (see Chapter Six), leading to the disruption of some old relationships, the development of new ones, or major restructuring in already existing ones. However, even where continuity prevails, inevitable shifts occur: subtle nuances, changed meanings, greater or lesser importance, more or less intensity. Whatever upheavals occur, be they large or small, in the relationships of the bereaved, they must adapt to these changes. That is, they must learn to deal with the reactions of others to their loss, their grief, their changed social status, and their needs; they must develop new attitudes toward their relationships that will allow for the ongoing gratification of their own needs; and they must contend with the potential loss of some relationships. This reconfiguration of both individual relationships and overall relationship patterns usually requires a major adjustment for the bereaved person.

Task 6: Developing an Integrated, Healthy Self-Concept and Stable World View. The task of achieving a stable new identity is one that necessarily occurs over an extended period of time. Most of us struggle with this task most seriously and for the most prolonged time period during adolescence. The search for identity following the death of one's spouse contains many of the same elements: uncertainty about who one is; a sense of incompleteness and instability; confusion about roles, social status, and self-worth (both positive and negative self-images); struggles with competing forces of dependency and autonomy; and a fluctuating sense of confidence about tackling the world. In the same way that one measures the accomplishments of a young adult as one who emerges from adolescence with a firm, stable sense of identity, so too can one assess the widowed person's emergence from the morass of personal confusion and diffusion into a newly evolved identity—a process that requires at least two years to complete. The person who emerges from his or her grief experience often feels a sense of "newness" and difference, at times rebirth, just as the newly "freed" young adult does.

Along with an altered identity, bereaved persons need to reestablish a stable world view, perhaps with a changed sense of purpose or meaning, a different direction, or new goals. The widowed person's world view—beliefs about the world and purposes in living—is understandably challenged or shaken by a spouse's death. A new set of beliefs often emerges only after a prolonged period of directionlessness, meaninglessness, and floundering. Even where the ultimate product does not look too different from what existed before the death, a period of disruption almost invariably precedes a return to stability.

Dimension-Related Interventions

Each of the dimensions of bereavement brings with it a unique configuration of changes, potential stressors, and challenges to the individual, who may respond in relatively adaptive or maladaptive ways. The bereaved may come to the attention of a professional under very different kinds of circumstances. A surviving spouse may seek professional help despite making a "good" adjustment, simply because the distress is so great that consultation seems warranted. Referrals may come from family members or friends, who feel that the bereaved person should not still be grieving so intensely after a year or should not spend so much time talking about the dead spouse. The family physician may be concerned about a depression that seems intractable or about recurrent infections that might be manifestations of ongoing stress. Regardless of the source of the referral, or the ostensible difficulty presented, the clinician's initial task is to make a thorough evaluation of the bereaved along each of the dimensions described (see Figure 1). The evaluation should include not only the changes that have occurred since the spouse's death but also a detailed developmental history, from which the clinician can determine the person's most adaptive levels of functioning in the areas covered in this book. What have been his responses to prior losses, separations, or other distressing occurrences? What means of coping have worked in the past when the person has been forced to deal with difficult stresses? Have there been episodes of physical or psychiatric illness? What kinds of conflicts have emerged in prior relationships? How have they been handled? Has this person achieved intimacy in relationships? Has he tolerated being dependent? Independent? How firm was her sense of identity before marriage? During the marriage? Such an assessment creates a baseline—although limited by the retrospective nature of the inquiry and the potential distortions created at a time where regressive influences may be great—from which the clinician can assess current regression and future progression. It may also serve as a point of reference for reassurance from the therapist about the bereaved person's capacity for adaptive functioning. Through the use of systematic assessment, the therapist will be able to identify problems as they occur in each dimension. The task of addressing these problems therapeutically can then proceed in a more organized and comprehensive fashion. The specific forms that therapeutic interventions can take are highly variable though still directed toward the identified problems. An examination of each of the dimensions will help to identify the specific therapeutic approaches applied in pursuing the "tasks" for each dimension.

Because of their intimate connection and interplay, the first two dimensions of grief (mental and emotional responses and coping mechanisms) will be considered together in examining the relevant therapeutic approaches to problems in each.

Coping with Mental and Emotional Changes

The Therapist. The first therapeutic consideration addresses aspects of the therapist. The person who has lost a spouse is seen as someone in great pain, highly vulnerable and needy. The responses of those who encounter such a person are either to back away and protect themselves or to reach out and try to help the grieving person. Some people are able to respond with care and compassion in such situations, yielding comfort and aid. Others might want to help but do not know how. These people—whether professionals or nonprofessionals—need first to understand, at least cognitively, the inner experience of the grieving person.

The paramount quality necessary for establishing a helping relationship with a grieving spouse is a tolerance for the many feelings and thoughts that are central to the experience of grief. The willingness of therapists to expose themselves to intense emotions, to become vulnerable to the often painful, fearful, or angry states with which the bereaved coexist, and to accept many thoughts and feelings that under most circumstances would be unacceptable to them—these are the means of access to the inner life of the bereaved. Such qualities allow therapists to hear when they listen. To understand at the deepest and most empathic level, one must achieve an identification with another person and take on the emotional burdens of very painful states. It is probably a mistake for therapists to protest that they will be unaffected by the pain of the bereaved. Such a statement means either that these therapists cannot help the bereaved or that they are fooling themselves. The most that therapists can say in such a situation is that they are willing to expose themselves and strong enough to bear the consequences. Therapists must also recognize that, unless they have experienced the same kind of loss, their empathy will be incomplete. One cannot extrapolate empathy.

Part of this capacity to tolerate the feelings of the bereaved and be available to them often involves a willingness to meet what are very exposed, intense, and primitive needs for dependency and

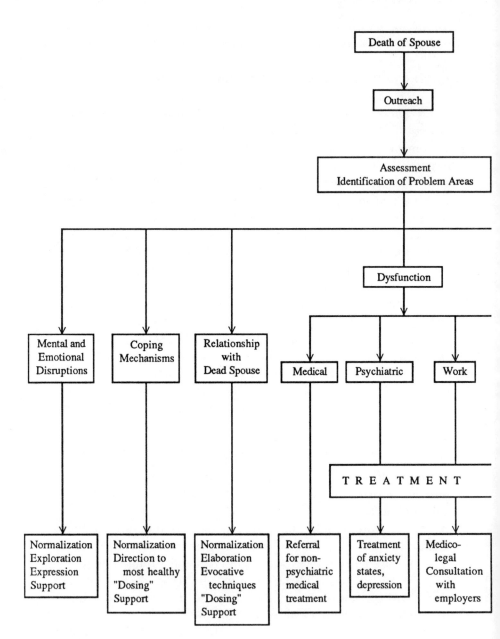

Figure 1. Multidimensional Approach to Treatment of
Dimension-Specific Problems.

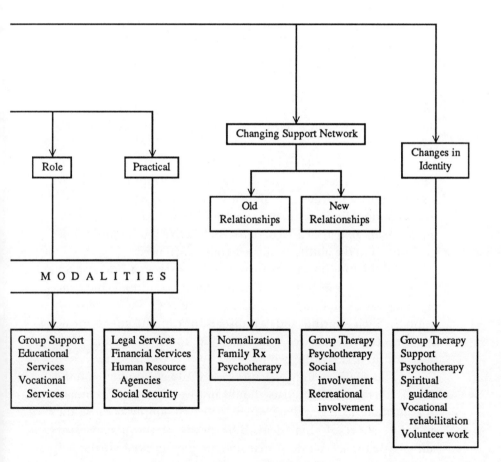

closeness. Such feelings can be frightening to others, causing them to withdraw lest they be "swallowed up." To immerse oneself in these feelings is seldom comfortable. However, although the bereaved may seem quite regressed at times, most healthy people will limit the degree to which they actually do attempt to "take over" their helpers. They are usually able to maintain sufficient control to prevent this from happening.

Few people would consider offering themselves as therapists without being willing and able to express warmth, caring, and respect toward others. These characteristics of support must be perceived by the bereaved before they are likely to allow the therapist to become "available" to them. These are qualities that most people can sense in others, although the bereaved are particularly vulnerable to ingenuousness in this area because of their intense needs. The "caring" need not be specific to the particular bereaved person at the onset, but the therapist must possess concern and respect for people in general. As the relationship develops, the concern, caring, and respect will become person-specific.

The therapist should be attuned to the needs of the grieving person. These needs may be diverse and shifting: a momentary need to express feelings may shift to a contrary need to move away from emotionality and then to yet another need for being alone, quiet, held, or cajoled. To help such a person requires both flexibility and the ability to suspend one's own needs.

In order to limit the bereaved person's sense of isolation and what seems like a great burden created by the continual emergence of images and emotions, therapists must be open about their own feelings. Such sharing and self-disclosure can encourage greater openness for the bereaved and contribute to the deepening of the relationship between the two.

The qualities and capacities described here apply to a rather "ideal" therapist. Therapists should not feel that they are unable to contribute to the welfare of the bereaved simply because they may fall short of this ideal. The needs of the bereaved are sufficiently broad and deep that they frequently need all the help they can get, in as many forms as are available.

Catharsis. The above description of the qualities of a helpful therapist suggests the importance of empathic listening as a therapeutic tool. The role of catharsis is universally accepted as paramount in the adaptive repertoire of the bereaved. Many cultures have developed institutionalized and ritualized mourning practices out of such wisdom. Catharsis among the bereaved serves, literally, to purge the body of its painful feelings, to release affects that build up within in a continuous way over time. It has been perceived as the safety valve in a hydraulic model where pressure builds up and seeks release lest there be a destructive explosion. While the validity of the model may not have been demonstrated, the press for catharsis among the bereaved has.

The therapist's presence and encouraging, supportive inquiry provide the sanction to and the direction of the catharsis. At times the pressure to talk, to cry, to express anger or guilt or longing is so great as to require almost no activity on the part of the therapist except to listen. The bereaved may expect little more than an empathic stance from the therapist—possibly because they implicitly or explicitly accept much of the turmoil as inevitable, unchangeable, or even desirable (symbolically as a demonstration of love for the dead). Under such circumstances the therapist's efforts to offer reassurance or comfort by whatever means are likely to be seen as means of deflecting the bereaved from their task of letting out their feelings.

An important task of the therapist who is helping the bereaved deal with the emergence of painful affects is continuous monitoring, either to help them open up more and express affect or to help them achieve some distance from their feelings when they seem overwhelming. There should be a mutual acknowledgment that the emotional pain of loss simply *exists,* that neither the bereaved nor the therapist can remove it even though certain maneuvers will lessen or remove its immediacy. Furthermore, aspects of this pain will *always* be present, now and in the future, and may be "tapped" either consciously and deliberately or incidentally by some trigger to which the person is exposed. Still, just as the pain of a physical wound diminishes with time, the awareness of this emotional reality serves as a buffer for both the bereaved and the therapist.

Normalization. A therapeutic "technique" that has potential benefits in every dimension of bereavement is "normalization,"
which translates into "understanding what is normal." By
discussions with a therapist, by reading, or by sharing personal
experiences in a group of other bereaved people, the bereaved gain
some cognitive appreciation of the process they are going through.
The primary benefits of normalization as it applies to coping with
the mental and emotional changes of grief are numerous.

First, it can help bring about a sense of order where there
was disorder. While the bereaved may be able to accept (though
not tolerate) the fact of their pain as something to be expected, the
intensity and unpredictability of their emotions, their intrusive
and disruptive thoughts and images, and their mental disorganization, distractibility, and confusion all give rise to the sense of
being out of control, even "going crazy." For many people this
aspect of their grief outweighs even the most painful of affects as
a disturbing influence. Evidence of their normality, while not
eliminating the disorder, provides tremendous relief and reassurance that they are not disintegrating. Thus reassured, they are
much better able to tolerate the disruption.

Second, normalization provides another level of relief for
many of the bereaved—relief from the sense of personal responsibility for their distress. Many people strongly believe that they
have directed themselves on whatever course they find themselves
by dint of their conscious or unconscious will, lifestyle, or
personal attributes. They have difficulty perceiving or accepting
the roles of things outside their control: social forces, genetics and
biology, or serendipity. In the extreme, of course, education is
impossible: the facts are always distorted to preclude the attainment of knowledge, and the belief goes on. For those who can be
influenced, an understanding of the relative universality or
normalcy of such disruptions can help to relieve them of the
additional burden of personal responsibility.

Third, particularly through reading, this process reinforces
the use of intellectualization and rationalization in helping the
bereaved achieve distance from their disruptive emotional states.
The mechanism by which this intellectualization is achieved is
unknown, but research on the lateralization of brain function

allows us to speculate that hemispheric dominance by the left side of the brain (used in linear, logical thinking) may temporarily override the influence of the right side, whose functions appear to include the experiences of emotions.

Finally, the education about bereavement can promote or enhance the freer expression of one's grief. Knowledge of the normalcy of certain experiences, such as anger or guilt, can give the bereaved permission to express such feelings where they may have been too embarrassed or guilty to do so otherwise. Learning that such expression may be beneficial, the person is further encouraged to express pent-up feelings. Reading about the experiences of others, the bereaved may become aware—cognitively—of feelings that they have repressed. Reading also can enable people, through identification and empathy, to reverse the process of intellectualization and "step inside" the emotional fabric of those in print. The experiences of others may "trigger" emotional responses in the reader, which may be very helpful. Some people, however, cannot bear to read or hear about grief experiences because the triggers create too much pain and must be avoided.

Dosing the Pain. The emotional pain associated with loss can be exquisite. An individual's capacity to tolerate such pain and his willingness to expose himself to it depends on several factors: the intensity of the pain; the impact of such pain on the individual's nervous system; prior experiences of exposure to such feelings, with assurance of survival; awareness of resources for emotional support; and belief in the importance of experiencing this pain. Whenever the intensity or impact is too great, when history has provided no success in coping with pain, when there are too few supports and an orientation toward "running," the bereaved will resort to avoidance wherever possible.

In the past, social, cultural, and religious ceremonies and rituals tended to force the bereaved to expose themselves on a regular and frequent basis to the realities of their loss, reinforcing the confrontation with the pain and providing sufficient experiences to "master" it—that is, to learn to tolerate it when one is exposed to it. Initially, the clinician dealing with the bereaved should determine whether the person has achieved this mastery. It is important to remember that the "task" of a bereaved person is not to be free of pain but to live with the pain, whether that be four months or four years after the spouse's death.

On a continuum from those who totally expose themselves to such pain and those who totally avoid it, most bereaved people are somewhere in between. The vicissitudes of living prevent people from having total control over possible triggers to which they may be exposed. Furthermore, the need to maintain ties with aspects of the deceased provides a source of repeated exposures to triggers. One consequence of these realities is that the bereaved are continuously "dosing" themselves in an approach-avoidance fashion in regard to painful stimuli. From a therapeutic standpoint, the bereaved appear to know what is best for them at a particular period, and over time I have come to trust their wisdom. However, the notion that the bereaved know what is best in dealing with their pain does not preclude a therapeutic role for the clinician—as long as the clinician is patient and willing to move at the rate that the bereaved person indicates he or she can tolerate.

The major principle of therapy that focuses on the pain of grief follows the maxim of dermatological therapeutics: "If it's wet, dry it. If it's dry, wet it." Because of the great variability in people's responses to their grief, I would modify this to a corollary that takes this range into account: "If it's too wet, dry it. If it's too dry, wet it."

Figure 2 presents a model of the forms of "pathological" grief as they have been described in the literature (Deutsch, 1937; Volkan, 1966; Brown and Stoudemier, 1983). It depicts both the "psychological" perturbations that are "too dry" (absent or inhibited grief) or "too wet" (hypertrophied grief) and the psychophysiological alterations that may lead to organic disease states. This model suggests that the driving force behind both of these mechanisms is separation anxiety.

If there are therapeutic problems in the earlier periods of grief, they generally are related to too much affect, the survivor's experience of being "too wet"; the separation anxiety, the pain of grief, and the impact of the loss are too great to bear. This hypertrophied grief seems too intense, too constant and enduring,

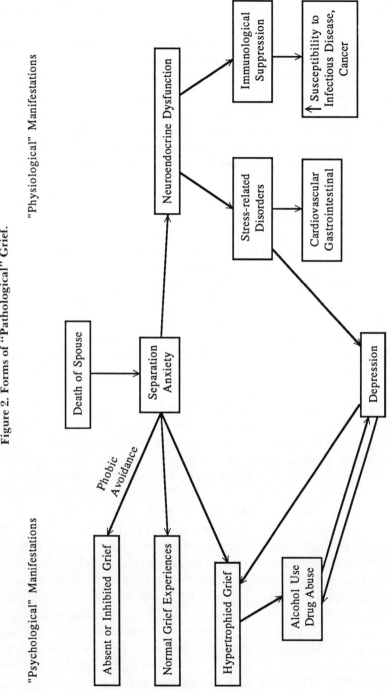

Figure 2. Forms of "Pathological" Grief.

"Psychological" Manifestations

"Physiological" Manifestations

impossible to escape for more than moments. Even the coping skills available to the bereaved provide inadequate protection from the pain. In such instances the stress of loss can be hazardous to the person's health through compromise of the cardiovascular, neuroendocrine, or immune system. These are circumstances where the family doctor prescribes sedative-hypnotics and anxiolytics and where the bereaved resort to alcohol or other drugs in efforts to sleep and to obliterate the overwhelming internal distress.

Too often clinicians may regard such a state as an opportunity to help deepen and elaborate on the pain. Such efforts may threaten the development of a therapeutic alliance, convincing the bereaved that the therapist does not understand their needs. Instead, the psychotherapeutic goals at such times of continuing, unremitting emotional distress should be to help protect the person from such a state in whatever ways seem feasible and responsible. The therapist's stance remains one of steady support and reassurance that the bereaved can survive such an onslaught. At the same time, the therapist examines the whole gamut of coping mechanisms that are possible sources of protection: denial, avoidance, distraction, rationalization, prayer, involvement, and so on. Such exploration may reveal adaptive mechanisms that have been underutilized or not even considered yet may provide a temporary haven. Frequently, useful defenses have not been utilized because of other barriers. For example, many of the bereaved might find distraction from their painful affects through involvement in a community activity, a class, a support group, or volunteer work but are too anxious, agitated, and fearful to leave their homes alone in such a state. Enlisting the support and practical help from family or friends necessary to follow through in such activity may seem overwhelming in itself. The therapist may need to help the bereaved deal with such barriers: by supporting them through their fears, by helping them enlist the help of others, or by soliciting those extra supports. Again, the therapist must be flexible: first, by assessing the grieving person's capacity to carry out certain functions; second, by being prepared to take a more active role for those who are too regressed or inhibited to act themselves. The clinician's recognition that the bereaved is in a state of temporary regression will allow him or her to be more active without fears of promoting permanent psychological disabilities. The subsequent therapeutic job of "cleaning up" after such a regression is much more often focused on dealing with the recovered person's embarrassment about his prior neediness than it is with weaning an overneedy person. Of course, the therapist will use developmental history as a partial guide, but, even then, characterological traits of dependency should not dictate keeping such a person at a distance.

When are the bereaved "too dry"? This question is difficult to answer because it may depend on "why" they are "dry." In rare instances a widowed person will be relatively dry because he or she had achieved a significant degree of detachment prior to the death of the spouse. A large number will appear to be dry because it is not their personality style to display painful emotions. They may always have used defenses of suppression, isolation, and intellectualization to close themselves off, both inside and outside, from emotions. Usually, when asked about painful affects, they will say that they feel them, but there may be little external evidence of their existence. A third form of dryness occurs where the bereaved person has successfully warded off all grief through a combination of stylistic traits and rigid avoidance. John (described in Chapter Three) displayed this form in its extreme. Variants on this absence of grief are forms of inhibited grief, where the bereaved are aware of having internal turmoil that they "know" is associated with their loss but where, despite their conscious efforts, they find themselves unable to cry or make contact with their grief.

The therapist's roles are quite different in each of these situations. Where there has been true detachment, prior to the death of a spouse, the lack of grief probably will not be perceived as a problem, and such a person is unlikely to present for help.

The question of how to intervene when a bereaved person reports grieving but where such grief is contained is a controversial one. There is a popular belief that the bereaved must cry a certain number of tears as a healthy response to their loss, something that is more easily accomplished by those who are expressive than those who are not. There are also popular beliefs among therapists of many backgrounds that showing one's feelings is healthy and "keeping things in" is not. These beliefs are yet to be supported by research, and I have seen too many healthy yet less expressive people make very good adjustments to their bereavement to feel any great obligation to change their style therapeutically. In such situations the major clinical consideration is still whether the person is able to experience the emotions, recognize them, and integrate them adaptively. Wearing such feelings on one's sleeve remains optional.

Where there is a true absence of grief or inhibited grief, the therapist's role is less equivocal. Wherever avoidance has been employed, the presumption is made that the person, consciously or unconsciously, believes that the exposed pain would be too great to bear. The person's total orientation is to prevent such pain from occurring, and, as with any phobic manifestations, the areas of circumscription can be narrow or broad, and the degrees of maladaptation necessary to maintain them can be lesser or greater. The person who is making a total effort to avoid pain will not readily accept any treatment that exposes him to it. It would be useful if the clinician could substantiate the perceived need for treatment with evidence of dire consequences for health if the individual is left untreated, but such evidence does not exist, and the therapist is left simply with conveying his or her own conviction about such a need. The situation is easier when the therapist is dealing with cases of inhibited grief. Usually these individuals recognize the need to experience their grief but are inhibited from doing so. There is conscious motivation to feel the pain despite the unconscious forces preventing it. Under such circumstances the therapist and patient can achieve the working alliance necessary to proceed.

How does the therapist "wet it"? Numerous technical approaches to eliciting grief have been described (Volkan, 1975; Melges and DeMaso, 1980; Mawson, Marks, Ramm, and Stern, 1981). While they have somewhat different perspectives about the nature of the problem, at a practical level these evocative techniques all rely on reestablishing emotional links with perceptual experiences in order to elicit the painful experiences and expressions of grief. The perceptual modes employed are verbal stimuli, visual imagery, and tangible reminders.

Verbal approaches often focus on the circumstances of death. The therapist reviews the events in great detail; looks for any evidence of emotional response to be elaborated; observes the person's difficulties in expressing affects; and, in general, uses stronger, more expressive, and more evocative language than the usually more neutral language of psychotherapy ("dead" versus "lost"; "excruciating" versus "difficult" or "painful"). The bereaved may themselves be aware of subjects that are especially painful to them, thus enabling the therapist to short-cut a more systematic investigation.

A more powerful approach to eliciting affect employs the use of directed imagery. These techniques are directed at bringing the dead spouse into the emotional life of the bereaved, and knowledge of their relationship will give clues to the most useful approach. The therapist may help the bereaved reminisce about poignant times in their married lives, soliciting scenes in which the dead spouse plays a prominent role. Greater immediacy may be attained through role playing, where the bereaved person pretends that the dead spouse is sitting in a chair and that the bereaved person is speaking to the spouse. Alternately, the surviving spouse may be asked to compose a letter to the dead spouse, reminiscing about past experiences or communicating a sentiment that had gone unspoken. At times the bereaved will be more capable of experiencing affect where it applies to others than to themselves; in such instances the imagery might focus on the impact of the loss on their children.

The most powerful evocative stimuli are likely to be the tangible representations of the deceased. The therapist can ask the bereaved person to bring to a session a picture of the dead spouse, alone or with the bereaved; an article of clothing or jewelry that has special meaning; old letters from the deceased; or other symbolic representations of the deceased. For those who are most avoidant, the cemetery may be the stimulus that produces the greatest emotional response. Therefore, the therapist may encourage the bereaved person to spend time at the grave, reminiscing, communicating, and in other ways making efforts to bring the dead to life.

The purpose of such techniques is to give the bereaved repetitive experiences with their grief and to desensitive them to the pain. The goal is a gradual development of mastery—not "getting it out once and for all" but learning to tolerate the emotional pain, so that the bereaved can have freer catharsis and can decrease the limitations that avoidance created in their emotional and day-to-day practical lives.

Other Affect-Specific Interventions. Therapeutic approaches to other grief-related affects take on the more typical characteristics of supportive and exploratory psychotherapies. In addition to the exploration of these affects, an understanding of their impact in the day-to-day lives of the bereaved, and their examination in a historical context, some interventions are affect specific.

Not all bereaved individuals experience anger; but for those who do, the anger can be tenacious and intense, reflecting the enormity of the loss. The therapist must treat this anger as a legitimate product of the immediate loss rather than as a derivative of earlier loss, failure, or other disappointment. Interpretations of other meanings should be reserved for a later period, when the more intense affect has subsided.

Guilt is another feeling that is not ubiquitous. While understanding its roots will go far in helping the bereaved relinquish guilt, the therapist can also take an active role in challenging the irrational beliefs that may be contributory. Where the person's stance remains punitive, the therapist may have that person call on the dead spouse to communicate the inappropriateness of the guilt or confer forgiveness. For some, this latter function may require contact with clergy.

Regrets about unfinished business with the deceased can be addressed through role playing, letter writing, or other directed imagery that allows the bereaved to complete their communications.

Where anxieties and fearfulness play a prominent role in the life of the newly widowed person, the therapist should be aware that these feelings may be warranted. Therefore, the customary reassurance and encouragement to confront feared situations must be tempered with a certain amount of reality-based caution. In fact, the bereaved may face real economic hardship, exploitation, and other rejections.

Apathy is seldom useful or productive to the bereaved, and the barrier to functioning often contributes to the person's already lowered self-esteem. Thus, the therapist must take a stance directed toward action in the face of apathy—probably somewhere between being a cheerleader and cattle prod.

Loneliness may become a long-term legacy of spousal bereavement. While learning to tolerate being alone and a certain amount of loneliness is probably useful and adaptive, continuing loneliness ought to be a spur to corrective action. Where there are psychological barriers to the development of relationships, the therapist can use the therapeutic relationship as a springboard for others. Again, sustained pressure by the therapist may be necessary, and direction toward support groups for the bereaved may be the most easily accepted form of contact for the newly bereaved. The therapist should also clearly identify the feelings of loneliness and not confuse them with simply "being alone." Being alone can be very constructive for the bereaved, and some balance between this utility and the pain of loneliness should be struck in the therapeutic efforts to help the bereaved reengage with others. Recognition of the survivor's need for some protective social withdrawal will also prevent premature pressure from the therapist. As in each area where pain is involved, the therapist should continuously monitor the competing and often conflicting needs created by internal discomfort and external realities.

Integrating the Continuing Relationship with the Dead Spouse

As noted earlier, the "task" here is not the relinquishment or decathexis of the dead spouse but the establishment of a form of continuing relationship that both satisfies the emotional need of the bereaved to maintain their ties and allows for grieving and living to proceed. Just what the configuration of this relationship is likely to become cannot be anticipated. The clinician should encourage the fullest expression of the grieving spouse's thoughts and feelings about the dead spouse. Recognizing the myriad forms that such continuing relationships can take, the therapist can elicit information about areas where the bereaved may feel reluctant to disclose their experiences. The clinician's assessment of the continuing relationship with the deceased can proceed in a straightforward and systematic fashion, conveying the normalcy of these phenomena. To stimulate further thoughts and emotions, the therapist can ask about the spouse's resting place, the patient's efforts to contact the spouse, experiences of communication or presences, ongoing manifestations of symbolic representations and living legacies, rituals, memories, and dreams. The use here of normalization can overcome concerns that the bereaved may have about their "strangeness" in communicating with the dead or hallucinating their presence. The matter-of-fact acceptance of such phenomena may sanction a freer relationship between the living and the dead, which can facilitate the integration of loss. Hollywood B-movies aside, there is little risk that the bereaved will suspend reality testing altogether and flee to a world of psychosis.

Most bereaved spouses find their own forms of communication and continuing contact with their spouses. Where there is a phobic avoidance of expression, the techniques described earlier can be used to desensitize the person and facilitate this process. Even after desensitization has occurred, the same evocative techniques—directed imagery, role playing, and reminiscing—can be useful tools in the ongoing therapeutic process.

Over time, traditional psychotherapeutic methods are employed to examine the spousal relationship as it existed before death, helping the bereaved person achieve a realistic perspective about the marriage and the dead spouse. The therapist must be patient, recognizing that ambivalence and angry feelings about the spouse and the marriage may be overshadowed by idealization in the early months after death. With each "reworking" of the issues, the bereaved person moves through successive stages of understanding and enlightenment, and the ongoing relationship with the spouse proceeds to evolve. This process of integration occurs over many years and should be conveyed thus by the therapist.

Maintaining Health and Treating Dysfunction

As described in Chapter Five, the bereaved are at high risk for stress-related medical and psychiatric disorders. Our current understanding of the nature of such risks is rudimentary, incomplete, and speculative. Figure 2, shown earlier, depicts the operational mechanisms presumed here to determine dysfunction both on psychological and physiological bases. Because of the increased medical morbidity, particularly during the first year of bereavement, the surviving spouse should have regular assessment by an internist, a general practitioner, or another primary care physician.

Stressors. The clinician needs to address any issue that is likely to be producing stress in the bereaved. Foremost among the numerous life stressors that may be contributing to possible risks after the death of a spouse are financial difficulties created by loss of income, accumulated medical bills, inadequate insurance, and the like. In addition, legal and administrative problems related to the disposition of an estate; filing for Social Security or veterans' benefits; complicated tax problems; and difficulties with decisions about where to live, how to invest, and even where to seek out advice can seem overwhelming to the newly bereaved. While the therapist may have limited expertise on any of these areas, he or she can be useful in three ways. First, in a general sense, therapists do have expertise in helping people cope with stressors. They can help them organize their thinking, give them perspective and reassurance, and support their efforts to confront anxiety-provoking situations. Second, the therapist can function as a resource person, directing those who seem unable to direct themselves to appropriate experts in finance, law, and social resources. Finally, the therapist may operate as an advocate for the bereaved person—for example, through direct intervention to assist in obtaining temporary disability leave from work where the bereaved person is too disorganized and confused to function adequately or where a continuing psychiatric disturbance, particularly depression, subsequently develops.

Depression and Anxiety. While as many as half of the bereaved experience some symptoms of depression during the first year after their spouse's deaths, an estimated 10-20 percent (Osterweis, Solomon, and Green, 1984) manifest a significant clinical depression, with dysfunction and symptomatology that meet criteria for the diagnosis of major depression according to the American Psychiatric Association's *Diagnostic and Statistical Manual of Mental Disorders (DSM-III)*. Although the efficacy of treating such depressions with antidepressant medication has not been established, since research has not been conducted in this area, there is no reason to think that such treatment would not be beneficial, and my clinical experience indicates that it *is* beneficial.

The clinician's major problem is to distinguish cases of "real" depression from those "depressoid" states associated with grief. Both conditions share the symptoms of grief as well as depression. In those major depressions that occur during bereavement, the grief symptoms may be intensified by the depression. The two criteria that I have used to diagnose a genuine depression are based primarily on features of the depression itself: (1) The depression has "a life of its own." That is, the depressive symptoms persist independently of the day-to-day events, the exposure to "triggers," or the internal psychological processes of the bereaved. These symptoms may worsen in response to these factors, but they will continue when these factors are "neutral." (2) Vegetative signs and symptoms persist beyond two months after the spouse's death. Vegetative signs and symptoms of depression—such as insomnia, anorexia with weight loss, depleted energy and easy fatigability, and psychomotor agitation—may be present as acute stress responses to the death of a spouse. Their persistence beyond the first two months strongly indicates that a clinical depression has evolved. Vegetative signs or symptoms that are less typical of acute stress reactions—hypersomnia, hyperphagia, and psychomotor retardation—also suggest the presence of clinical depression.

Aggressive treatment of such clinical depression is important for two reasons. First, treatment of the depression is likely to lower the risk of medical sequelae to which the depressed are vulnerable. Second, treatment of the depression will make the bereaved better able to cope with their grief. They will have more resources available to them to carry on with the tasks of life as well as to tolerate the temporary and limited regressions forced on them by their grief.

At a more speculative level, the argument has been presented (Shuchter, 1982a) that antidepressants may have a place in the therapeutic armamentarium not just for treating the more clear-cut major depressions associated with grief but also for cases of hypertrophied grief, where its action may be useful primarily for lowering separation anxiety (see Figure 2).

At present, the place for anxiolytics and sedative-hypnotics has been and will likely continue to be based on the expressed intensity of need. Where the bereaved, particularly in the early weeks and months, are having great difficulty in tolerating the suffering brought about by their grief, in spite of their best efforts to cope with it, few medical practitioners would withhold humane relief in the form of such medications. While such use is easier to sanction when it helps with sleep or limits the dysfunction that anxiety may wreak on performance, it takes a die-hard believer in the usefulness of suffering to make a case for abstinence. The therapist should be working to help the bereaved find the most adaptive forms of alternately experiencing and containing their grief, but short-term and limited use of anxiolytics (and perhaps low-dose antidepressants) sometimes may be necessary.

Alcoholism. Alcoholism is another psychiatric disorder for which the bereaved are at great risk. The utility of small amounts of alcohol for sleep, diminishing anxiety, and obliterating ruminative thinking predisposes the grieving survivor to find comfort in drinking, at times leading to gradual escalation and eventually to degrees of uncontrolled or obligatory consumption. Alcoholism may also mask other disorders, particularly depressive or anxiety disorders, which have more specific, more efficacious, and safer treatments. At greatest risk are those bereaved who are recovering alcoholics or who have strong family histories of alcoholism. An essential component of any assessment is a careful and persistent inquiry about alcohol use and potential abuse. Where there is suspicion of alcoholism, vigorous pursuit of this question should extend to family and friends, since the individual is likely to be rationalizing its use and denying its relevance. Aggressive treatment is important to prevent the potentially severe consequences of alcoholism among the bereaved. Escalation of drinking can lead to an intensification of grief, precipitation of secondary depression, and great impairment of function. Any efforts to treat alcoholism among the bereaved, regardless of one's therapeutic inclinations, should be done in conjunction with the person's involvement in Alcoholics Anonymous.

The sense of entitlement "permits" the bereaved numerous other indulgences that may be detrimental to their health. Abuses of drugs, cigarettes, and food are all quite common. Aside from any ongoing supportive therapy that addresses issues specific to bereavement, these special problems are probably best addressed in problem-specific treatment programs—for example, Overeaters Anonymous.

Adapting Successfully to Altered Relationships

The therapeutic approach to problems arising from the relationships of the bereaved is simple: Figure out what is wrong and help to fix it. Beyond this general principle, the clinician is faced with innumerable possibilities where difficulties can arise for the bereaved. Each has unique characteristics and a variety of potential solutions.

Family. The impact of death is greatest within the immediate family, especially where there are young children. Having the family meet together with the therapist can be enormously helpful when family members are struggling with issues of competing grief; variable capacities to grieve or to tolerate the grief of others; lack of role definitions in the family; and the difficulties of parceling out the already diminished emotional and material resources. In this context the clinician can encourage greater communication of individuals' struggles as well as mutual concerns about the impact of the family's loss. Expressions of grief in one member can foster the same in others or, through understanding, provide for mutual support. Where there are older children or grown children, family therapy sessions can explore these children's efforts to assume the role of protector of the surviving parent or to limit the parent's expressions of grief. Working with other family members in this context can help the bereaved tackle other tasks that may have seemed overwhelming in the face of their loss. If communication is inhibited, the clinician can use his or her knowledge of the problems that people in such circumstances experience to initiate or stimulate discussion.

Family conflicts sometimes can be dealt with more effectively in individual psychotherapy. There are difficult decisions that many parents feel they must make by themselves, without their children's or other family members' involvement. Such decisions may have been made in conjunction with the spouse who has died, and the therapist may be utilized as a sounding board to think through such decisions in a setting that does not compromise the decision maker's sense of autonomy. The surviving spouse may want to explore negative, conflictual feelings about a child or parent or sibling without exposing the other person directly to such feelings. Using knowledge about how others respond to the death of a parent, child, or sibling, the therapist may be able to offer sufficient understanding and perspective to the bereaved that they will be in a good position to deal with the intrafamilial problem by themselves.

Friends. Distance is created between the bereaved and their friends when the friends cannot comprehend or empathize with the experiences of the bereaved and therefore may avoid them. In these instances the friends may be unable to tolerate their own uncomfortable feelings, or they do not know what to say or do and are reluctant to make the bereaved more uncomfortable. At the same time, they may not recognize that their avoidance in itself can cause great pain. Another manifestation of such limited empathy is the intolerance of friends for the bereaved person's expressions of grief. These friends may make it clear that emotional displays are unacceptable to them, or they may constantly try to distract the bereaved person. (Certainly, the effort to distract may be a gesture of caring when it is part of a larger repertoire of responses, including empathic listening and emotional support.)

The therapeutic approaches to such relationship problems can be multifaceted. Education of the bereaved about "normal," though not "desirable," responses of others to grief can help them gain greater perspective, and at least help them see that the disruption of their relationship is not something they have "caused." When they understand the difficulties that others may have in dealing with grief, the bereaved can either voluntarily relinquish their active expressions of grief, if they feel that the other person cannot tolerate such feelings, or they can approach the other person and enlist his support—pushing through his resistance to their pain—with the goal of being able to share more of themselves. As in the family, there may be some use in bringing the friend to a therapy session, to capitalize on the therapist's resources in opening up such communications. Therapist and patient must recognize that sometimes such relationships cannot be repaired. The patient then must learn to deal with yet another loss and must actively pursue more available relationships. The relationship with the therapist may provide a temporary shelter but should not, in the long run, replace relationships in the "real" world.

Another source of potential disruption of friendships comes from within the bereaved, where distance is created by internal forces: protective withdrawal, envy, or the belief that others *cannot* understand. The therapist's task is initially to help the bereaved recognize such forces as temporary states of mind. When bereaved persons are in such a state, they may spurn even the most persistent efforts of loved ones; and everyone who deals with them, including the therapist, may have to wait patiently, at times for weeks or even months, for these internal forces to subside. The bereaved person may find it easier to resume contact with others in a setting where these "others" seem to be "in the same boat." This theme will be discussed later in this chapter, in the section on support groups.

Romance and Remarriage. A frequent source of anxiety and inhibition for the bereaved is the prospect of developing heterosexual relationships. This may become an issue long before the person is actually "ready" emotionally to embark on such a course.

The pressure to be reinvolved or remarried can come from many sources: from within, as a response to loneliness and the anticipation of a future alone; from family, friends, or therapists who believe that a romantic involvement is necessary for the person's well-being; from those who feel that small children need two parents; or from those who may have romantic feelings toward this person. A therapeutic task here can be to help the bereaved sort out their feelings from their own and others' expectations, so that they can proceed in their own best interest.

Even where the bereaved person feels "ready" to become involved with someone, there are problems to be faced: the anxieties of dating, the pangs of guilt, the fears of repeating a loss or enduring another illness, and the conflicts intrinsic to the relationship itself.

Avoidance of dating or even "exposure" may stem from the real culture shock of a more open and sexually free society or from the doubts about one's desirability and consequent fears of rejection. The role of the therapist may require at one time exploring the historical contexts of such concerns and, at another point, offering support to face such fears slowly in stepwise fashion.

Concerns that the bereaved will betray the dead spouse may create both a sense of guilt and a worry that involvement with a new partner will mean the loss of the original mate—a loss that is unacceptable. The therapist can reassure the bereaved person that romantic involvement does not require "giving up" one's first love, that feelings about both can coexist. The therapist may also contribute support to existing belief systems, in which reinvolvement or remarriage is seen as a testimony to the success of a first marriage. One should not, however, press one's own belief in remarriage as the only healthy adaptation to bereavement. This is not only an unrealistic expectation but a contradiction to the reality that living as a single person can be gratifying and productive.

Remarriage can bring with it all the marital problems generally encountered by clinicians. In this study there seemed to be very few, however. By their very longevity (average over twenty years), these marriages suggested the capacity either to choose well or to accommodate well, or both. The experience of loss frequently contributes to the person's marital adaptability. There is often a greater appreciation for what one has, a greater acceptance of the other person's foibles, and a consequent willingness to be flexible. Nevertheless, problems in communications and expectations do arise, for which couples therapy may be appropriate. Family therapy can also be employed in remarriages where "blended" families create competing loyalties and other conflicts.

Sexual Problems. The sexual problems most frequently encountered are those associated with anxiety and inhibitions. Performance anxiety in men, resulting in erectile dysfunction, and anorgasmia in women can be treated with simple reassurance combined with perseverance and open communication between the sexually involved couple. Persistent sexual difficulties may reflect conflict about the bereaved person's dead spouse or ongoing conflict with the new partner and may require further exploration as well as the application of standard behavioral and communication strategies used to treat sexual dysfunction.

Consolidating an Evolving Identity

There are several important contributions that the therapist can make in helping the bereaved deal with their changing identity and belief systems. Initially, a crucial precondition to offering help is a thorough understanding of this dimension of grief. The therapist must recognize the early regression for what it is and communicate such to the bereaved. The therapist must also be able to maintain a conviction about the bereaved person's adaptive capacities, a feat made difficult by the strong regressive pull on the therapist of the grieving person's feelings of helplessness, hopelessness, and inadequacy. The intensity and power of such feelings cannot be underestimated, and the therapist's exposure to these affects may not be duplicated in many other clinical situations. Communicating this knowledge and conviction to the bereaved is a difficult task, but this therapeutic stance may need to be sustained over an extended period of time to provide the support necessary to prevent further demoralization in the bereaved.

Where the bereaved find their lives meaningless or directionless, they will seek direction and advice from the therapist. While clinicians may have different views of what constitute adaptive directions, the most supportive stance is usually to communicate repeatedly that the bereaved will be quite capable of making decisions or taking actions when they are "ready," and that until that time they should probably defer any decisions or actions that are not essential. During this period the bereaved are likely to be operating almost solely on the principle of "what hurts least is best," and impulsive actions whose goals are the anticipated relief of pain are likely to occur. At such times they may require greater support and more active direction by the therapist toward safety or the prevention of irreversible actions such as changing jobs or selling homes.

As the bereaved emerge from the period of greatest regression, the changes in identity, personal growth, and attitudinal shifts generally proceed spontaneously and effectively. The therapist then becomes more of a mirror, reflecting such changes and supporting behaviors that will promote further growth through the bereaved person's excursions into new relationships, new careers, and new ways of thinking about himself and the world. This mirror should be "real," demonstrating the therapist's genuine joy, pride, and enthusiasm for the bereaved person's growth.

Support Groups for the Bereaved

The Widow-to-Widow program developed by Silverman (1969, 1970), in the late 1960s has evolved into the prototype for mutual support groups in this country and Great Britain; this model has been adopted by the American Association of Retired Persons in establishing its Widowed Persons' Service, with branches throughout this country. The efficacy of such support groups has been established in several studies (Barrett, 1978; Vachon and others, 1980; Videka-Sherman, 1982). These programs

provide continuing support services for the bereaved as a significant public health intervention strategy.

My personal experience with such groups began in 1980,
when my participation in developing a group for widows and
widowers was solicited because of my already established clinical
research interest in bereavement. In cooperation with the Jewish
Community Center of San Diego and through the tireless and
efficient efforts of a staff worker, Louisca Seidel Sachs, herself a
recent widow, and many other widowed volunteers, the nonsectar-
ian Widowed Persons' Resource Group was established and has
been in operation for six years. During the first two years, I served
as a facilitator of group therapy sessions and consultant to the
organization, and the subsequent two years as supervisor to the
psychiatric residents who became the facilitators.

The organizational structure was developed to address the
multiple levels of need experienced by the bereaved. Meetings were
held in a large multipurpose room on a weekly basis. Those who
wished to discuss their thoughts and feelings met from 6 to 7 P.M.
in a small group in a corner of the large room. The group varied
in size from five or six up to twenty or more people. Like any other
therapy group, this group operated as a forum for examining
bereavement experiences. People were free to speak or only listen.
The group served as the point of entry to the larger organization
for the newly bereaved, but its membership was self-determined
and many of its stable members might consist of men and women
well beyond their first year of bereavement. The focus of this
group was variable but generally oriented to the emotional turmoil
of the newly bereaved, their efforts to understand and cope with
their experiences, and their efforts to provide support and
reassurance to one another. Every aspect of their grief was open for
discussion. Members of the group showed great respect for the
pain that each experienced and the needs to talk about such
feelings or sit quietly and listen. Themes initiated by one person's
internal press were developed throughout the group as it examined
variations of these experiences and the different means of coping
with them. The therapist's task was as a facilitator, although this
task was frequently assumed by other members of the group. The
only formal structure or direction given to the group was a ritual

that evolved early in its development. At the end of every group meeting, each member, including the therapist, was "obligated" to describe something positive that was happening in his or her life. This was done for two reasons: first, to maintain a reassuring perspective on the regression that many people experienced in their day-to-day lives; and second, to provide a transition from the intense atmosphere of the small group to the social atmosphere of the large group.

The large-group meeting of thirty to forty people followed the small-group meeting and lasted for two hours. There were widely varying agendas for this meeting. Its primary purposes were social, recreational, and educational. Coffee, tea, and cookies were served (purchased by the $1 weekly optional donations of the members). Speakers were invited to discuss such topics as health, bereavement, self-help, and writing wills and other legal matters. Parties, outings, and dinner shows were organized and the internal organizational officers selected. Once a month the group had either a potluck at this time or went out as a group to eat.

From among the membership, those who had completed their earliest periods of turmoil within the small group volunteered to become resources for new members. These men and women contacted potential new members and helped make arrangements for their coming to meetings. Transportation was a frequent problem for the elderly and for those who did not drive or were fearful of going out alone at night. The availability and cooperation of most people in the organization precluded almost anyone's missing meetings for those reasons. As new members joined the group, they were offered the phone numbers of "veterans" to contact whenever they felt it necessary. In addition to functioning as facilitator of the small group, I was also a consultant available to any of the group members who had special concerns about another person. During the large-group meetings, I was frequently consulted by individuals, often for the evaluation of depression, and regularly referred group members for medical and psychiatric services in the community.

The benefits of such an organization are multiple. For a great number of bereaved, participation in the small group constitutes their only access to people who understand them or accept their feelings, thus providing them with their only means of catharsis. The awareness that others have gone through the same experiences and have come out not only intact but often stronger provides great reassurance that they are not "going crazy." At the same time, the uniqueness of their loss is respected and supported, and they are made to feel important. Participants also can share practical information—for instance, on how to apply for Social Security and veterans' benefits or how to find a trustworthy auto mechanic. Organized social and recreational activities with a growing extended family can help structure a life that may seem relatively empty. Exercising one's social skills occurs more easily in an atmosphere of support without the sexual demands experienced in other settings. Yet to be determined is the relative therapeutic efficacy of support groups in contrast to individual therapy for the bereaved. Clearly, there is considerable overlap in their functions in dealing with most of the dimensions of grief.

Therapeutic Impact of the Study

While this study was phenomenological in nature, the process of accumulating data entailed many aspects that parallel what might occur in therapy. Subjects were interviewed regularly and repeatedly over time by an experienced, concerned person whose task was to explore their inner experiences. They often developed a close relationship with the interviewer—either my research assistants or me.

Our research subjects' responses to specific inquiries about the value of their participation confirm the observations that their involvement in the study was useful to them, although our design precluded any independent corroboration of this conclusion. Our subjects' descriptions of their perceived benefits and definitions of what was therapeutic provide at least a "consumer's" view of what can contribute to their sense of well-being.

A majority of subjects found it helpful to talk about their inner experiences, to confront them, and sort through them with another person.

Beth: "It was a chance to talk to someone about a specific thing that I didn't have a chance to talk to anyone else about so specifically."

Linda: "Bringing it out, you cry awhile and then you laugh and it just kind of cleans the cobwebs out and brings your emotions to the surface. It's a release."

Sharon: "The questions you ask make me think, and that's helped me to see certain things."

Perry: "It was indirect psychotherapy which I wouldn't have gotten."

People identified the support they felt from the contact with the interviewer and referred to my research assistant as someone who felt like a friend.

Linda: "It was helpful to think that somebody cares."

Many of the bereaved achieved a sense of altruism and mastery by being able to contribute to the benefits of others by their participation in research.

Gloria: "My first thought was 'Boy, this is the pits. If I can do anything to help anybody in the future, I'd like to do it.'"

Ralph: "That whole premise [contributing] I liked. I think if I was told, 'Maybe you ought to sit down with a psychologist because your wife has died and you may have some problems coming up,' I probably would have said no."

The nature of the inquiry, through interviews and question-naires, provided a form of normalization as our subjects extrapolated from our questions.

Susan: "When I would take the forms home and sit and look at them and fill them out, I'd think, 'These things are obviously happening to other people or they wouldn't be down on this form. It's not just me and that's good.'"

Many people felt that their experience over time gave them an excellent opportunity to observe their progress in dealing with their grief and enhanced their sense of growth and mastery.

> *Phyllis:* "It was an excellent signpost on the road. . . . I would be answering them the same, and then all of a sudden I realized I'm not answering these questions the same as I did three months ago."

> *Bobbi:* "I walked in one day and saw the widow sign on the door, and the word seemed so foreign to me, and that gave me a measure of how far I'd come."

Our subjects' responses to the study were not always positive. Several people dropped out—usually early in their participation—because they found the inquiry too painful. Others found the confrontation with painful stimuli helpful. As time went on, a number of people indicated that they had looked forward to their interviews during the periods of greatest pain but found themselves dreading them as they achieved greater relief and distance: interviews would dredge up what they wanted behind them.

The subjects of this research have not been its sole therapeutic beneficiaries. Those of us who have been intimately involved with this group of courageous people have reaped many rewards. We have had the opportunity to observe one of life's great dramas unfold before us many times, yielding a depth of understanding of human nature for which we feel privileged. Through our experiences with other people's grief, we have had the chance to reexperience and further integrate our own losses. We have developed greater patience and tolerance for life's difficulties and a greater sense of appreciation for life's beauty and fragility. We have shared the intimacy of others and have had the opportunity to contribute to their lives. I hope that the understanding of grief imparted by this book will offer the same possibilities to others.

 Appendix

Description of the
Bereavement Study

Research Instruments

The purpose of this study was to examine the course of spousal bereavement prospectively, using a multidimensional approach. A battery of semistructured interviews and self-administered questionnaires was developed. These are outlined here.

1. Initial Assessment Structured Interview

    Demographic data
    Description of nature and circumstances of spouse's death
    Description of reactions to spouse's death
          Emotional and mental reactions
          Psychosocial circumstances and impact of the death
          Dealing with children and their responses
    Past development
          Nature of marital relationship
          History of losses and responses
          Responses to major development milestones
          History of relationships
    Past psychiatric history
    Family psychiatric history
    Medical history, including current medications
    Drug and alcohol history
    Hamilton Depression Scale
    Research Diagnostic Criteria for Depression

2.   San Diego Widowhood Project Questionnaire—a self-
     administered 14-page, 269-item questionnaire

   Name, address, age, sex, marital status, children, religion,
     ethnicity
   Occupation
   Educational level
   Monthly income
   Number of people in home now/prior to death
   Church attendance now/prior to death
   Social activities now/prior to death
   Availability of a confidant
   "Nervous breakdown" now/prior to death
   Counseling or therapy now/prior to death
   Number of physician visits in past year/year prior to death
   Number of hospitalizations in past year/year prior to death
   Record of medications now/prior to death
   Alcohol consumption now/prior to death
   Smoking habits now/prior to death
   Presence of the following grief-related experiences:
             Preoccupation with thoughts of deceased spouse
             Clear visual memory of the deceased
             Sense of spouse's continued presence
             Tearfulness
             Visual image of deceased
             Voice of deceased
             Irritability and anger
             Feelings of restlessness
             Tension
             Social withdrawal
             Numbness
             Difficulty in accepting the fact of loss
             Avoidance of situations, articles of clothing, pictures,
                or other things that would serve as reminders of the
                deceased
             Worry about loneliness
             Depression
             Awakening during the night

      Ideas of guilt or self-reproach regarding death of spouse

      Anger at others felt to be responsible for spouse's death

      Apathy

Personal estimation of overall adjustment to widowhood

Holmes and Rahe Life Events Scale (42 items)

Beck Depression Inventory (21 items)

Hopkins Symptom Checklist (52 items)

Weissman Social Adjustment Scale (60 items)

Zung Depression Scale

3. Interim History Interview—a semistructured interview to elicit the following information:

Major life events since last interview

Emotional and mental reactions to the death

Ways of coping with distress

Continuing relationship to dead spouse

Difficulties in functioning

Changes in relationships

Self-perceptions

Research Design

    Research subjects were to be interviewed (initial assessment interview) approximately one month after the death of their spouses; at that time also, they were asked to fill out the self-administered questionnaire. At subsequent intervals subjects would be given the interim history interview and the self-administered questionnaire, as well as the structured interviews for the Hamilton Depression Scale and the Research Diagnostic Criteria for Depression. The intervals—at 4, 7, 10, 13, 16, 19, 22, 25, 37, and 49 months after the death—were selected in order to obtain data every three months for the first two years, yet miss the anniversary dates of the death, a period that would likely distort the data (Parkes, 1972).

Subject Selection

Approximately 350 newly bereaved men and women were identified through the San Diego County Department of Public Health Vital Records. They were contacted by letter at three weeks with a follow-up phone call a week later, inviting their participation in a study on the phenomenology of bereavement. Selection criteria limited the participants to English-speaking men and women, age sixty-five or under, who lived within the city of San Diego proper. The exclusion criteria were based on the geographical and language constraints of the researchers and the decision to avoid, if possible, the physical health complications of an elderly population. Current studies by the San Diego Widowhood Project are now focused on this older population.

Participation

Seventy subjects participated in the study. Sixty of the subjects were interviewed and completed questionnaires at one month, and another ten began at four months. Compliance with the interviewing and completion of questionnaires was variable.

Month	1	4	7	10	13	16	19	22	25	37	49
Questionnaires	60	58	43	49	43	50	43	47	48	36	27

There were generally a few more interviews completed for any time period than questionnaires completed because of the length of the questionnaire. Reasons given for noncompliance and dropout from the study included moving, "being too busy," and getting "too upset" by participation.

Demographic Data

Age: Mean: 50; Median: 52; Range: 24–66; <35: 11 percent;
             36–45: 9 percent; 46–55: 49 percent; 55–66: 31 percent
Sex: Female: 70 percent ($N = 49$); Male: 30 percent ($N = 21$)
Education: <H.S. grad.: 12 percent; H.S. grad.: 19 percent;
                 Some college: 40 percent; College grad.: 29 percent

Religion: Protestant: 56 percent; Catholic: 19 percent;
             Jewish: 9 percent; None: 7 percent; Other: 9 percent
Race: Caucasian: 87 percent; Black: 4 percent;
             Latino: 2 percent; Native American: 7 percent;
             Asian-Pacific: 0 percent
Family's monthly income at the time of death: Men: $2,118;
             Women: $1,982; All subjects: $2,028

Frequencies of Grief-Related Experiences

The following data represent the frequencies of our research subjects' responses to a series of grief-related items selected as representative of the different dimensions of grief contained in the self-scored questionnaire. The reader is advised to approach these with caution on several counts. First, the descriptive phenomenology contained in the body of this book is based primarily on observations made through interviews, not on questionnaire data. Our subjects are acting as their own controls over time, but there is no other control group. Also, no attempt is made here to analyze the significant dropout rate or the variability of participation of our subjects over so long a period of time. Detailed analyses of these limitations and other data analyses are the subjects of current papers being prepared for submission to scientific journals. With these caveats the data are presented for the reader's interest. The figures in Table 1 represent the percentage of respondents endorsing an item.

As can be seen in Table 1, many areas of grief-related experiences are inadequately "covered" by components of the questionnaire used in the study. As mentioned earlier, the questionnaire contained 269 items, only some of which are utilized in Table 1 for illustration. The descriptive data from interviews are obviously much more complete and clinically richer than the data from questionnaires. Both are subject to methodological limitations in establishing the validity of observations made here. The descriptive data from this study have been used to develop a self-administered questionnaire that is more comprehensive in its focus on grief-related experiences and covers each of the many dimen-

Table 1. Grief-Related Experiences over Time.

	Percent of Subjects Endorsing Each Item										
	1 mo.	4 mo.	7 mo.	10 mo.	13 mo.	16 mo.	19 mo.	22 mo.	25 mo.	37 mo.	49 mo.
Emotional and Mental Responses											
Numbness	29%	9%	2%	0%	9%	2%	0%	3%	2%	0%	4%
Tearfulness	73	62	56	35	42	28	26	20	23	14	17
I cry more than I used to	60	44	33	10	21	10	7	6	4	6	15
Guilt	27	19	14	10	21	8	5	0	2	3	0
I feel I am being punished	7	2	5	6	2	8	0	0	2	3	4
Anger at others felt responsible	12	9	9	4	5	8	9	9	6	8	8
Tension	50	29	49	25	28	26	23	26	25	28	42
Feelings of restlessness	53	35	35	20	23	26	23	20	21	17	20
Depression	33	26	33	14	26	26	19	15	21	17	13
Awakening during night	48	43	33	31	30	24	28	17	29	17	32
Spells of terror or panic	7	7	7	8	7	6	7	6	2	14	8
Feeling lonely	56	36	48	22	28	30	19	25	21	17	20
Worry about loneliness	37	21	26	16	16	22	14	13	21	8	4
Apathy	17	7	9	12	9	6	7	9	8	6	0
Mind is going blank	15	12	17	4	9	11	14	11	10	11	12
Trouble concentrating	22	15	17	6	14	11	14	11	10	11	12
Continuing Relationship with Dead Spouse											
Difficulty accepting loss	42	31	21	6	16	8	2	9	8	3	0
Preoccupation with thoughts of deceased	63	50	49	25	33	20	19	9	23	11	17
Clear visual memory of deceased	68	53	56	41	40	42	35	35	38	31	21
Sense of spouse's continued presence	37	26	21	10	16	18	14	11	13	8	4
Avoiding reminders of deceased	23	19	7	8	12	10	5	8	8	3	4
Visual image of deceased	27	22	26	8	12	16	21	11	13	11	17
Voice of the deceased	12	7	5	4	5	4	2	4	6	3	0
Health and Work Function											
Physician visits past year	7	5	4	6	4	5	6	5	6	6	6
Medications (any psychotropic)	40	28	26	24	26	22	20	15	10	8	16

Alcohol (more than one drink per day)	16	14	16	12	9	18	26	17	19	22	8
No smoking	52	61	62	56	71	54	64	61	64	69	72
I can do my work about as well as before	48	67	63	75	74	75	70	63	67	78	65
Mean monthly income											
Men ($2,118 prior to death)	$2,007	$2,180	$2,069	$2,100	$2,621	$2,238	$2,850	$2,633	$2,261	$2,530	$2,874
Women ($1,982 prior to death)	$1,102	$1,058	$1,130	$1,411	$1,273	$1,317	$1,397	$1,383	$1,453	$1,936	$2,211
Do not have thoughts of killing myself	77	95	88	92	91	94	95	93	92	92	81
Have thoughts but wouldn't kill myself	17	2	9	2	9	4	5	6	10	8	11
Would like to kill myself	0	0	0	2	0	0	0	0	0	0	0
Relationships											
Social withdrawal	13	10	12	10	16	12	14	7	13	8	13
Out socially three or more times in past month	62	74	76	75	81	75	64	74	68	64	72
Get along well with relatives	98	100	100	100	100	100	100	100	100	100	100
At least one confidant	92	91	93	90	91	90	93	96	91	94	96
Interested in dating	47	53	37	67	52	53	64	60	58	52	60
Dated in past two weeks	23	28	19	33	21	29	35	28	35	30	18
Still enjoy sex	49	50	40	61	47	56	57	70	55	64	70
Living with someone of opposite sex	4	4	8	13	22	15	19	16	16	24	40
Remarried	1	1	5	6	9	12	11	13	8	17	23
Identity and World View											
Critical of myself for weakness or mistakes	41	25	35	25	19	18	21	22	33	26	37
I hate myself	0	0	0	2	0	0	0	2	0	0	0
Disgusted with self	7	2	7	2	2	6	2	2	2	3	7
Disappointed with self	20	19	23	15	21	8	19	20	25	20	22
Feel discouraged about the future	25	19	23	10	21	12	16	13	15	20	18
Encouraged about the future	77	76	70	83	79	86	82	89	87	81	74
I get as much satisfaction as I used to	41	51	49	60	67	63	63	70	67	69	67
My life is pretty full	85	91	83	96	93	92	83	91	88	94	87
Overall Adjustment											
Good or excellent	55	71	63	74	77	71	79	85	81	78	80
Mean score (1 = poor, 2 = fair, 3 = good, 4 = excellent)	2.6	2.8	2.8	2.8	3.0	2.9	3.1	3.1	3.2	3.2	3.2

sions of grief more fully. It is now being field-tested on a larger bereaved population.

Considerations of methodology aside, most of the data in Table 1 demonstrate that the most intense disruptions of grief occur early in the process and gradually subside, although usually they do not disappear. Some elements of grief may remain as the continuing legacy of a process that is integrated into the lives of the bereaved. This book is a testimony to the vicissitudes of those grief experiences.

Bibliography

General References

Bowlby, J. *Attachment and Loss.* Vol. 1: *Attachment.* London: Hogarth Press, 1969.

Bowlby, J. *Attachment and Loss.* Vol. 3: *Sadness and Depression.* New York: Basic Books, 1980.

Glick, I. O., Parkes, C. M., and Weiss, R. *The First Year of Bereavement.* New York: Basic Books, 1975.

Lopata, H. Z. *Widowhood in an American City.* Cambridge, Mass.: Schenkman, 1973.

Lopata, H. Z. *Women as Widows: Support Systems.* New York: Elsevier Science, 1979.

Osterweis, M., Solomon, F., and Green, M. (eds.). *Bereavement: Reactions, Consequences, and Care.* Washington, D.C.: National Academy Press, 1984.

Parkes, C. M. *Bereavement.* London: Tavistock, 1972.

Parkes, C. M., and Weiss, R. S. *Recovery from Bereavement.* New York: Basic Books, 1983.

Raphael, B. *The Anatomy of Bereavement.* New York: Basic Books, 1983.

Schoenberg, B., and Gerber, I. (eds.). *Bereavement: Its Psycho-Social Aspects.* New York: Columbia University Press, 1975.

Phenomenology of Grief

Bowlby, J. "Separation Anxiety." *International Journal of Psycho-Analysis,* 1960, *41,* 89–113.

Caine, L. *Widow.* New York: Morrow, 1974.

Heyman, D. K., and Gianturco, D. T. "Long-Term Adaptation by the Elderly to Bereavement." *Journal of Gerontology,* 1973, *28,* 359–362.

Krupp, G. R., and Klingfield, B. "The Bereavement Reaction: A Cross-Cultural Evaluation." *Journal of Religion and Health,* 1962, *1,* 222–246.

Lindemann, E. "Symptomatology and Management of Acute Grief." *American Journal of Psychiatry,* 1944, *101,* 141–149.

Parkes, C. M. "The First Year of Bereavement: A Longitudinal Study of the Reaction of London Widows to the Death of Their Husbands." *Psychiatry,* 1970, *33,* 444–467.

Pollock, G. H. "Anniversary Reactions, Trauma and Mourning." *Psychoanalytic Quarterly,* 1970, *34,* 347–371.

Weiss, R. S. (ed.). *Loneliness: The Experience of Emotional and Social Isolation.* Cambridge, Mass.: MIT Press, 1974.

Zisook, S., Devaul, R. A., and Click, M. A. "Measuring Symptoms of Grief and Bereavement." *American Journal of Psychiatry,* 1982, *139,* 1590–1593.

Zisook, S., and Shuchter, S. "Time Course of Spousal Bereavement." *General Hospital Psychiatry,* 1985, *7,* 95–100.

Impact on Health and "Pathological Grief"

Bartrop, R., and others. "Depressed Lymphocyte Function After Bereavement." *Lancet,* 1977, *1,* 834–836.

Board, F., Persky, H., and Hamburg, D. A. "Psychological Stress and Endocrine Functions: Blood Levels of Adrenocortical and Thyroid Hormones in Acutely Disturbed Patients." Psychosomatic Medicine, 1956, *18,* 324–333.

Bornstein, P. E., and others. "The Depression of Widowhood After Thirteen Months." *British Journal of Psychiatry,* 1973, *122,* 561–566.

Brown, J. T., and Stoudemier, G. A. "Normal and Pathological Grief." *Journal of the American Medical Association,* 1983, *250,* 378–382.

Clayton, P. J. "Mortality and Morbidity in the First Year of Widowhood." *Archives of General Psychiatry,* 1974, *30,* 747–750.

Clayton, P. J. "The Sequelae and Nonsequelae of Conjugal Bereavement." *American Journal of Psychiatry,* 1979, *136,* 1530–1543.

Clayton, P. J., Halikas, J. A., and Maurice, W. L. "The Depression of Widowhood." *British Journal of Psychiatry,* 1972, *120,* 71–78.

Clayton, P. J., Herjanic, M., Murphy, G. E., and Woodruff, R. A. "Mourning and Depression: Their Similarities and Differences." *Canadian Psychiatric Association Journal,* 1974, *19,* 309–312.

Cox, P. R., and Ford, J. R. "The Mortality of Widows Shortly After Widowhood." *Lancet,* 1964, *1,* 163–164.

Deutsch, H. "Absence of Grief." *Psychoanalytic Quarterly,* 1937, *6,* 12–22.

Engle, G. "Sudden and Rapid Death During Psychological Stress." *Annals of Internal Medicine,* 1971, *74,* 771–782.

Freud, S. *Mourning and Melancholia.* In J. Strachey (ed.), *The Standard Edition of the Complete Psychological Works of Sigmund Freud.* Vol. 14. London: Hogarth Press, 1957. (Originally published 1917.)

Helsing, K. J., and Szklo, M. "Mortality After Bereavement." *American Journal of Epidemiology,* 1981, *114,* 41–52.

Hofer, M. A. "Relationships as Regulators: A Psychobiological Perspective on Bereavement." *Psychosomatic Medicine,* 1984, *46,* 183–197.

Hofer, M. A., Wolff, C. T., Friedman, S. B., and Mason, J. W. "A Psychoendocrine Study of Bereavement. Part I: 17-Hydroxycorticosteroid Excretion Rates of Parents Following Death of Their Children from Leukemia." *Psychosomatic Medicine,* 1972, *34,* 481–491.

Hofer, M. A., Wolff, C. T., and Mason, J. W. "A Psychoendocrine Study of Bereavement. Part II: Observations on the Process of Mourning in Relation to Adrenocortical Function." *Psychosomatic Medicine,* 1972, *34,* 492–504.

Jacobs, S., and others. "Bereavement, Psychological Distress, Ego Defenses, and Adrenocortical Function." Paper presented at meeting of the American Psychosomatic Society, New York, March 1984.

Kraus, A. S., and Lilienfeld, A. M. "Some Epidemiological Aspects of the High Mortality Rate in the Young Widowed Group." *Journal of Chronic Diseases*, 1959, *10*, 207-217.

Levav, I. "Mortality and Psychopathology Following the Death of an Adult Child: An Epidemiological Review." *Israeli Journal of Psychiatry and Related Sciences*, 1982, *19*, 23-38.

MacMahon, B., and Pugh, T. F. "Suicide in the Widowed." *American Journal of Epidemiology*, 1965, *81*, 23-31.

Maddison, D. C., and Viola, A. "The Health of Widows in the Year Following Bereavement." *Journal of Psychosomatic Research*, 1968, *12*, 297-306.

Parkes, C. M. "Effects of Bereavement on Physical and Mental Health: A Study of the Medical Records of Widows." *British Medical Journal*, 1964a, *2*, 274-279.

Parkes, C. M. "Recent Bereavement as a Cause of Mental Illness." *British Journal of Psychiatry*, 1964b, *110*, 198-204.

Rees, W. "The Hallucinations of Widowhood." *British Medical Journal*, 1971, *4*, 37 ff.

Rees, W., and Lutkins, S. G. "Mortality and Bereavement." *British Medical Journal*, 1967, *4*, 13-16.

Reich, P., De Silva, R. A., Lown, B., and Murawski, B. J. "Acute Psychological Disturbance Preceding Life-Threatening Ventricular Arrhythmias." *Journal of the American Medical Association*, 1981, *246*, 233-235.

Schleifer, S. J., and others. "Suppression of Lymphocyte Stimulation Following Bereavement." *Journal of the American Medical Association*, 1983, *250*, 374-399.

Shuchter, S. R. "The Depression of Widowhood Reconsidered." Paper presented at meeting of the American Psychiatric Association, Toronto, May 15-21, 1982b.

Shuchter, S. R., Kirkorowicz, C., Zisook, S., and Risch, C. S. "The Dexamethasone Suppression Test Responses in the Acutely Bereaved." *American Journal of Psychiatry*, 1986, *143* (7).

Siggins, L. D. "Mourning: A Critical Survey of the Literature." *International Journal of Psychoanalysis*, 1966, *52*, 259-266.

Vachon, M. L. S., and others. "Correlates of Enduring Stress Patterns Following Bereavement: Social Network, Life Situation, and Personality." *Psychological Medicine,* 1982, *12,* 783–788.

Volkan, V. D. "Normal and Pathological Grief Reactions—A Guide for the Family Physician." *Virginia Medical Monthly,* 1966, *93,* 651 ff.

Young, M., Benjamin, B., and Wallis, G. "The Mortality of Widowers." *Lancet,* 1963, *2,* 454–456.

Impact of Grief on Relationships

"The Bereaved Family." *Annals of the American Academy of Political and Social Sciences,* 1932, *169,* 184–190.

Clayton, P. J. "The Effects of Living Alone on Bereavement Symptoms." *American Journal of Psychiatry,* 1975, *132,* 133–137.

Cleveland, W. P., and Gianturco, D. T. "Remarriage Probability After Widowhood: a Retrospective Method." *Journal of Gerontology,* 1976, *31,* 99–102.

Eliot, T. D. "The Adjustive Behavior of Bereaved Families: A New Field for Research." *Social Forces,* 1930, *8,* 543–549.

Lopata, H. Z. "The Social Involvement of American Widows." *American Behavioral Scientist,* 1971, *14,* 41 ff.

Marris, P. *Widows and Their Families.* London: Routledge & Kegan Paul, 1958.

Pihlblad, C. T., and Adams, D. L. "Widowhood, Social Participation and Life Satisfaction." *International Journal of Aging and Human Development,* 1972, *3,* 323–330.

Schlesinger, B. "The Widow and Widower and Remarriage: Selected Findings." *Omega,* 1971, *2,* 10–18.

Silverman, S. M., and Silverman, P. R. "Parent-Child Communication in Widowed Families." *American Journal of Psychotherapy,* 1979, *33,* 428–441.

Vachon, M. L. S., and others. "Correlates of Enduring Stress Patterns Following Bereavement: Social Network, Life Situation, and Personality." *Psychological Medicine,* 1982, *12,* 783–788.

Vollman, R. R., Ganzert, A., Picher, L., and Williams, W. V. "The

Reactions of Family Systems to Sudden and Unexpected Death." *Omega,* 1971, *2,* 101–106.

Walker, K. N., MacBride, A., and Vachon, M. L. S. "Social Support Networks and the Crisis of Bereavement." *Social Science and Medicine,* 1977, *11,* 35–41.

Sociocultural Aspects of Grief

Blauner, R. "Death and Social Structure." *Psychiatry,* 1966, *29,* 378–394.

Bowman, L. *The American Funeral.* Westport, Conn.: Greenwood Press, 1973. (Originally published 1959.)

Mitford, J. *The American Way of Death.* New York: Simon & Schuster, 1963.

Stannard, D. E. *Death in America.* Philadelphia: University of Pennsylvania Press, 1974.

Grief and Identity

Horowitz, M., Wilner, N., Marmar, C., and Krupnick, J. "Pathological Grief and the Activation of Latent Self-Images." *American Journal of Psychiatry,* 1980, *137,* 1157–1162.

Lopata, H. "Self-Identity in Marriage and Widowhood." *Sociological Quarterly,* 1973, *14,* 407–418.

Pollock, G. H. "Mourning and Adaptation." *International Journal of Psychoanalysis,* 1961, *42,* 341–361.

Pollock, G. H. "The Mourning-Liberation Process and Creativity: The Case of Käthe Kollwitz." *Annual of Psychoanalysis,* 1982, *10,* 333–354.

Anticipatory Grief

Aldrich, C. K. "Some Dynamics of Anticipatory Grief." In B. Schoenberg and others (eds.), *Anticipatory Grief.* New York: Columbia University Press, 1974.

Clayton, P. J., Parilla, R. H., Jr., and Bieri, M. D. "Methodological Problems in Assessing the Relationship Between Acuteness of Death and the Bereavement Outcome." In J. Reiffel and others (eds.), *Psychosocial Aspects of Cardiovascular Disease: The Life-Threatened Patient, the Family, and the Staff.* New York: Columbia University Press, 1980.

Gerber, I., and others. "Anticipatory Grief and Aged Widows and Widowers." *Journal of Gerontology,* 1975, *30,* 225-229.

Treatment Interventions

Barrett, C. J. "Effectiveness of Widows' Groups in Facilitating Change." *Journal of Consulting and Clinical Psychology,* 1978, *46,* 20-31.

Gerber, I., Wiener, A., Battin, D., and Arkin, A. M. "Brief Therapy to the Aged Bereaved." In B. Schoenberg and I. Gerber (eds.), *Bereavement: Its Psychosocial Aspects.* New York: Columbia University Press, 1975.

Hollister, L. "Psychotherapeutic Drugs in the Dying and Bereaved." *Journal of Thanatology,* 1972, *2,* 623-629.

Jacobs, S., and Ostfeld, A. "The Clinical Management of Grief." *Journal of the American Geriatrics Society,* 1980, *28,* 331-335.

Maddison, D. C., and Raphael, B. "Normal Bereavement as an Illness Requiring Care: Psychopharmacological Approaches." In I. K. Goldbert, S. Malitz, and A. H. Kitscher (eds.), *Psychopharmacologic Agents for the Terminally Ill and Bereaved.* New York: Columbia University Press, 1973.

Mawson, D., Marks, I. M., Ramm, L., and Stern, R. S. "Guided Mourning for Morbid Grief: A Controlled Study." *British Journal of Psychiatry,* 1981, *138,* 185-193.

Melges, F. T., and DeMaso, D. R. "Grief Resolution Therapy: Reliving, Revising, and Revisiting." *American Journal of Psychotherapy,* 1980, *34,* 51-70.

Parkes, C. M. "Bereavement Counseling: Does It Work?" *British Medical Journal,* 1980, *281,* 3-6.

Parkes, C. M. "Evaluation of a Bereavement Service." *Journal of Preventive Psychiatry,* 1981, *1,* 179-188.

Raphael, B. "Preventive Intervention with the Recently Bereaved." *Archives of General Psychiatry,* 1977, *34,* 1450-1454.

Rogers, J., and others. "A Self-Help Program for Widows as an

Independent Community Service." *Hospital and Community Psychiatry*, 1980, *31*, 844–847.

Shuchter, S. R. "Antidepressant Treatment of Grief Reactions." Paper presented at meeting of the American Psychiatric Association, Toronto, May 15–21, 1982a.

Shuchter, S. R. "How the Family Physician Can Help Patients Adjust to the Death of a Spouse." *Medical Aspects of Human Sexuality*, 1984, *18*, 30–54.

Silverman, P. R. "The Widow-to-Widow Program: An Experiment in Preventive Intervention." *Mental Hygiene*, 1969, *53*, 333–337.

Silverman, P. R. "The Widow as Caregiver in a Program of Preventive Intervention with Other Widows." *Mental Hygiene*, 1970, *54*, 540–547.

Silverman, P. R. *If You Will Lift the Load, I Will Lift It Too: A Guide to Developing Widow-to-Widow Programs.* New York: Jewish Funeral Directors of America, 1976.

Silverman, P. R., and Cooperband, A. "On Widowhood: Mutual Help and the Elderly Widow." *Journal of Geriatric Psychiatry*, 1975, *8*, 9–27.

Silverman, P. R., MacKenzie, D., Pettipas, M., and Wilson, E. W. (eds.). *Helping Each Other in Widowhood.* New York: Health Science Press, 1974.

Suomi, S. J., and others. "Effects of Imipramine Treatment of Separation-Induced Social Disorders in Rhesus Monkeys." *Archives of General Psychiatry*, 1978, *35*, 321–327.

Vachon, M. L. S., and others. "A Controlled Study of Self-Help Intervention for Widows." *American Journal of Psychiatry*, 1980, *137*, 1380–1384.

Videka-Sherman, L. "Effects of Participants in a Self-Help Group for Bereaved Parents: Compassionate Friends." *Prevention in Human Services*, 1982, *1*, 69–77.

Volkan, V. D. "Re-Grief Therapy." In B. Schoenberg and I. Gerber, (eds.), *Bereavement: Its Psychological Aspects.* New York: Columbia University Press, 1975.

Worden, J. W. *Grief Counseling and Grief Therapy: A Handbook.* New York: Springer, 1982.

Index